THEORY OF PROFANE LOVE AMONG THE ARABS: THE DEVELOPMENT OF THE GENRE

NEW YORK UNIVERSITY
STUDIES IN NEAR EASTERN CIVILIZATION
NUMBER 3.

ALSO IN THIS SERIES

NUMBER I: F. E. Peters, Aristotle and the Arabs

NUMBER II: Jacob M. Landau, Jews in Nineteenth-Century Egypt

THEORY OF PROFANE LOVE AMONG THE ARABS: THE DEVELOPMENT OF THE GENRE

LOIS ANITA GIFFEN

NEW YORK/NEW YORK UNIVERSITY PRESS
LONDON/UNIVERSITY OF LONDON PRESS LTD.
1971

Library of Congress Catalog Card Number 74-133017
ISBN: 8147-2951-7

NEW YORK UNIVERSITY STUDIES IN NEAR EASTERN CIVILIZATION

The participation of the New York University Press in the University's new commitment to Near Eastern Studies—building on a tradition of well over a century—will provide Americans and others with new opportunities for understanding the Near East. Concerned with those various peoples of the Near East who, throughout the centuries, have dramatically shaped many of mankind's most fundamental concepts and who have always had high importance in practical affairs, this series, New York University Studies in Near Eastern Civilization, seeks to publish important works in this vital area. The purview will be broad, open to varied approaches and historical periods. It will, however, be particularly receptive to work in two aspects of near Eastern civilization that may have received insufficient attention elsewhere but which do reflect particular interests at New York University. These are literature and art. Furthermore, taking a stand that may be more utilitarian than that of other publications, the series will welcome both translations of important Near Eastern literature of imagination, and of significant scholarly works written in Near Eastern languages. In this way, a larger audience, unacquainted with these languages, will be able to deepen its knowledge of the cultural achievements of Near Eastern peoples.

R. Bayly Winder
Richard Ettinghausen
General Editors

PREFACE

This study was intended as a contribution to both the literary history of the Arabic language and the intellectual history of the Islamic Middle Ages, for these Arabic works on the theory of profane love are not literary in any narrow sense of the word. They concern themselves not only with literary tradition and literary and social fashions, but also with psychology, philosophy, cosmology, theology, ethics, practical piety, Islamic Law, and the science of Tradition—Ḥadīth. Though I have written primarily for the Arabist and Islamicist, or the reader at least somewhat familiar with the Arabic language and the Islamic milieu, I hope to attract other readers who may have a special interest in this timeless and universal topic and may be familiar with its treatment in the writings of Classical Antiquity or Medieval and Renaissance Europe.

As the subtitle indicates, this is a study of the development of the genre, a tradition of writing on the subject of profane love—human, earthly love, its nature, causes, and vicissitudes. From this, and from the Introduction, the reader will understand that we are speaking of a substantially coherent group of twenty-odd essays and books written over a nine hundred year period and not anything so vague as "the ideas of the Arabs about love," wherever they may be found. I have provided some notes in the Appendix on the relevance of some writings on love which I cannot by definition include in the genre. Here I should mention that I would like to have taken cognizance of J.-C. Vadet's recently published book, *L'esprit courtois en Orient dans les cinq premiers siècles de l'hĕgiré*, but it was necessary to complete my revisions for the press before I had an opportunity to see it.

The desirability of studying one or more of these works on love and its relationship to others was an idea first suggested to me by Professor Seeger A. Bonebakker in the fall of 1962. From my first research to the final writing, he was always ready to share his experience, to guide, and to lend encouragement, giving unstintingly of his time. Great as my debt is to him, we would both acknowledge that this study has as its foundation the work and teaching of the late Professor Joseph Schacht, for without the thorough background of the most unusual sort which he gave his students in Arabic and Islamic Studies, it would have been impossible for me to undertake a work of this scope and kind. In a more specific sense, I owe him a debt for his support in the project from the beginning. On several occasions, he lent books from his private library that would otherwise have been difficult to come by, and he offered valuable corrections or passed on bits of helpful information from time to time.

I am grateful to a number of friends, former teachers, colleagues, and others who contributed suggestions about style or substance. If their left hands have forgotten what their right hands have done, let them know that I shall not forget. When I was making the final changes for this revised version, Professors Gustave E. von Grunebaum and Jaroslaw Stetkevych kindly contributed particularly valuable information on several points. Final responsibility for error is in all cases mine, of course.

The names of libraries—Süleymaniye, Top Kapı, Aya Sofya, Şarkiyât Enstitüsü, Bursa Orhan Cami, Ankara Millî Kitaplık, Dil, Tarih ve Cografya Fakültesi, Ẓāhirīya, Dār al-Kutub al-Miṣrīya, Faculté de Lettres and Dār al-Kutub al-Waṭanīya (Tunis), Zaitūnīya, Ambrosiana, Leiden Rijksuniversiteit, Chester Beatty—evoke memories of persons whose kindness smoothed the rough path. I am most grateful also to the Turkish Ministry of Education for microfilms of manuscripts from their Süleymaniye, Aya Sofya, and Bursa Libraries, as well as to the directors of the Top Kapı Saray, the Biblioteca Reale di Torino, the Tübingen Universitäts Bibliothek, and the Chester Beatty Library for microfilms. However, I should like to note that I also had the opportunity to make use of the original manuscripts, except in the case of the Torino *Kitāb az-Zahra* and the Tübingen *Rauḍat al-Muḥibbīn*. Therefore, I have noted these two in the Bibliography as microfilms but not the others.

Special thanks are due to the Nederlands Instituut voor het Nabije Oosten, the Hollanda Tarih ve Arkeoloji Enstitüsü, their director Professor Dr. A. A. Kampman, and their staffs for their hospitality. It was at these institutes in Leiden and Istanbul that I found a needed home and an ideal atmosphere for work during much of the year 1966. Much of the research and writing for this study was supported by a fellowship and travel grant from the Foreign Area

Fellowship Program of the American Council of Learned Societies and the Social Science Research Council. Later, a grant from the Research Fund of the New York University Graduate School of Arts and Sciences enabled me to publish the first, mimeograph edition of this study which appeared under the title *The Development of the Arabic Literature on the Theory of Profane Love: An Historical Study*. This was done as a step toward revision and wider publication in the present form.

CONTENTS

PAGE

PREFACE v

INTRODUCTION xi

PART 1. SURVEY OF THE AUTHORS AND THEIR WORKS

Two Essays of Jāḥiẓ 3
An Anonymous and Untitled Essay on Love containing a quote from Aḥmad b. aṭ-Ṭayyib as-Sarakhsī . . . 5
Muḥammad b. Dā'ūd's *Kitāb az-Zahra* 8
Al-Washshā''s *Kitāb al-Muwashshā* 13
Al-Kharā'iṭī's *I'tilāl al-Qulūb* 15
Al-Marzubānī's *Kitāb ar-Riyāḍ* 16
Al-Ḥuṣrī's *Kitāb al-Maṣūn fī Sirr al-Hawā al-Maknūn* . 21
Ibn Ḥazm's *Ṭauq al-Ḥamāma fi 'l-Ulfa wa 'l-Ullāf* . . 23
Ja'far b. Aḥmad as-Sarrāj's *Maṣāri' al-'Ushshāq* . . 25
Ibn al-Jauzī's *Dhamm al-Hawā* 27
Aḥmad b. Sulaimān al-Kisā'ī's *Rauḍat al-'Āshiq wa Nuzhat al-Wāmiq* 30
Shihāb ad-Dīn Maḥmūd's *Manāzil al-Aḥbāb wa Manāzih al-Albāb* 31
Mughulṭāi's *Wāḍiḥ al-Mubīn fī Dhikr Man Ustushhida min al-Muḥibbīn* 33
Ibn Qayyim al-Jauzīya's *Rauḍat al-Muḥibbīn wa Nuzhat al-Mushtāqīn* 34
Ibn Abī Ḥajala's *Dīwān aṣ-Ṣabāba* 38
Al-Biqā'ī's *Aswāq al-Ashwāq fī Maṣāri' al-'Ushshāq* . . 41
Dā'ūd al-Anṭākī's *Tazyīn al-Aswāq bi Tafṣīl Ashwāq al-'Ushshāq* 42
The Anonymous *As'ār al-Aswāq fī Ash'ār al-Ashwāq* . . 45
Mar'ī b. Yūsuf's *Munyat al-Muḥibbīn wa Bughyat al-'Āshiqīn* 46
As-Salaṭī's *Ṣabābat al-Mu'ānī wa Ṣabbābat al-Ma'ānī* . . 48

PART 2. THE CONTENT AND FORM OF THE WORKS

Chapter

I. The Elements or Raw Materials of the Arabic Theory of Profane Love 53
II. The Evolution of Form and Content in These Works . 67
III. The Discussion of Terms and Their Use 83

PART 3. CENTRAL DOCTRINAL OR ETHICAL ISSUES

I. The Martyrs of Love 99
II. The Great Divide: The Two Senses of "*Hawā*" and the Corollary Issues of *Ghaḍḍ an-Naẓar* vs. the *Naẓar Mubāḥ* 117

CONCLUSION 133

APPENDIX 141

Remarks on the Character and Relevance of Some Writings Not Treated in This Study.

A Chapter in the *Aṭ-Ṭibb ar-Rūḥānī* of ar-Rāzī (Rhazes) 141
An Account of a Learned Discussion of Love in Mas'ūdī's *Murūj adh-Dhahab* 142
The *Risālat Māhīyat al-'Ishq* of the Ikhwān aṣ-Ṣafā' . 143
The *Risālat aṣ-Ṣadāqa wa 'ṣ-Ṣadīq* of Abū Ḥayyān at-Tauḥīdī 144
Ibn Sīnā's *Risāla fī Māhīyat al-'Ishq* 145
A Chapter on Love in Nuwairī's *Nihāyat al-Arab fī Funūn al-Adab* 146

Table I. The Life Spans of the Authors in Chronological Relationship to One Another 148
Table II. Suwaid b. Sa'īd as Common Transmitter of the Traditions on the Martyrs 149

BIBLIOGRAPHY AND ABBREVIATIONS 153

INDEX 163

INTRODUCTION

Though love and the vicissitudes of lovers are themes which have always found a large place in the literatures of the world, discussions of the nature of love, its causes, its varieties, and its possible courses, are relatively much less frequent. In Arabic, though, as in some other languages, far outnumbered by *dīwāns* of poetry or tales about love, there exist a significant number of works on the theory of love, sacred and profane. Since, in the Islamic world, the religious motive has usually outstripped all others in stimulating the production of books, the works on the theory of mystical love far outnumber those on the theory of profane (human) love. Indeed, ethical, religious, or even mystical considerations have a place in the writings on profane love.

Most of the interest among modern scholars in the Arabic works on the theory of profane love dates from 1914, when D. K. Petrof published the first edition of the Arabic text of the *Ṭauq al-Ḥamāma*, The Dove's Neck Ring,[1] of Ibn Ḥazm al-Andalūsī from the unique manuscript in Leiden. Its appearance prompted an examination of its significance for Spanish Arabic literature and history, and led to a new interest in other books to which it could be compared or to which it bore a relationship. Ignacz Goldziher (*ZDMG*, LXIX [1915], 192–207) in his review of the Petrof edition made some brief remarks about other Arabic works on love, some profane, some mystical in their orientation. However, the lion's share of attention has always centered on the *Ṭauq al-Ḥamāma* because of its particular qualities as well as its significance for the history of Spanish literature in general and studies on the troubadors in particular. Emilio García Gómez, who since 1934 has been one of the principal contributors to the study of this type of work, has written several articles on the *Ṭauq al-Ḥamāma* and on its proven or possible relationship to certain other books, most of them on the theory of profane love.

1. Books and articles mentioned or alluded to in the Introduction will not be footnoted. They may be found in the Bibliography.

A. R. Nykl's translation of the *Ṭauq* into English in 1931, though somewhat awkward, had the great merit of making the book accessible to non-orientalists and—most importantly—to specialists in the European Middle Ages and Renaissance interested in cultural relations with the Islamic world. Nykl performed a double service because he prefaced his translation with an essay on the connections between Spanish Arabic and troubador poetry. The wide interest aroused by his book can be seen in the numerous reviews which appeared afterward in the scholarly publications of both orientalists and specialists in the European Middle Ages and Renaissance.

Translations and studies of the text benefited increasingly from revisions and emendations to the Arabic text proposed in learned reviews and articles, especially those by Ignacz Goldziher, William Marçais, Carl Brockelmann, Leon Bercher, and E. Lévi Provençal. A Russian translation by A. Salie came out next (1933), followed by a German one by Max Weisweiler (1941), an Italian translation by Francesco Gabrieli (1949), and, in the same year, a new Arabic edition with interleaved French translation was published by Leon Bercher. Next to appear were a new oriental edition by Ḥasan Kāmil Ṣayrafī (1950), a Spanish translation by Emilio García Gómez (1952), and an English translation by Arthur Arberry (1953).

However, Ibn Ḥazm's book was not the sole Arabic work on love to get attention during these years. Aḥmad 'Ubaid of Damascus published an edition of Ibn Qayyim al-Jauzīya's *Rauḍat al-Muḥibbīn*, The Garden of Lovers (1930), and Alois R. Nykl, with Ibrāhīm Tūqān, brought out an edition of Muḥammad b. Dā'ūd's *K. as-Zahra*, The Book of the Flower (1932), only one year after the appearance of Nykl's translation of the *Ṭauq al-Ḥamāma*. After these events, Hellmut Ritter thought the time ripe to call attention to this type of book as a special branch of literature. He published (*Der Islam*, XXI [1933], 84–109) an annotated two-part bibliography of the more important Arabic and Persian works on profane and on mystical love. His article was widely noticed, and among the twelve works on profane love, all in Arabic, Ritter listed several which had not previously been discussed in this connection. It is less well known that in the introduction to his edition (1959) of the *Mashāriq Anwār al-Qulūb* (Where the Light Breaks Forth in Men's Hearts), a book on the theory of mystical love by 'Abd ar-Raḥmān b. Muḥammad al-Anṣārī b. ad-Dabbāgh, he gave a revised version of his earlier list of works on the theory of profane love. His own interest and attention has centered largely on the writings on mystical love. Of his many contributions to their study, one thinks immediately of his *Das Meer der Seele*, published in 1955.

The theory of mystical love has in general received more attention over the years than the theory of profane love. Though smaller in number, the works dealing with profane love merit more attention as a group than they have gotten to date. They are important not only in the general history of Arabic literature, but also within the larger framework of the comparative history of literature. They deal with a subject of broad human concern, one close to the experience of every man. Its issues are deeply entwined with the most important values in life. It seems therefore that a study of these Arabic works would reveal something of the social, intellectual, and religious milieu of the Islamic world, both in its flowering and in its decline.

Doubts have sometimes been voiced as to whether the works on the theory of profane love, which are rather various in character, can be treated as a single group. I hope to dispose of such doubts in this study. It became clear to me in the course of my preliminary research that there were genetic relationships between these works which justified—indeed required—their study as a group. Their authors appear to have been clearly aware of themselves as contributors to a distinct literature on the subject. They speak of some of their predecessors, cite them, take material from them, or attack them.

Under the ground rules or assumptions upon which modern literary study proceeds, I think that we do not need to be timid in treating these works as a distinct branch of literature, since we can demonstrate not only their common content but also their historical or genetic relationships to each other in many cases. I think we may even call them a genre, though I have qualified this term because it may not apply in the same way to Arabic literature as it does in Western literature. One difficulty in the transfer of terms from one literary tradition to another is that what is "literature" in one tradition is not "literature" in the other. Indeed, all that Western scholars of the Islamic world (e.g. Gibb, Nicholson, and Brockelmann) have called "Arabic literature," "Persian literature," etc. would not be "literature," in the strict sense, in the eyes of modern scholars of Western literatures. To them, the distinguishing traits of "literature" are fictionality, invention, or imagination. This is intended as a descriptive not an evaluative distinction. What is not "literature" is classified as rhetoric, philosophy, political pamphleteering, theology, economics, and so forth.[2] However, this view of literature is based upon the canons of taste prevailing in Europe, where, since the Renaissance, the role of the imagination has been exalted in literary theory. Among the Arabs, imagination ranked low as a desideratum in literary effort. By such modern Western standards, the Arabic works with which we are concerned here would contain a mixture of "literature" and "non-literature" and the purpose for which they were written would be considered "non-literary." However, modern literary theorists assure us that the study of "non-literature" can and does pose problems of esthetic analysis, stylistics, or composition similar to, or the same as, those posed by "literature."[3] With that assurance in mind, perhaps we can look to modern literary theory for guidance on the question of whether or not these Arabic works on the theory of profane love constitute a "non-literary kind." (In "literature," the proper term would be "genre" or "literary kind.") Modern genre theory is descriptive and neither limits the number of possible kinds nor prescribes rules to authors. It supposes that the traditional kinds may be mixed and produce a new kind. "It sees that genres can be built up on the basis of inclusiveness or 'richness' as well as that of 'purity' (genre by accretion as well as by reduction)." Rather than emphasizing the distinction between kind and kind, it is interested both in the uniqueness of each work and in the common denominator within a kind.[4]

To make even a preliminary study of the character of the Arabic literature on the theory of profane love as a whole forces one

2. René Wellek and Austin Warren, *Theory of Literature*, 2nd ed. (New York: Harcourt, Brace, and World, 1955), 15.

3. Wellek and Warren, 15.

4. Wellek and Warren, 225.

to gather together if possible all the extant works devoted to the subject. Obviously, not all the extant Arabic works on this subject have yet been brought to light or identified as such. Therefore, the researcher must try to find works not previously known or recognized as belonging to this category and to assign them their proper historical place. I am happy that I was able to put my finger on a few new ones, at least two of them of some importance, not previously described as having a place in this group.[5]

The standards by which I decided which works should be included in the group studied here were relatively simple, though sometimes hard to apply in individual cases. The work must be chiefly about profane love and chiefly about "theory." Here "theory" covers two types of material: (1) Discussion of the essence, nature, names, causes, and kinds of love and the differences between them. (2) The *aḥwāl* of the lovers, literally, their "circumstances," a term used by the Arab authors themselves and which will be discussed further.

The word "theory" was not, as far as I know, used by the writers of these books to designate their contents. They described the contents in more specific terms. It is a usage of modern times, employed by Goldziher, Ritter, and Von Grunebaum among others. It has also been used with reference to European works on love of a similar nature, as in the title of the book *Renaissance Theory of Love* by John Charles Nelson. Other terms have been used, however, or might be proposed, though none seem so broad in connotation. "Philosophy of love," if used in its stricter sense, is the name for just one of the ingredients of this literature. Employed in the loose sense of the word, it makes an acceptable name for some of what comes under "theory." ʿAbd al-Laṭīf Sharāra published a book entitled *Falsafat al-Ḥubb ʿind al-ʿArab* which is a discussion of the Arab "philosophy of love" in the loose sense of the word, i.e. how the Arabs, past and present, have viewed love and women. "Psychology of love" and "phenomenology of love" are also parts of Arab "love

5. The more important were Marzubānī's *Kitāb ar-Riyāḍ* and Ḥuṣrī's *Kitāb al-Maṣūn*. Two others were the anonymous *Asʿār al-Aswāq fī Ashʿār al-Ashwāq* and Salaṭī's *Ṣabābat al-Muʿānī*. Discussion of these is included in Part 1.

theory." "Theories" of love, the plural, are also part of the content of these books on theory of love, much as we can have under the broad label of "theoretical physics" or "physical theory" many theories about the functionings of the universe, observed as physical phenomena. The term "nature of love" also covers only a fraction of the subject matter, that usually referred to by the authors as *māhīyat al-ʿishq* or *ḥaqīqat al-ʿishq*. The "art of love" has been used in connection with this subject, but it has several drawbacks. In the first place, "art" has the connotation of being the opposite to "theory," being the application of what is known in theory, though perhaps the art of love may be discussed in a theoretical way. The subtitle of Arberry's translation of the *Ṭauq al-Ḥamāma* was "The Art and Practice of Arab Love," which is not a particularly accurate description of the contents of the book, for over half the chapters deal not with what the lover should do, but with what happens to him, or to the two lovers, or to their love. There is a certain ambiguity, also, as to what is meant by "love" in the phrase "art of love." The English and German translators of Nafzāwī's *Rauḍ al-ʿĀṭir* (commonly called "The Perfumed Garden"), once characterized by Brockelmann as "ein sehr obscönes Buch über die Liebe," also used the words "Arab art of love" and "arabische Liebeskunst" in their subtitles.[6]

My first interest in this subject was in the development of this group of works from the point of view of the history of literature, but practical considerations seemed to demand a more limited focus. Therefore, for a time in my earlier research I turned my attention to the place of Ibn Qayyim al-Jauzīya's *Rauḍat al-Muḥibbīn* in this literature, because it seemed to be important in certain respects. As I slowly became better acquainted with the character and

6. Such ambiguities or disagreements about what is meant by the "art of love" existed among the Arabs themselves, of course. Al-Aṣmaʿī, the famous philologist (who will be discussed later) was reported, in one of several versions of the following anecdote, to have asked a bedouin lady: "What do you consider as *ʿishq* among your people?" " 'Necking' and embracing and caressing and conversation," she replied. "And how is it with you people?" When al-Aṣmaʿī described what the city Arabs did, she exclaimed, "My dear young man! That isn't *ʿishq*! That is seeking to beget a child." (See *Rauḍa*, 84.)

development of this literature as a whole, Ibn al-Qayyim and his book seemed to recede somewhat in importance but were, on the other hand, more correctly appreciated for their *faḍā'il,* or merits. I saw him less as an original thinker and more as one who brought out the essence of Arabic theory of profane love, composing a book that in several respects is the culmination of this literature. I became increasingly convinced of the fruitlessness, and indeed, the impossibility, of analyzing the character or place of any one work in this group before the outlines of the history of this literature were made clear, something that had never been done. In fact, it has not been shown that it *has* a history or even that it has some coherence as a literature.

The particular nature of these works requires that we gain an idea of their overall development as a group and their individual variety before we can understand the value or interest of any one particular work. With few exceptions, the authors are compilers to a greater or lesser degree. The basic materials of their books are sentences and paragraphs collected out of earlier written works or taken down from oral sources and passed on intact. It is what they do with these materials that is interesting. The old Arabic metaphor of "the necklace" for a literary work is apt here. Simply put, many of the authors are selecting beads out of older necklaces and restringing them with some new ones to create a certain effect. We must see how much is familiar in a work and how much is different in content, treatment, and viewpoint. Then some works can be seen as isolated or unique in certain respects, while at the same time showing the marks of the developing tradition, or some points of connection with it.

This study aims to demonstrate the essential unity and continuity of this group of works and its main lines of development in form and content from the third/ninth century to the eleventh/seventeenth century. It will describe at least briefly the character of individual works and some of the more important connections, similarities, and oppositions between them. Some of my conclusions will have to be tentative and many details will remain for future investigation, but I hope that my findings will prove a first step in the right direction and a sound basis for further study.

PART 1

SURVEY OF THE AUTHORS AND THEIR WORKS

I

SURVEY OF THE AUTHORS AND THEIR WORKS

TWO ESSAYS OF JĀḤIẒ

The famous writer Abū 'Uthmān 'Amr b. Baḥr al-Jāḥiẓ (ca. 160/776–255/868 or 869)[1] left us two essays dealing with *'ishq*. In contrast to most of the literature, they are original in that they present primarily the author's own thought, rather than a body of material selected and commented upon. The short "Risāla fi 'l-'Ishq wa 'n-Nisā'," [2] Treatise on Passionate Love and Woman, discussed the meaning of *'ishq* as a word, and its proper use, demonstrating that passionate love, *'ishq*, is a feeling evoked in men by women and by nothing else, and that a man's love for his womenfolk takes

1. *GAL*, G. I, 152–53; S. I, 239–247. Charles Pellat, art. "al-Djāḥiẓ," *EI²*, and *Le milieu baṣrien et la formation de Ǧāḥiẓ* (Paris: Adrien-Maisonneuve, 1953). Two dates separated by a virgule as they are here represent the Muslim *hijrī* (A.H.) date followed by the Christian (A.D.) date.

2. Abū 'Uthmān 'Amr b. Baḥr al-Jāḥiẓ, "Risāla fi 'l-'Ishq wa 'n-Nisā'," *Majmū'at Rasā'il* (In one vol. with *Kitāb al-Bukhalā'*; Cairo: Maṭba'at al-Jumhūr, 1323/1905), 161–169. For an English translation, abridged, of this essay and the "Risālat al-Qiyān," see Charles Pellat, ed., *The Life and Works of Jāḥiẓ*, translated from the French of Pellat by D. M. Hawke ("The Islamic World;" Berkeley and Los Angeles: University of California Press, 1969). The original French edition, and a German translation from the French by Walter W. Müller, *Arabische Geisteswelt* ("Bibliothek des Morgenlandes") are both published by Artemis Verlag of Zürich, 1967.

priority in his life and scale of values. Thus his title, unlike many in Arabic literature, indicates exactly the nature of what he has to say: he is proving the specific relationship between *ʿishq* and woman. He also has other important remarks to make on the subject of *ʿishq*, as we shall see later.

His remarkable "Risālat al-Qiyān,"[3] The Treatise on Singing Girls, is a longer and more sustained discussion of love as the subject is related to the pleasures and perils of the entertainments offered by the *qiyān*. In the midst of his shrewd analysis of these professional givers of pleasure, the responses of their clients, and the factors at work there, he takes time out to distinguish more clearly than he did in the "Risāla fi ʾl-ʿIshq wa ʾn-Nisāʾ" the difference between *ḥubb*, *hawā*, and *ʿishq* and the relationship between them.

The occasion for the essay on *qiyān* and love was created by the attacks of some orthodox Sunnites whom Jāḥiẓ contemptuously refers to as "*Ḥashwīya*." These were not the crude anthropomorphists later designated by that name, but learned religious conservatives.[4] In their eyes, Jāḥiẓ and his friends were libertines and sinners because they owned and enjoyed the professional singers and dancers. Jāḥiẓ defends the licitness of such pleasure and undertakes to show the ridiculousness of his opponents' viewpoint, demonstrating the discrepancy between the standards of conduct they demand and the known conduct of the most exemplary early Muslims where women were concerned. Here, in the first Arabic writings we have on the theory of profane love, Jāḥiẓ takes a position on those ethical questions which never ceased to exercise his successors and were, indeed, to form the chief area of controversy down through the history of this literature. Every writer reveals an attitude toward these matters, whether by his choice of material or by what he himself says or, sometimes, what he refrains from saying.

3. Al-Jāḥiẓ, "Risālat al-Qiyān," *Thalāth Rasāʾil*, ed. J. Finkel (Cairo: Maṭbaʿat as-Salafīya, 1382/1962–63), 54–76. Charles Pellat, "Les esclaves-chanteuses de Ǧāḥiẓ," *Arabica*, X (1963), 121–147. (A French translation with notes.) The *qiyān* seem to have been a popular topic for essays in the third century. As-Sarakhsī wrote one as we shall see, and so also did al-Washshāʾ, neither extant as far as I know.
4. See Pellat, *Arabica*, X (1963), 130, n. 1, and *EI* and *EI²* *s.v.* "Ḥashwīya."

AN ANONYMOUS AND UNTITLED ESSAY ON LOVE CONTAINING A QUOTE FROM AḤMAD B. AṬ-ṬAYYIB AS-SARAKHSĪ

This essay, comprising only three closely written folios,[5] is said by its author to be unprecedented. It sets out to analyze the meaning, essence, nature, and cause of love. The author has had the perspicacity to see that any discussion of the essence and meaning of love must proceed from some clear concept of the nature of man and what faculties there are within man that are involved in loving. Part of the variety and confusion of ideas about love in this literature on profane love stems from the fact that if the authors have clear notions about the nature and psychological structure of man, they do not usually have much to say about it. They use certain terms such as *nafs*, *rūḥ*, *qalb*, *ʿaql*, and *ḥiss* in their own ways. Given the large variety of theories about these matters current at various times in the Islamic world,[6] it is not surprising that many of the statements about love do not seem to be based upon common premises. This anonymous writer first explains some of his premises. In a few sentences, he outlines man in terms of soul, spirit, mind, senses, imagination, memory, and so forth. In his eyes, the *nafs nāṭiqa* (reasoning soul) of the philosophers, the *rūḥ* (soul) of the theologians, and the *qalb* (heart) of the mystics are the same, and this is the part of man which loves and is loved. After this beginning, the essay proceeds in the form of an imagined dialogue: "And if you ask, . . . then I would say, ..."

Franz Rosenthal once called attention to this essay, part of a *majmūʿa*, because of the fragment from a work of Aḥmad b. aṭ-Ṭayyib as-Sarakhsī that he found at its conclusion. He discussed the fragment but not the essay itself, except for its subject and the claim of the anonymous author that he was the first to write in this

5. Top Kapı Saray, Ahmet III 3483, folios 238a–240b.

6. See E. E. Calverly, art. "Nafs," *EI*[1] and *SEI*.

vein.[7] Rosenthal mentions several of the most interesting titles in the manuscript which are dated by their copyists. This anonymous essay on love also contains a date, I believe. The date A.H. 769 (A.D. 1367–1368), written out, can be made out on the last line of folio 240b, but I have not been able so far to decipher the copyist's name.[8]

The original character of the essay, except for the single quote from as-Sarakhsī, gives the impression that the essay is a relatively early one. Among later writers on love, there was a strong tendency to quote predecessors rather than to formulate their own views. A careful analysis by someone thoroughly familiar with the varieties of Islamic philosophy and their historical development might at least identify the man's allegiances, but my inquiries to date in that direction have not produced any conclusions.

The quotation on love from Aḥmad b. aṭ-Ṭayyib as-Sarakhsī (c. 218–222/833–837 to 286/899) that comes at the end of the essay is said to be from the *Tathbīt Amr an-Nujūm wa Ajzā' al-Ḥikma wa Asrā(r)?*[9] *an-Nafs*. Rosenthal is reasonably certain that this is to be identified with the book entitled *Kitāb Arkān al-Falsafa wa Tathbīt Aḥkām an-Nujūm,* mentioned by Ibn Rustah, though he expresses mild surprise that a discussion on love should have been found in a work that presumably dealt mainly with astrology. In the books on the theory of profane love and on friendship, however, we often find theories detailing how love is determined by the position and movements of the stars and planets. They decide who shall be soul-mates, and, some say, determine the character of their love. Therefore, it would not be strange to find a discussion of love in the pages of a book dealing with astrology.

7. Franz Rosenthal, "From Arabic Books and Manuscripts VIII: As-Sarakhsī on Love," *JAOS*, LXXXI (1961), 222–24. Though listed as a *majmū'a* at the library, the MS is not a *majmū'a* in the proper sense of the word, since it is made up of a number of short MSS of different dates bound together.

8. He is also the copyist of folio 241, containing a fragment of an essay in Persian, which seems to break off at the end of that folio. The next folio has been left blank.

9. The problematic word in the MS looks like "*isrā'*" (folio 240a, line 17). Rosenthal transcribes it as above, "*asrār*" with a question mark (*JAOS*, LXXXI [1961], 223). A few lines from this same passage occur in somewhat altered form in *Wāḍiḥ*, 41.

Briefly, as-Sarakhsī's words have to do with a theory of how two souls who love each other and aspire to the strongest kind of union can achieve this. Physically, both being within living bodies which are their instruments but which also separate them, they can achieve this only approximately. Kissing offers the nearest contact with the soul of the beloved, because it is the mouth and nostrils which carry the breath which has had recent contact with his nature and the powers of his soul. "Therefore the soul seeks the beloved through the mouth, kissing and deriving through the nostrils the breath coming from the beloved . . . so that the two substances are united and the two powers be joined."[10] They may also encounter one another through the pores of the skin, as they embrace each other. This recalls a much more complicated theory attributed by Ibn al-Jauzī to "*ḥukamā' al-awā'il*" (the philosophers of the Ancients), probably some Hellenistic source, which details the physiology of the process whereby *'ishq* is engendered when two persons who love one another breathe one another's breath or swallow a drop of one another's saliva while kissing. It traces the received substance through the body and accounts for its effect.[11] Beyond these means, as-Sarakhsī suggests the union of the two souls through the uniting of their two wills and seems to think that this is the most sure kind of union.

Aḥmad b. aṭ-Ṭayyib as-Sarakhsī,[12] probably born in Sarakhs as his name indicates, was a pupil of al-Kindī, the "philosopher of the Arabs," and a *rāwī* (oral transmitter) from al-Kindī, as was Muḥammad b. Dā'ūd, the author of the *Kitāb az-Zahra*.[13] There is a strong likelihood that they knew each other. As-Sarakhsī wrote a *Kitāb al-'Ishq*, which has not survived and which Rosenthal thinks is almost certainly of philosophical content and not an *adab*

10. Rosenthal, *JAOS*, LXXXI (1961), 223. Arabic text in MS Ahmet III 3843, folio 240b.

11. *Dhamm al-Hawā* (Cairo: Dār al-Kutub al-Ḥadītha, 1381/1962), 305.

12. See Rosenthal, *Aḥmad b. aṭ-Ṭayyib as-Sarakhsī* ("American Oriental Series," Vol. 26; New Haven: American Oriental Society, 1943), which contains all known information about him and surviving fragments of his writings, otherwise all lost.

13. Louis Massignon "Notion de 'l'essentiel Désir'," *Opera Minora*, ed. Y. Moubarac (Beirut: Dar al-Maaref-Liban, 1963), II, 248, citing aṣ-Ṣūlī, *Akhbār Abī Tammām*, 65.

book, presumably because of Sarakhsī's reputed eminence as a philosopher.[14] According to Ibn Abī Uṣaibiʿa's *ʿUyūn al-Anbā'*, as-Sarakhsī wrote a *Kitāb al-Qiyān*, The Book of Singing Girls.[15] If he did write such a book, he makes a third with al-Washshā' in the third century. As-Sarakhsī was in charge of the *ḥisba* in Baghdad before the end of his life, and so we know that he moved both among the leading scholars of the day and among the most powerful officials of the caliph in a time of great luxury and lavish worldly entertainments. He would have been as well qualified as any man to comment upon the *qiyān*, perhaps inspired by the older Jāḥiẓ but taking his own approach. Where the caliph's personal or state secrets were concerned, it is possible that he knew too much, for after he had become a favorite, Muʿtaḍid suddenly ordered all his possessions confiscated and had him thrown in prison, where he died mysteriously on an unknown day and in an unknown manner.

MUḤAMMAD B. DĀ'UD'S "KITĀB AZ-ZAHRA"

Abū Bakr Muḥammad b. Dā'ūd al-Iṣfahānī (255/868–297/910),[16] son of the founder of the Ẓāhirī school of jurisprudence, was gifted with a precocious intelligence and a sure memory. At the death of his father in 270/883, when Ibn Dā'ūd was scarcely sixteen, he succeeded his father as head of the Ẓāhirīs. Those who thought it

14. Rosenthal, 55, citing *Murūj*, VIII, 179–180.

15. Rosenthal wonders whether it is actually "*Kitāb al-Qiyān*" or whether it should be read "*Kitāb al-Qiyās*," The Book of Analogical Reasoning. (Rosenthal, 55, citing Ibn Abī Uṣaibiʿa, I, 215.)

16. *GAL*, S. I, 249–250. *Murūj*, VIII, 254–55; *Ta'r. Bagh.*, V, 256–63; Yāfiʿī, *Mir. al-Jan.*, II, 228–30; b. Khall., II, 681. See also the recent article, "Ibn Dāwūd," *EI*², by J.-C. Vadet.

In transliterating the name "Dā'ūd" thus, I follow the injunction that it must be pronounced thus with the long *a*, the *hamza*, and long *u* regardless of how variously it is written in the manuscript sources, often without the *hamza*. See W. Wright, *A Grammar of the Arabic Language* (Cambridge: Cambridge University Press, 1955), I, 18D.

ridiculous that a mere adolescent should take on such a responsibility were soon won over, having been convinced of his sagacity.[17] The titles of some of his works on Islamic law and Ẓāhirī doctrine are preserved for us though the works themselves have not survived. Among them were scholarly polemics against several persons, including Ibn Jarīr aṭ-Ṭabarī, the famous historian and legal scholar.[18]

As one of the two chief jurisconsults of the city of Baghdad at the time when the Vizier Ibn al-Furat resolved to arrest and try al-Ḥallāj, Ibn Dā'ūd was called upon for a *fatwā* (formal legal opinion). He concluded that it would be licit to put al-Ḥallāj to death for heresy, an opinion that gained increasing support as time went on.[19] The other jurist, Ibn Suraij, chief of the Shāfi'ites in Baghdad, declined competence in the case. Thus, Ibn Dā'ūd played a role in bringing about the execution of the mystic, although the event did not actually take place until twelve years after his own demise.

In his own lifetime, as well as afterward, Ibn Dā'ūd was considered to be as much a learned literary figure as a jurisprudent. His *Kitāb az-Zahra*, The Book of the Flower, achieved great fame while he was alive. In testimony to this, there are a number of literary traditions in which he is addressed in the street or in a learned disputation, and asked a question about a phrase or verse of his in the *Kitāb az-Zahra*.[20] Ibn Dā'ūd dedicated the book to a dear friend, not named, for whom he felt a fervent and sincere affection but who he felt was treating him badly. As was common knowledge at the time, this friend was Muḥammad b. Jāmi' aṣ-Ṣaidalānī.[21] Ibn Dā'ūd describes his book as a kind of ideal boon companion (*nadīm*) which will respond to Ibn Jāmi''s every mood.

17. See the anecdote describing how his wisdom was put to the test, *Ta'r. Bagh.*, V, 256.
18. *Murūj*, VIII, 255; *Fihrist*, 217.
19. The possible reasons for his stand are discussed by Massignon, *La Passion d'al-Hallāj* (Paris: Paul Geuthner, 1922), I, 161–182 and *Opera Minora*, II, 249, but see my remarks on Massignon's interpretation below, in Part 2, Chap. 11, n. 8.
20. *Ta'r. Bagh.*, V, 259–261; *al-Maṣūn*, folio 50b.
21. See *Maṣāri'*, II, 223. *Ta'r. Bagh.*, V, 260,

He intends in the first fifty chapters to deal with the successive aspects of love, its principles, vicissitudes, and states, and in the last fifty with various other themes for poetry.[22]

Besides this, he asks God that the attractive contents might change the views of those who reject passionate love, *hawā*, and bring them to a proper understanding of it, so that no rational and intelligent person might henceforth feel obliged to condemn it nor any *imām* (here: religious leader) speak against it. Nevertheless, he says, this is not one of those articles of belief which are established only by proofs. Rather, an affinity for this sort of love is something characteristic of persons distinguished by the gentleness of their natures and the harmony of their souls. One who is like them will excuse them, and one who is not of their kind will speak harshly of them. So, though he hopes his beautiful book will help the reader to see *hawā* in a positive light, he suspects that only those who are capable of loving in this way will understand.[23]

The *Kitāb az-Zahra* is a large book. The fifty chapters on love amount to 366 well-filled manuscript pages. It is perhaps just as well for the modern reputation of the book that Nykl did not know that the second half was extant when he undertook to edit the first half as a work on love. The first half deserves to stand alone as a complete work in itself; it is more attractive without the second half, which has little relation to the half on love.

According to the traditional account, quoted many times in the books on love theory, Ibn Dā'ūd became a "martyr of love," killed by pure but violent yearning for his friend. This report, which became a controversial document in the later discussions on the ethics of love and the "martyrs of love," was given by a close friend, Nifṭawayh, who said:

> *I went in to see Muḥammad b. Dā'ūd al-Iṣbahānī during the illness in which he died and I said to him, "How do you feel?" He said, "Love of you-know-who has brought upon me*

22. Abū Bakr Muḥammad b. Abī Sulaimān Dā'ūd al-Iṣfahānī, *Kitāb al-Zahrah*, The First Half, ed. A. R. Nykl in collaboration with Ibrāhīm Ṭūqān ("Studies in Ancient Oriental Civilization," No. 6; Chicago: University of Chicago Press, 1932), 4.
23. *Zahra*, 4–5.

what you see!" So I said to him, "What prevents you from enjoying him, as long as you have the power to do so?" He said, "Enjoyment has two aspects: One of them is the permitted gaze and the other is the forbidden pleasure. As for the permitted gaze, it has brought upon me the condition that you see, and as for the forbidden pleasure, something my father told me has kept me from it: He said, [here follows a chain of transmitters] '. . . the Prophet said . . . "He who loves passionately and conceals his secret and remains chaste and patient, God will forgive him and make him enter Paradise," ' " . . . . and [says Nifṭawayh, after repeating some verses which Ibn Dā'ūd recited to him on that occasion] he died that very night or perhaps it was the next day.[24]

A. R. Nykl thought that Ibn Dā'ūd's "philosophy of love" as expressed in the *Kitāb az-Zahra* was much weaker than that of Ibn Ḥazm, author of the *Ṭauq al-Ḥamāma*. He pointed out that Ibn Ḥazm had the advantage of greater maturity and more experience of life when he wrote his book, whereas Ibn Dā'ūd was but a youth when he wrote his *Kitāb az-Zahra*.[25] However, one must bear in mind that the authors plainly set out to write two very different types of book. The *Kitāb az-Zahra* is mainly an anthology of poetry on love containing critical comment, passages about the psychology of love and its pathology, and theories about its origin. In contrast, the *Ṭauq al-Ḥamāma* is primarily a prose work on the theory of profane love—how love begins and progresses, how a love affair is conducted, and how it may end—with occasional selections of poetry illustrating the subject under discussion.

In Nykl's view, the principal value of the *Kitāb az-Zahra* is that it is a well-chosen collection of excellent verses on one subject, love,[26] culled from earlier and contemporary poets. As an anthology (and

24. *Ta'r. Bagh.*, V, 262.
25. Nykl says, "not much over twenty years of age." (*Zahra*, foreword, 7.) However, in *Ta'r. Bagh.*, V, 259, Ibn Dā'ūd is quoted as saying that he began to write it while he was still a school boy ("*wa 'anā fī 'l-kuttāb*"), and that his father reviewed most of it, thus dating that much of it no later than his sixteenth year, when his father died.
26. At the time that he prepared his edition, Nykl thought that Ibn Dā'ūd had never written the second half of his book, *not* about love. Later, it came to light. See Carlo A. Nallino, *O.M.*, XIII (1933), 490, and Nykl, *al-Andalus*, IV, (1936), 147–54.

dated about A.D. 890), it stands in time between the *Kitāb al-Ḥamāsa* of Abū Tammām and that of al-Buḥturī and the *Kitāb al-Aghānī*.[27] What distinguishes the *Kitāb az-Zahra* from other works of that period, besides its special subject, is that Ibn Dā'ūd subjects some of the verses to comment and literary criticism.

Some of the poetry is his own, hidden under the pseudonym *ba'ḍ ahl hādhā al-'aṣr*, though he may have used other pseudonyms, too.[28] In it, he constantly complains of his friend's ill treatment of him. As poetry, some of it is excellent. His prose, however, is another matter. Says Nykl:

> *I cannot say much in favor of Ibn Dâwoud's prose, unless we assume that it has been seriously tampered with by copyists. It does present a good many examples of sonorous* saj' *[rhymed prose], but too often it is hopelessly muddled as to thought and logic. He evidently wishes to appear very deep, but only succeeds in being obscure.*[29]

Nevertheless, one must agree with Louis Massignon that the book is "précieux pour la connaissance de la vie sentimentale de ce temps: rien ne peut mieux nous dire quelle était à Baghdad l'opinion des esprits lettrés et cultivés, sur ce sujet perdurable qu'est l'amour."[30]

It is also important in the history of the literature on the theory of love. Muḥammad b. Dā'ūd lived in that time when Arabic literature burst into full flower under the competing influence of Hellenism, Persian tradition, and orthodox reaction against these two. From his above-mentioned remarks about those who condemn *hawā* and from other things which he has to say in his introduction, we know that he is carefully considering what the conservative theologians will say when they see his book. As to Hellenism, he is the first of the Arabic writers on love theory (whose work we have) to quote the opinions of Greek thinkers. He cites at length from Plato, Ptolemy, Galen, and an unnamed physician, undoubtedly

27. See *Zahra*, Foreword, 2.
28. See *Murūj*, VIII, 255.
29. *Zahra*, Foreword, 5.
30. Massignon, *Passion*, I, 173.

Greek.[31] The arrangement and content of the book did more to set a pattern for later books on love than has generally been recognized or admitted.[32]

AL-WASHSHĀ'’S “KITĀB AL-MUWASHSHĀ”

We have only meager information on Abū ’ṭ-Ṭayyib Muḥammad b. Aḥmad b. Isḥāq al-Washshā’ al-A‘rābī (ca. 246/860–325/936).[33] It is not even certain whether the *laqab* “al-Washshā’” belonged to him or to his father. The few biographical sources and even the Leiden manuscript of the work are inconsistent on this point.[34] The nickname “al-Washshā’,” meaning “vendor of richly variegated cloth,” may have been applied to the author in a metaphorical sense, and it is even possible that he received this name from the title of his book. The second *laqab* “al-A‘rābī” seems to indicate that he was of bedouin extraction.[35] That he studied with some of the most distinguished grammarians of that day is indicated in the *Kitāb al-Muwashshā* when he quotes directly Tha‘lab and al-Mubarrad, the principal scholars of the rival schools of Kūfa and Baṣra. Judging from the character of the works attributed to him, he seems to have been more a writer of belles-lettres than a grammarian, since his works of the former type outnumber the latter about four

31. Most of these are found in *Zahra*, 15–19. I cannot say whether he is correct in his attributions or accurate in his quotations. After Ibn Dā’ūd, such statements attributed to Greek or Hellenistic sources are common in such works. In some cases the same statement has been attributed to several different sources. An example of this is one of these quotations in the *Kitāb az-Zahra*, attributed to “a physician” (p. 17). See also Part 2, Chap. 1, n. 26.

32. See beginning of Part 2, Chap. 11.

33. *GAL*, G. I, 124; S. I, 189. *Fihrist*, 85; *Ta’r. Bagh.*, I, 253; *Irshād*, VI, 277–78; Suyūṭī, *Bughya*, 7.

34. See Rudolph E. Brünnow, ed., *K. al-Muwashshā* (Leiden: E. J. Brill, 1886), Introd., iii–iv.

35. Brünnow, iii–iv.

to one.[36] Though he got his living by teaching in an elementary school in Baghdad, he was invited to give lectures in the caliph's palace.

The book sets forth what the man of polite education, the *ẓarīf* or the *adīb*, should know.[37] The first thirteen chapters deal with the two most essential qualities of polite behavior: *adab* (chapters 1–9), and manly honor, *murūwa* (chapters 10–12),[38] but most of the book encompasses the subject of *ẓarf*, a comprehensive ideal of elegant, civilized conduct. The *ẓarf/adab* ideal imposes standards of decency, manners, and emotional behavior. An integral part of this code were the concepts of idealized and chaste (ʿUdhrī) love. About one-third of the book, chapters 15–22, deals directly with the subject of love, and much of the rest is concerned with prescribing the conduct, dress, ornament, and food which will convey the proper impression or message to others—associates, friends, or the beloved. The conventions of idealized love underlie or color the most mundane relationships and social activities.[39] Herein lies the significance of the book. It reveals the connection between the first writings on the theory of profane love and the code of social conduct in the centers of power and culture, a code based upon civilized and chivalrous love—I would like to say "courtly love," but the term was invented for a later European phenomenon, and has even been questioned recently as a proper term there.[40]

The first to suggest (in 1951) that this book should be treated primarily as a book on profane love and studied in connection with the other works in this group was García Gómez, who proposed some possible connections and parallels between the text of the *K. al-*

36. Brünnow, iv–v, citing *Fihrist*, 85.
37. See M. F. Ghazi, "Un groupe social: 'Les Raffinés' (Ẓurafā')," *Studia Islamica*, XI (1959), 39–71.
38. Not to be confused with the pagan ideal denoted by the same word. See Gustave von Grunebaum, *Medieval Islam*, 2nd ed. (Chicago: University of Chicago Press, 1953), 254.
39. Parallels could readily be found in modern social conventions, entertainment media, advertising practice, and so on.
40. See E. Talbot Donaldson, "The Myth of Courtly Love," *Ventures: Magazine of the Yale Graduate School*, V, No. 2, pp. 16–24.

Muwashshā and that of the *Ṭauq al-Ḥamāma.*[41] He thought that up to that time it had been treated as a book on elegant manners and had not been recognized for what it is, essentially, a book on love.[42] However, it ought to be noted that Von Grunebaum, though saying nothing about its position vis-à-vis other books, recognized fully its significance as a manual of love à la mode, for he used it as such in his *Medieval Islam,* a book first published in 1946.[43] Nevertheless, García Gómez was right, apparently, in complaining that in the long span of time—almost three generations—since Brünnow's edition appeared, scholars had largely neglected the *Kitāb al-Muwashshā* and it had remained inexplicably obscure.

AL-KHARĀ'IṬĪ'S "I'TILĀL AL-QULŪB"

Both as an author and as a man, Abū Bakr Muḥammad b. Ja'far al-Kharā'iṭī as-Sāmarrī (d. 327/938)[44] seems cloaked in the obscurity of time. His *I'tilāl al-Qulūb* more than anything else, seems to have fixed him in the memories of the scholarly community. Biographical sources report that he was originally "from the people of Surra Man Ra'ā (Sāmarra)," but exactly where and when he was born we do not know. He lived in Syria for some time, they say, went to Damascus in 325, and died in 'Asqalān in 327.

His *I'tilāl al-Qulūb,* The Malady of Hearts, is a work of modest size, the only complete manuscript of it, Ulu Cami 1535, being a book of only 125 folios. Al-Kharā'iṭī was a contemporary of Muḥammad b. Dā'ūd and of al-Ash'arī, the theologian (d. 324/935), and his book no doubt represents the response of the pious and orthodox to the

41. See García Gómez, "Un precedente y una consecuencia del 'Collar de la Paloma,' " *al-Andalus,* XVI (1951), 309–23, on *Kitāb al-Muwashshā.*

42. García Gómez, *And.,* XVI (1951), 309–10, 313–14.

43. See Von Grunebaum, 256, 311–12.

44. *GAL,* S. I, 250. *Ta'r. Bagh.,* II, 139–40; Sam'ānī, 192a–b; *Sh.Dh.,* II, 309; *Irshād,* VI, 464; Ṣafadī, Teil 2, 296.

conduct and writings of persons like Ibn Dā'ūd. Al-Kharā'iṭī is one of those religious leaders, mentioned by Ibn Dā'ūd, who condemn *hawā*. Chapter Seven of his treatise is, in fact, entitled "On the Condemnation of *Hawā* and the Following of It."[45]

The book is largely a collection of traditions, very short anecdotes, and verses on the subject of the malady of love, gathered for the guidance and edification of the reader. It is worth noting that the author lived about two generations after the compilers of the six canonical books of traditions, in a period when innumerable compilations of Ḥadīth[46] were being produced. It is therefore possible that al-Kharā'iṭī was not the first to write a book on love based on Ḥadīth, but his is the first to come to light. Four centuries later, Ibn al-Jauzī, Ibn Qayyim al-Jauzīya, and Mughulṭāi cite him as an authority on love theory. The resemblance between the structure of his book and that of later books, particularly Ibn al-Jauzī's *Dhamm al-Hawā*, is also worth examining.[47]

AL-MARZUBĀNĪ'S "KITĀB AR-RIYĀḌ"

Abū 'Abd Allāh (or Abū 'Ubaid Allāh) Muḥammad b. 'Imrān b. Mūsā al-Marzubānī (296–7/909–10—384/993 or 378/987),[48] son of the representative of the governor of Khurāsān, was born at the court at Baghdad in the same year that Ibn Dā'ūd, author of the *Kitāb*

45. MS Ulu Cami 1535, folios 12a–13a.
46. The term "Ḥadīth" usually means the formal traditions reporting the doings and sayings of the Prophet. See *EI*², *s.v.* The verbal text of the account (*matn*) is preceded by the *isnād*, the names of the chain of persons who transmitted the report. In some contexts, we will speak also of the collecting of another kind of tradition (in Arabic usually *khabar*, pl. *akhbār*, which can also mean Ḥadīth, however). These are brief accounts of the sayings or doings of someone collected for their literary or historical interest and also accompanied by *isnāds*.
47. See Part 2, Chap. 11.
48. *GAL*, S. I, 190–91. *Ta'r. Bagh.*, III, 135; *Fihrist*, 132–33; *Irshād*, VII, 50–52; b. Khall., No. 619 (I, 642); Sam'ānī, 521a; Ṣafadī (in introduction to Teil 1); *Sh.Dh.*, III, 11.

az-Zahra, died. Al-Kharā'iṭī and al-Washshā' were older contemporaries who died when al-Marzubānī was young. He specialized in *akhbār* (probably the transmission of historical and biographical information) and the collecting and relating of literary traditions. In his doctrinal views, he was a Mu'tazilī. Only a few of his many works have come down to us and of these his *Mu'jam ash-Shu'arā'* is most familiar to modern scholars, largely because it has been published and is a useful reference work.[49]

Al-Marzubānī used to work at his own home, which was sometimes thronged with as many as fifty scholar-guests staying with him. He was a prodigious writer, and it was reported that he used to sit all day with a bottle of ink and a bottle of *nabīdh* (date wine) in front of him, dipping his pen in the one and sipping from the other. Once, when Aḍūd ad-Daula, who regarded him highly, asked how he was, al-Marzubānī replied, "How would a person feel who was between two long-necked bottles?"[50] 'Alī b. Ayyūb al-Qummī, who related many traditions on his authority, said that he was regarded by some as a better stylist than Jāḥiẓ.[51]

Among the scholars from whom al-Marzubānī collected traditions were Abū Bakr b. Duraid and Abū 'Abd Allāh Nifṭawayh,[52] bosom friend and *rāwī* of Ibn Dā'ūd, the author of the *Kitāb az-Zahra*,[53] as well as Muḥammad b. Yaḥyā aṣ-Ṣūlī.[54] Among those who received traditions from him or exchanged them with him were Abū 'Umar Muḥammad b. al-'Abbās b. Ḥayawayh al-Khazzāz and Abū Bakr b. Shādhān. These names are among those occurring very frequently in *isnāds* throughout the literature on the theory of profane love.

49. Ed. F. Krenkow (Cairo, 1354/1935). It might be noted (see *GAL*) that al-Marzubānī made a large collection of the compositions of women poets, *Ash'ār an-Nisā'*, of which only one section seems to have survived in a Cairo manuscript.

50. "Kaifa ḥāl man huwa bain qarūratain?" (*Ta'r. Bagh.*, III, 136.) In evaluating this story, one should keep in mind that the author of this account, al-Khaṭīb al-Baghdādī, was orthodox and did not like the Shi'ite and Mu'tazilite tendencies attributed to al-Marzubānī. Thus he might tend to quote unfavorable rumors or stories about al-Marzubānī.

51. See *Ta'r. Bagh.*, III, 135. I am so far unable to identify this particular al-Qummī, though his name may be found throughout the *Maṣāri'* as a transmitter.

52. Ibn Duraid: *GAL*, G. I, 111; S. I, 172–74. Nifṭawayh: *GAL*, S. I, 173, n. 2, 184.

53. See *Ta'r. Bagh.*, III, 135.

54. *Maṣāri'*, *passim*. *GAL*, G. I, 143; S. I, 218–19.

The *isnād* of the famous story about the "martyrdom" of Ibn Dā'ūd, for example, reads, "'Alī b. Ayyūb al-Qummī on the authority of Ibn Shādhān, Ibn Ḥayawayh, and al-Marzubānī [all three] on the authority of Nifṭawayh, who said . . . ."[55] In the *Maṣāri' al-'Ushshāq*, written about a century later, al-Marzubānī appears frequently as the third authority (backwards in time) in a chain of transmitters. He should not be confused with Abū Bakr Muḥammad b. Khalaf b. al-Marzubān al-Muḥawwalī,[56] who died when al-Marzubānī was eleven or twelve years old and who appears perhaps three times as often in the same position as the third authority in an *isnād*. Both men related traditions to Ibn Ḥayawayh.

Not only does al-Marzubānī's name occur regularly as an oral transmitter of materials on love and lovers, but there are three quotations I have found in later works on love attributed to a written work of his called the *Kitāb ar-Riyāḍ*,[57] or in other places the *Kitāb al-Mutayyamīn*.[58] As far as I know, no work carrying either of these titles is extant, but Ibn an-Nadīm in his *Fihrist* gives a *K. ar-Riyāḍ* among the works of al-Marzubānī, indicating it as a book of 3,000 pages (!), the only one he wrote on love. It contained the stories told about the *mutayyamīn*, those enslaved by love, amongst the pre-Islamic poets, the Islamic poets, and those whose lives spanned both periods. In it, al-Marzubānī also speaks of *ḥubb* and its ramifications, its beginning and its end, what the philologists say about its names, its types, and the derivations of

55. *Ta'r. Bagh.*, V, 262. I have not yet succeeded in identifying Ibn Shādhān.

56. *GAL*, G. I, 125; S. I, 189–90. The true identities of the two men and the frequency and consistency of their appearance might not be instantly apparent to the casual reader of the *Maṣāri'*, because their names appear in a number of shortened forms, combining different elements of them. Thus, al-Marzubānī appears as Muḥammad b. 'Imrān, Abū 'Ubaid Allāh Muḥammad b. 'Imrān, Muḥammad b. 'Imrān al-Marzubānī, etc. Ibn al-Marzubān appears as Muḥammad b. Khalaf, Abū Bakr b. al-Marzubān, etc.

57. Shihāb ad-Dīn Maḥmūd b. Sulaimān b. Fahd, *Manāzil al-Aḥbāb* (Leiden Or. 1069), folio 23b.

58. 'Alā' ad-Dīn Abū 'Abd Allāh Mughulṭāi, *Al-Wāḍiḥ al-Mubīn fī Dhikr Man Ustushhida min al-Muḥibbīn*, ed. O. Spies ("Bonner Orientalistische Studien," 18. Heft; Stuttgart: W. Kohlhammer, 1936), 33. Muḥyī ad-Dīn b. Taqī ad-Dīn Abū Bakr as-Salaṭī, *Ṣabābat al-Mu'ānī wa Mathābat al-Ma'ānī* (Chester Beatty 4990), folio 17b.

these names, with quotations from the poetry of those three classes of poets as textual evidence.[59] It seems clear from this description of the *K. ar-Riyāḍ* that it is the same work sometimes referred to later as the *K. al-Mutayyamīn*, a name which gave a better indication of the contents than the original name, which is rather vague. There have been many a "*rauḍa*" and "*riyāḍ*" in the titles of Arabic books dealing with nearly every subject.

Ibn an-Nadīm's description suggests that the work belongs to the category which we call theory of profane love. It conforms to the pattern found in the majority of the works which we will discuss. It contains both (1) a discussion of such matters as the nature, kinds, and names of love and (2) the *aḥwāl* (circumstances) of the lovers, at the very least the *aḥwāl* of being a poet and a *mutayyam* and belonging to one of the three time categories given to poets, i.e., pre-Islamic, Islamic, or living in the late pre-Islamic and early Islamic times. Occupation or status in life, which was presumed to make one susceptible to certain types of love, was one type of *ḥal* grouping for the stories of lovers. Others were degrees of love or outcomes—to be a *mutayyam* was to have reached a certain very advanced stage—and categories of time such as the Jāhilīya (pre-Islamic) or "men of our time."

The conclusion that the *K. ar-Riyāḍ* had a place in the succession of works we are considering in this study is supported by a consideration of the three fragments I have found. Each is typical of the subject matter of the books on the theory of profane love. The fragment found in Mughulṭāi's *Al-Wāḍiḥ al-Mubīn* reads:

> *And in the* Kitāb al-Mutayyamīn *of al-Marzubānī: Someone said to Zuhair al-Madīnī, "What is* 'ishq?" *He said, "Madness and submissiveness, and it is the malady of refined people* [ahl aẓ-ẓarf]." *And he* [*al-Marzubānī, probably*] *said, "A person ardently in love looked at his beloved and violent emotion overcame him and he fainted, so someone present asked a learned man, 'What happened to him?' He said, 'He looked at the one he loved and his heart dilated greatly and then the body*

59. *Fihrist*, 133.

was agitated by the great dilatation of the heart.' So someone said to him, 'We love our children and our spouses and nothing like that happens to us.' He answered, 'That is the love that comes from the mind [maḥabbat al-'aql, *or rational love*], *but this is the love that comes from the soul* [maḥabbat ar-rūḥ, *or spirited love*].' "[60]

The quotation in Shihāb ad-Dīn Maḥmūd's book, *Manāzil al-Aḥbāb*, reads, "And al-Marzubānī in the *Kitāb ar-Riyāḍ* relates via several different chains of transmitters on the authority of Ibn 'Abbās, on the authority of the Prophet—on him be blessing and peace—who said, 'He who loves and remains chaste and keeps it a secret and dies, dies a martyr.' "[61] Besides the fact that this immediately indicates that the *K. ar-Riyāḍ* also dealt with the "martyrs of love," a prominent subject in this literature, it was this mention of the title of Marzubānī's book that led me to look in the *Fihrist*, in the first place, and to relate the description found there to the other fragments from al-Marzubānī and to the evidence which I had found in other texts of his importance as an oral transmitter of material on love theory. I think, therefore, that there can be no reasonable doubt about the character and contents of the *K. ar-Riyāḍ*, or *K. al-Mutayyamīn*.

A third fragment, in the form of an extract from an immense list of Arabic words for love or for the emotions connected with it, occurs in al-Ḥuṣrī's *Kitāb al-Maṣūn* and will be dealt with later in connection with the discussions of terminology found in these books. This is an area in which the *Kitāb ar-Riyāḍ* seems to have led the way for later works.[62] There is every indication that its content and arrangement influenced its successors also.[63] Even if we never discover a copy of this book, I believe we can be certain of its fundamental importance in the development of this literature.

60. *Wāḍiḥ*, 33. Cf. *Rauḍa*, 141; *Maṣāri'*, I, 12; *Tazyīn*, I, 60–61; *K. al-Muwashshā* (Brünnow ed.), 69. Given also in somewhat abbreviated form without identification of the source in *Dhamm*, 295.
61. *Manāzil* (Leiden Or. 1069), folio 23b.
62. See Part 2, Chapter III.
63. See Part 2, Chapter II.

AL-ḤUṢRĪ'S "KITĀB AL-MAṢŪN FĪ SIRR AL-HAWĀ AL-MAKNŪN"

Abū Isḥāq Ibrāhīm b. 'Alī b. Tamīm al-Ḥuṣrī (died after 413/1022)[64] was a Maghribī, a contemporary of the Spanish author Ibn Ḥazm. He was born in Qairawān and died in al-Manṣūra, both within the bounds of present-day Tunisia. We know little about him, though he is reputed to have been a poet. He dedicated (c. 450/1058) an anthology of belles-lettres, entitled *Zahr al-Ādāb*, to one Abū al-Faḍl al-'Abbās b. Sulaimān. He had heard that Abū al-Faḍl had gone on a book-buying expedition to the East and suggested that this new anthology would obviate the need for any other books, thus saving him much trouble. While this is pure hyperbole, it is a useful collection and has fortunately survived.

Such grandiose claims could not be made for the *Kitāb al-Maṣūn fī Sirr al-Hawā al-Maknūn*, What Has Not Been Revealed (or, What Has Been Preserved) About the Secret of Hidden Love. It is a much smaller work and deals, as the title would suggest, with certain aspects of profane love: particularly, chaste love and the question of whether one ought to, or can, keep one's feelings a secret. While structurally it is a simple anthology, having no chapter headings or apparent plan of organization, its subject matter is theory of profane love. This work has not up to this time been identified as belonging to the works on the theory of profane love. Yet, it has some importance as a link in the transmission of material from the writers of the third and fourth centuries to later authors.

One reason, perhaps, that this work was not easily recognized or studied in this connection long ago is that it was described in the catalog of De Goeje and Houtsma as being the same sort of work as the *Zahr al-Ādāb*, which was known to be a general anthology of

64. *GAL*, G. I, 267–68; S. I, 472–73. b. Khall., 15; *Irshād*, I, 358–60. See also the recent article, "al-Ḥuṣrī," in *EI*² by Ch. Bouyahia.

belles-lettres.[65] On reading that inaccurate description (which was taken over by Brockelmann), one might conclude that the *K. al-Maṣūn fī Sirr al-Hawā al-Maknūn* was another of those many Arabic titles with words like "secrets" and "love" in them which had little or nothing to do with either.

The book contains many quotes from Jāḥiẓ. Whether these are all from his extant writings, I cannot say at this moment.[66] There is also much material from Abū Bakr b. Duraid (d. 321/933), who was important as a *rāwī* of material on love,[67] but none of whose *adab* works were specifically on the subject of love theory, so far as I know. Anecdotes and poetry by and about Muḥammad b. Dā'ūd, author of the *Kitāb az-Zahra*, are very frequent. There are many other names, including al-Marzubānī's, among the sources of the book, and some may prove like al-Marzubānī to be of interest in the early history of this literature. The *K. al-Maṣūn* was in turn used by later writers on love, directly or indirectly and with or without acknowledgment. Fortunately, the authors of the *Manāzil al-Aḥbāb* and the *Al-Wāḍiḥ al-Mubīn* mention it as the source of their long lists of Arabic words for love, an item which became almost a regular feature of books on love, thus indicating to us the relationship of the *K. al-Maṣūn* to those later works. Al-Ḥuṣrī himself, as was mentioned earlier, said that he took the list from al-Marzubānī, one of those pieces of evidence that, together with all the rest, leads us to a proper appreciation of that fourth century author and his *Kitāb ar-Riyāḍ*.

65. M. J. De Goeje et M. Th. Houtsma, *Catalogus Codicum Arabicorum, Bibliothecae Academiae Lugduno-Batavorum* (Leiden: E. J. Brill, 1888–1907), Vol. I, 276.

Just before this revised edition was ready for the press, I found that Ch. Bouyahia had recently given an accurate description of the contents of the *K. al-Maṣūn*, though he did not link it with any of the other works on the theory of love as I do here. See art. "al-Ḥuṣrī," *EI*².

66. It would be difficult to ascertain this, since most editions of works by Jāḥiẓ have no index and therefore do not permit quick identification of the passages attributed to this author.

67. See note 52 and text.

IBN ḤAZM'S "ṬAUQ AL-ḤAMĀMA FI 'L-ULFA WA 'L-ULLĀF"

Abū Muḥammad ʿAlī b. Aḥmad b. Saʿīd b. Ḥazm (383/993–456/1064)[68] was the son of a high court official in the service of the ʿĀmirids al-Manṣūr (Almanzor) and his son al-Muẓaffar, regents for the last Umayyads in al-Andalus. The fall of the ʿĀmirids resulted in the house arrest of Ibn Ḥazm's father, who died four years later, in A.D. 1012. The next fifteen years, as the Umayyad and Ḥammūdid pretenders struggled for the throne, were chaotic. Before he was thirty, Ibn Ḥazm was twice vizier to Umayyad pretenders in Valencia and Cordova, had seen battle, and had been in prison at least three times. By 418/1027, he had settled in Jativa, where he wrote the *Ṭauq al-Ḥamāma*, and, according to most sources, he kept out of political life after that. He began to write a great deal, especially in the fields of tradition and theology. Originally a Shāfiʿite, he became an enthusiastic Ẓāhirī. As such, he was almost isolated, and he came into sharp conflict with his contemporaries, who did not share his views. A famous saying had it that the pen of Ibn Ḥazm was like the sword of al-Ḥajjāj (the notorious Umayyad governor of Iraq) in sharpness. His original way of applying Ẓāhirī tenets to theology, which led him to make the charge that al-Ashʿarī, Abū Ḥanīfa, Mālik, and other great authorities had been heretics, caused the same charge to be leveled against him.

His two belletristic works, the *Risāla fī Faḍl al-Andalus*, which we know only through Maqqarī,[69] and the *Ṭauq al-Ḥamāma*, seem to have been written in Jativa sometime about 418/1027 after he

68. *GAL*, G. I, 400; S. I, 694. C. van Arendonk, art. "Ibn Ḥazm," *EI Suppl.* and *SEI*. R. Arnaldez, art. "Ibn Ḥazm," *EI*². Miguel Asín Palacios, *Abenházam de Cordoba y su historia crítica de las ideas religiosas*, Vol. I (Madrid: Tip. de la "Revista de archivos," 1927). Additional bibliography and biographical sources in García Gómez, tr., *El Collar de la Paloma* (Madrid: Sociedad de Estudios y Publicaciones, 1952), Apéndice I.

69. Aḥmad b. Muḥammad al-Maqqarī, *Analectes sur l'histoire et la littérature des Arabes d'Espagne*, ed. R. Dozy, *et al.* (Leiden: E. J. Brill, 1855–61), II, 109–121.

ended his last term in prison.[70] Whether or not he had become a convinced Ẓāhirī before he wrote them is uncertain.[71] Ibn Qayyim al-Jauzīya, writing about three centuries later, thought that he was and attributed certain shocking attitudes which Ibn Ḥazm displayed in his *Ṭauq al-Ḥamāma* to his stubborn adherence to Ẓāhirī doctrines.[72]

The *Ṭauq al-Ḥamāma* as we know it has come down in a single manuscript at Leiden[73] which is not the complete work but an epitome, made by a rather careless copyist. Since we have no way of knowing how much of the original was pruned out, we can only discuss the work as it stands today, after the efforts of numerous scholars have emended some of its mistakes and elucidated most of its obscurities. As was emphasized earlier in contrasting this book with the *Kitāb az-Zahra,* the *Ṭauq* is primarily a prose work in which the passages of poetry take a place subservient to the prose text. Their role is to illustrate and to summarize his views. Ibn Ḥazm quotes much of his own poetry, which is not the finest. If it was only some of these verses that the copyist left out, perhaps the book has not lost much. In any case, the work is widely regarded as a masterpiece, even in its present condition, and a monument of the culture of Muslim Spain. Through it, one gains entry into the intimate

70. This is Van Arendonk's dating. A. R. Nykl, in the introduction to his English translation of the *Ṭauq, A Book Containing the Risala Known as the Dove's Neckring about Love and Lovers* (Paris: Paul Geuthner, 1931), p. lvii, puts the date of composition in 412–13/1022. García Gómez accepts Nykl's dating. See introduction, *El Collar de la Paloma,* 25.

71. See Van Arendonk (*EI* article cited in note 68) and Goldziher, *ZDMG,* LXIX (1915), 201 ff. Apparently, the transmission of Ẓāhirī doctrine to Spain and to Ibn Ḥazm in particular was through one Ibn Saʿīd al-Ballūṭī, a scholar only ten years younger than Ibn Dāʾūd, author of the *Kitāb az-Zahra* and head of the school of the Ẓāhirīs after the death of his father, the founder. The pupil of Ibn Saʿīd, Aḥmad b. M. b. al-Jasūr, became the teacher of Ibn Ḥazm. Both men were poets of some ability and the older was especially interested in the love poetry of ʿUmar b. Abī Rabīʿa. This is brought out by Von Grunebaum, speaking of the transmission not only of the Ẓāhirī *madhhab* but the "growth in Andalus of a love concept akin in several respects to that of courtly love . . . possibly to be explained by the influence of the cultural tradition of the Ẓāhirīs . . . not that of Avicenna." (*JNES* XI [1952], 237.)

72. See Part 3, Chap. 11.

73. Leiden, Warneriana 461.

life of Cordova of the fifth/eleventh century. The author proceeds in a rational manner to describe the essence and nature of love, its possible causes, symptoms, and accompaniments, its checks, frustrations, and perils. He closes with moral and religious observations.

The *Ṭauq al-Ḥamāma* is one of the few Arabic works which, when translated, is attractive to the Western non-specialist reader. (Unfortunately, none of the other books on the theory of profane love would be equally attractive.) Ibn Ḥazm is a sharp and witty observer of the human scene. In keeping with the Arabic tradition of literature on love, he also portrays the tragedies of love, including some of the bitter ones of his own life. The immediacy of the book's appeal is due partly to the fact that the author writes mostly about the Andalusians of his own day, many of them individuals whom he knew personally, telling colorful, even risqué, stories about them. His personal and brisk prose style is untypical of the Arabic literature on this or almost any subject and for this García Gómez has an interesting explanation.[74] It is also, I believe, un-Islamic in the sense that the conduct portrayed in it as acceptable runs counter to some standards of conduct considered proper by much of the orthodox Islamic world.[75] It is ironic that it is these two unusual aspects of the book that make it so appealing to the modern reader.

JA'FAR B. AḤMAD AS-SARRĀJ'S "MAṢĀRI' AL-'USHSHĀQ"

Abū Muḥammad Ja'far b. Aḥmad b. al-Ḥusain as-Sarrāj al-Qārī (417/1026–500/1106),[76] a prominent *ḥāfiẓ* (memorizer of the Koran or Ḥadīth) and religious scholar of his time, was born in Baghdad. He traveled to Egypt and Mecca several times and once lived in Ṣūr (Tyre), but near the end of his life he returned to his

74. See Part 2, Chap. 11.
75. See Part 3, Chap. 11.
76. *GAL*, G. I, 351; S. I, 594. b. Khall., I, 134 (not 311 as given in *GAL*); *Irshād*, II, 401–5; *Bughya*, 211.

home city. On his travels, he collected many of the traditions about love which appear in this book, The Calamities of Lovers, which is his most famous work.[77] He gives *isnāds* for most traditions, sometimes adding the place and date that he received a particular tradition from the latest authority. The latest such date given is 455/1063. How soon after that the book was written down we do not know, though it was sometime before A.H. 493. Al-Biqāʿī, who, four centuries later, based his *Aswāq al-Ashwāq* upon as-Sarrāj's *Maṣāriʿ al-ʿUshshāq*, gives in his introduction a certificate of transmission, or reading certificate, for the *Maṣāriʿ* going back to Shuhda bint Aḥmad b. al-Faraj b. ʿUmar. She said that as-Sarrāj transmitted it to them (herself and others), reading the text aloud from his own copy in 493.[78]

In 446/1054, while he was a young man studying in Mecca, he took down a number of literary traditions from Abū Bakr Muḥammad b. Aḥmad al-Ardistānī who transmitted traditions from Abū al-Qāsim al-Ḥasan b. Muḥammad b. Ḥabīb, known elsewhere sometimes as an-Nīsābūrī, who wrote the *ʿUqalāʾ al-Majānīn* (The Wise Madmen).[79] Some of the stories from the *ʿUqalāʾ al-Majānīn*, those having to do with lovers, reappear in the *Maṣāriʿ al-ʿUshshāq*. Paul Loosen, who first detected the connection between the two men, showed that as-Sarrāj was the actual redactor of the Escurial manuscript of Nīsābūrī's work.[80]

The *Maṣāriʿ al-ʿUshshāq* is a treasure house of the kind of definitions, anecdotes, stories, and verses from which the later,

77. It is the only work mentioned by title in Ibn Khallikān, who says that as-Sarrāj wrote some "wondrous" books, among them the *Maṣāriʿ al-ʿUshshāq*. Yāqūt mentions it first. Certainly among Arabic books on love, this has been one of the most famous.

78. Süleymaniye Kütüphanesi, Haci Beşir Ağa 552, folio 4a. Shuhda bint Aḥmad died A.H. 574. See b. Khall. (Cairo edition, 1948), II, 172–73, No. 276.

79. *GAL*, S. I, 254. Al-Ḥasan b. Muḥammad an-Nīsābūrī, *ʿUqalāʾ al-Majānīn* (Damascus, 1343/1924).

80. Paul Loosen, "Die Weisen Narren des Naisābūrī," *ZA*, XXVII (1912), 193. Ritter in 1933 listed the *ʿUqalāʾ* as indirectly belonging to the works on the theory of profane love but did not include it in his 1959 list. (Both lists are cited in the Introduction.)

more systematic books on love theory were composed. In fact, almost the entire contents of this book were rearranged to serve as the basis for several compilations. As-Sarrāj's book was a straight anthology, one item recited after the other in no particular scheme or order. The book was artificially divided into twenty-two *juz'*, or parts, each one prefaced by three verses composed by the author, incorporating the words "*maṣāri' al-'ushshāq*" and reiterating the theme of what love did to its victims. Some of its victims were smitten by mystical rapture, caused by the hearing of a verse of the Koran or a sermon, for example. Hence, to some degree it is also a source book for Arab ideas of mystical love.

IBN AL-JAUZĪ'S "DHAMM AL-HAWĀ"

Abu 'l-Faraj 'Abd ar-Raḥmān ibn al-Jauzī (510/1116–597/1200),[81] was born at Baghdad of a family who considered themselves descendants of the caliph Abū Bakr. His father took pains to give him the best education possible and left him moderately wealthy. However, he sold his inheritance and invested it all in his library. He was himself a prolific writer, and in this his reputation was exceeded later only by that of as-Suyūṭī. Like as-Suyūṭī, however, he was more often a compiler than an original author. This is largely true of the *Dhamm al-Hawā*, certainly, though to say that is not to disparage the contribution of the book or to minimize what he put of himself and his own knowledge and ingenuity into it. Most of the literature on the theory of profane love consists of compilations in one sense or another.

81. His full name: Jamāl ad-Dīn Abu 'l-Faraj 'Abd ar-Raḥmān b. Abī 'l-Ḥasan 'Alī b. Muḥammad b. al-Jauzī. *GAL*, G. I, 500–506; S. I, 914–20. *Sh.Dh.*, IV, 329–31; b. Khall., 343; Suyūṭī. *Interpr.*, 17, No. 5. See also the editor's introduction to *Dhamm al-Hawā*, ed. Muṣṭafā 'Abd al-Wāḥid (Cairo: Dār al-Kutub al-Ḥadītha, 1381/1962), 3–27.

Ibn al-Jauzī did not spend all his time writing books, however. He was also interested in practical religion and took up preaching with great success. In Mecca and in Baghdad he preached to throngs in the street or to gatherings in homes. Ibn Jubair on his travels in the East heard him twice in 1185 at Baghdad, once out of doors and once before the caliph and his harem.[82] Ibn al-Jauzī claimed at the end of his life to have turned 100,000 men and 10,000 young people to a pious life.

This bent for practical piety and for the writing of voluminous books are both evident in his *Dhamm al-Hawā* (The Condemnation of Lust/Passionate Love). Here is the preacher and spiritual physician expounding the evils and dangers of passionate cravings for anything and unbridled sexual lust in particular. He was prompted to write the book, he says, by the anguished complaints of one tortured by *hawā*, who came to him asking for treatment for his malady. Ibn al-Jauzī's first words to him were both cheering and stern:

> *You would not have complained to me of your disease, if there were not some glimmer of soundness left in you upon which we may hope to rebuild your health. So, hurry to take your medicine, and stick strictly to your diet . . . If you sink deeper into delirium and do not bear with your treatment, you will trouble both me and yourself . . .you should know that for your sake, to bring about your safe recovery and health, I came down off the hill of dignity in this book to the low point of cheapening myself by speaking of* [*some of*] *those things which are set forth here.*[83]

The *Dhamm al-Hawā* is, in effect, two books: a book on *hawā* (up to Chapter Thirty-Four), followed by a book on *ʿishq*. There is a cleavage between the two subjects which Ibn al-Jauzī never

82. Ibn Jubair, *Riḥla*, ed. M. J. De Goeje ("E. J. W. Gibb Mem. Series," Vol. V, 1907), 220 ff.
83. *Dhamm*, 1.

succeeded in reconciling and which he perhaps never perceived clearly himself.[84] The book is made up heavily of traditions—*ḥadīth* from the Prophet and early Muslims, other pious traditions or anecdotes, and literary traditions—most of them provided with long chains of transmitters. If there is more than one version available, he gives every acceptable one. In some chapters this means paragraph after paragraph of names of *rāwīs* with a few golden words coming at the end, possibly the same words each time.

Among the topics discussed in the first half of the work are the nature of *hawā* and why it is usually blameworthy, the nature of the reason or rational soul (*ʿaql*), its superiority over the lower nature (*nafs*), and the necessity of being guided by the *ʿaql* and fighting the lusts of the *nafs*. Other subjects are the mechanism of temptation, avoiding occasions of temptation, and how to combat their onslaught and divert one's energies to praiseworthy preoccupations and pleasures.

In the latter half of the book, which ought to have been entitled *Dhamm al-ʿIshq*, he gives the now traditional material on the nature and cause of passionate love and discusses whether it is blameworthy or praiseworthy. Then he deals with the reward of chaste conduct, the illness, madness, and so forth that befall the *ʿāshiq* (lover), and the stories, mostly tragic, told of famous poet-lovers and ʿUdhrī lovers.[85] These are followed by chapters painting the very blackest side of *ʿishq*, repeating stories of individuals whom it drove to fornication, incest, murder, and suicide or who were themselves slain or who died by slowly wasting away. These stories are part of the therapy he offers to this anonymous sufferer: Read and shudder, and beware, lest the same unspeakable things befall you. The book ends with many "remedies" or "medicines" for *ʿishq*, depending on the need of the sufferer, and collected advice and admonitions.

84. Further discussion of this follows in Part 2, Chap. III.

85. The celebrated lovers of the tribe of ʿUdhra, "who, when loving, die." The adjective "ʿUdhrī" is also applied to love which is like theirs in intensity and purity. See *EI*, *s.v.* "ʿUdhra" and "ʿUdhrī."

AḤMAD B. SULAIMĀN AL-KISĀ'Ī'S "RAUḌAT AL-'ĀSHIQ WA NUZHAT AL-WĀMIQ"

We know nothing about Aḥmad b. Sulaimān b. Ḥumaid al-Kisā'ī ash-Shāfi'ī[86] except that he dedicated this book to the Ayyūbid ruler al-Malik al-Ashraf Abu 'l-Muẓaffar Mūsā b. Saif ad-Dīn Abū Bakr, who controlled Ba'albak and Damascus from about 626, and who died in late 634 or early 635/1237.[87] Therefore, the author may have been a Syrian. The unique manuscript of his book, Ahmet III 2373, in Top Kapı Saray, İstanbul, was finished 22 Sha'bān 769. The copyist signed his name in a secret number code with diacritical marks, so even this shred of information is denied us.[88]

In the dedication and introduction, the author discusses his reasons for writing the book: "The thing most likely to gain the favor of kings is the branch of *adab*; what serves them best is the stories of the *ẓurafā'* (refined people), Arab and non-Arab; and the finest stories written and the best traditions collected are those dealing with love and lovers and the memorable deeds of the *ahl al-hawā* (those passionately in love)." He tells the reader that he has examined earlier books on the subject and found them to fall short in one of two respects. Their authors either discussed love and its types without addressing themselves to the *aḥwāl* of those in love, or they gave the *aḥwāl* of the lovers without proper treatment of the essence or meaning of love and its division into types or degrees. In his view, none of these authors seemed to perceive that the two aspects of the subject must share equally in any complete treatment.

> *... so I made it my concern to do what they neglected to do. I made the book an introduction to what needs an introduction, topic by topic, and I included verses from the Koran, traditions from the Prophet, wise anecdotes, witty stories, and fine poetry.*

86. *GAL*, S. I, 599; S. II, 909.
87. Zambaur, 97–98.
88. I have not been able to solve the code. Neither of the two keys for solving Bāṭinī secret codes which I came upon in MS Caprotti 183, a notebook of E. Griffini, in the Ambrosiana, Milan, fit this particular code.

I eliminated the isnāds *for fear of being lengthy, redundant, boring, and vexatious. I called it the Garden of the Ardent Lover and the Pleasure Garden of the Tender Lover.*[89]

SHIHĀB AD-DĪN MAḤMŪD'S "MANĀZIL AL-AḤBĀB WA MANĀZIH AL-ALBAB"

Shihāb ad-Dīn Abu 'th-Thanā' Maḥmūd b. Sulaimān (or Salmān) b. Fahd (644/1246–725/1325),[90] was born in Aleppo and moved with his father to Damascus in 654, when he was ten years old. After an excellent education by some of the leading scholars of the day, he served in several posts as a Ḥanbalī judge. The talents for which he was remembered, however, were his superb prose style, his excellent poetry, and his calligraphy. Ibn Rajab, who would have been a youth when Shihāb ad-Dīn died an old man, says that he spent altogether half a century in the Dīwān al-Inshā' (chancellery of state) of Cairo and its counterpart in Damascus, and was also *kātib as-sirr* (secretary of state, chief of the Dīwān al-Inshā')[91] in Damascus some thirty years.

He is reported to have been the author of about three volumes of poetry and thirty of prose. Among the existing works by him is one on the art of writing letters, *Ḥusn at-Tawassul fī* (or *ilā*) *Ṣinā'at at-Tarassul,* with examples supposedly drawn from his official correspondence. The *Manāzil al-Aḥbāb* was the first of several important books on the theory of profane love written in the late seventh/thirteenth and eighth/fourteenth centuries. It can be credited with influencing at least two of the three books written just after it by men of the next generation.

89. Top Kapı Saray, Ahmet III 2373, folio 1b.
90. *GAL,* G. II, 43; S. II, 42–43. Shaukānī, 295–96; Ibn Rajab, *K. adh-Dhail 'alā Ṭabaqāt al-Ḥanābila,* II, 378 (No. 487); *D.K.,* IV, 324–26; *Fawāt,* II, 287; *Sh.Dh.,* VI, 69.
91. See *EI*², *s.v.* "Dīwān."

It is very possible that Ibn al-Qayyim, author of the *Rauḍat al-Muḥibbīn*, knew him, perhaps well. Both were Damascenes and Ḥanbalīs, although Shihāb ad-Dīn Maḥmūd belonged to the generation of Ibn al-Qayyim's father. Four verses by Shihāb ad-Dīn Maḥmūd appear in the *Rauḍat al-Muḥibbīn*, but Ibn al-Qayyim does not mention the *Manāzil al-Aḥbāb*.

Mughulṭāi, another contemporary of Shihāb ad-Dīn, knew the *Manāzil al-Aḥbāb* and used passages from it for his book on the Martyrs of Love, *Al-Wāḍiḥ al-Mubīn fī Dhikr Man Ustushhida min al-Muḥibbīn*,[92] both material credited specifically to Shihāb ad-Dīn and some originally from other authors who are quoted in the *Manāzil al-Aḥbāb*.[93] Ibn Abī Ḥajala, also of the same century but younger than Mughulṭāi or Ibn al-Qayyim, names Shihāb ad-Dīn Maḥmūd twice in the first few paragraphs of his *Dīwān aṣ-Ṣabāba*[94] and expresses his esteem for the book.

The *Manāzil al-Aḥbāb wa Manāzih al-Albāb*, which might be translated The Campsites of the Lovers and the Gardens of Hearts, is a book of only modest length, manuscripts of it averaging about 80 to 150 folios, depending on the format.[95] After a few introductory words, the author speaks of the merit of those who love one another in God or for God's sake, a familiar topic in these works, since there are traditions from the Prophet on this subject.[96] After speaking of the necessity of a golden mean or moderation in love and hate, he gives several sections on the *aḥwāl* of the lovers: poets who became famous for *ʿishq* in the pre-Islamic period, the *ʿishq* to which the members of the tribe of ʿUdhra fell victim, those who became martyrs of love, those who were ensnared by love from the first glance, the

92. Introduced in the following section.
93. See Part II, Chap. 3 for evidence that he took the list of words for love, which he says comes from al-Ḥuṣrī's *K. al-Maṣūn*, through the *Manāzil*, not directly.
94. Introduced below.
95. There are two more MSS to add to those listed in *GAL*: Tunis, Bibliothèque de la Faculté des Lettres 2792 (= ʿAbdalīya [or Aḥmadīya] collection, formerly in the Zaitūna, for which there exists a printed catalog) and Ambrosiana, Caprotti H48, which I encountered among those MSS for which there exists only the handwritten, partial catalog in notebooks of E. Griffini.
96. See A. J. Wensinck, *A Handbook of Early Muhammadan Tradition* (Leiden: E. J. Brill, 1927), *s.v.* "Love."

ʿishq of kings and how their love differs from that of the bedouin Arabs, and the passion of youth and the preference for one's first love.

After this come discussions of the causes of *hawā* according to the scholars, the nature of *ʿishq*, those who praise *hawā*, and those who condemn it and depict it as a terrible thing. The last sections are mainly on chasteness: chasteness and what follows from it, its rationale, restraining one's *nafs* from its passion or concupiscence, what men of recent times say in praise of decency and chastity, keeping one's love a secret in spite of the certitude of gaining the beloved if it were revealed, and having compassion for those afflicted with *hawā* and helping them to quench its fire.

MUGHULṬĀI'S "KITĀB AL-WĀḌIḤ AL-MUBĪN FĪ DHIKR MAN USTUSHHIDA MIN AL-MUḤIBBĪN"

ʿAlāʾ ad-Dīn Abū ʿAbd Allāh Mughulṭāi b. Qilīj b. ʿAbd Allāh al-Ḥanafī al-Ḥikrī was born ca. 690/1291 and died 762/1361.[97] Judging by the name Mughulṭāi, he may have been of Turkish descent.[98] He specialized in tradition, genealogy, and biography and was a contemporary of Ibn Qayyim al-Jauzīya, having been born only about a year before him. After the death of Ibn Sayyid an-Nās[99] in 734/1334, Mughulṭāi was appointed to fill his place as professor of the science of Tradition in the Madrasat aẓ-Ẓāhirīya in Cairo. For some reason his appointment was not popular, or he personally was not popular. Local people tried to discredit Mughulṭāi and to make fun of him. The biographical sources imply that he was appointed

97. *GAL*, G. II, 48; S. II, 47–48. *D.K.*, IV, 352; *Sh.Dh.*, VI, 197; Shaukānī, II, 312–13; b. Taghr., Vol. V, Pt. I, 179.
98. For the meaning of the proper name "Mughulṭāi," see *Ein türkisch-arabisches Glossar*, ed. M. Th. Houtsma (Leiden: E. J. Brill, 1894), 29. This glossary is based upon a unique Leiden MS dating from the century in which Mughulṭāi was born.
99. *GAL*, G. II, 71–72; S. II, 77.

because a good word had been said in his behalf to the Sultan by an influential advisor.[100]

Whether these difficulties had anything to do with his books or whether it was some petty academic power struggle or jealousy, we do not know. At any rate, in 745, when Khalīl b. Kaikaldī al-ʿAlāʾī,[101] a Shāfiʿī traditionist and son of a Turkish soldier, came to Cairo, Mughulṭāi's book came to his attention one day in the book market, whether by accident or someone's design it is not clear. When he learned that it contained a story unfavorable to ʿĀʾisha, the Prophet's wife, he took offense and brought a case against Mughulṭāi before a Ḥanbalī court. As a result, Mughulṭāi was rebuked and imprisoned for a time. It is reported that local book dealers took the book off the market after that incident.

Al-Wāḍiḥ al-Mubīn fī Dhikr Man Ustushhida min al-Muḥibbīn,[102] literally, The Clear and Eloquent in Speaking of Those Lovers Who Became Martyrs, is an alphabetically arranged dictionary containing the accounts of those who died of pure but tragic love. It is prefaced with a long introduction discussing the problem of the reliability of the traditions from the Prophet which say that those who die of chaste love are martyrs. Mughulṭāi shows that some versions of the tradition are reliable. After that he presents many pages of definitions and words for love, theories of its cause, and opinions of philosophers and physicians.

IBN QAYYIM AL-JAUZĪYA'S "RAUḌAT AL-MUḤIBBĪN WA NUZHAT AL-MUSHTĀQĪN"

Shams ad-Dīn Abū ʿAbd Allāh Muḥammad b. Abī Bakr b. Ayyūb b. Saʿd b. Ḥarīz az-Zarʿī ad-Dimashqī (691/1272–751/1350),

100. *D.K.*, IV, 352; *Sh.Dh.*, VI, 197.
101. *GAL*, G. II, 64; S. II, 68.
102. See O. Spies, "Al-Mughulṭāʾī's Specialwerk über 'Martyrer der Liebe'," *Festschr. Kahle*, 145–55. Spies published an edition of the first half of the book ("Bonner Orientalistische Studien," herausg. von P. Kahle u. W. Kirfel, Heft 18; Stuttgart: W. Kohlhammer Verlag, 1936).

In addition to the two İstanbul MSS in *GAL* (on which the Spies edition was based) there is one at Yale University, MS Landsberg 77.

was known as Ibn Qayyim al-Jauzīya, because his father was the *qayyim* of the Jauzīya, a madrasa in Damascus founded in 652 by Muḥyī ad-Dīn Yūsuf, the well-to-do son of Ibn al-Jauzī.[103] Besides his studies under famous scholars of the time, he studied *farā'iḍ* (inheritance law) at his father's knee. Later, Ibn al-Qayyim became *imām* of the Jauzīya and his own son succeeded him at that post after his death. Four of his contemporaries, fellow Damascenes, have given us a small amount of biographical information about him. Therefore we are fortunate in having more accurate information on him than on most of these writers. These contemporary sources are Dhahabī (c. 696/1293–748/1348) in his *Mukhtaṣar,*[104] Ṣafadī (c. 696/1293–764/1363) in his *Wāfī bi 'l-Wafayāt,* Ibn Kathīr (701/1301–774/1373) in his *Al-Bidāya wa 'n-Nihāya,* and Ibn Rajab (709/1309–795/1393) in his *Dhail 'alā Ṭabaqāt al-Ḥanābila.* Later writers of *ṭabaqāt*

103. *GAL,* G. II, 105–107; S. II, 126–28. On "*qayyim,*" a rather vague term for an office whose functions seemed to vary from place to place, see J. Pedersen's article "Masdjid" in *EI*[1] or *SEI.*

I have not found the Jauzīya Madrasa on any map or in any modern architectural description of Damascus. However, it is included in 'Abd al-Qādir b. Muḥammad an-Nu'aimī's *Ad-Dāris fī Ta'rīkh al-Madāris,* ed. Ja'far al-Ḥusnī ("Maṭbū'āt al-Majma' al-'Ilmī al-'Arabī;" Dimashq: Maṭba'at at-Taraqqī, 1370/1951), II, 29 ff., where the history of its founding and the biographies of scholars attached to it are given. The passages from the *Mukhtaṣar* of al-'Almāwī translated with notes in H. Sauvaire's "La description de Damas," *JA,* 3rd series, III–VII (1894–96) are an extract from this *Ad-Dāris.* (See *GAL,* G. II, 133, 360.) The recent history of the Jauzīya Madrasa, to 1930, is sketched briefly in a note (p. *'ain,* note 2) by the editor of the *Rauḍat al-Muḥibbīn.* Now (1966) the remnants have been torn down to make space for an air raid shelter and only what may be a *mihrāb* of the Jauzīya adheres yet to the outside of an adjacent wall. A dyer's business operates in the traditional manner next to it.

104. *Apud* Ibn Rajab, Ibn Ḥajar al-'Asqalānī, and Shaukānī. Most likely this refers to *Al-Mukhtaṣar al-Muḥtāj ilaihī min Ta'rīkh al-Ḥāfiẓ Abī 'Abd Allāh M. b. Sa'īd b. M. b. ad-Dubaithī.* However, the one volume of this work which has appeared in print (ed. Muṣṭafā Jawād; Baghdad: Maṭbū'āt al-Ma'ārif, 1371/1951) does not contain a biography of Ibn al-Qayyim. According to the list of known works attributed to adh-Dhahabī, given in pages 11–15 of Muṣṭafā Jawād's introduction, there were a number of titles beginning with "*Al-Mukhtaṣar.*" It is also possible that one of the abridgments which Dhahabī made from his *Ta'rīkh al-Islām* is what is meant. However, neither of the two available to me, the *Ta'rīkh al-Awsaṭ,* otherwise known as *Al-'Ibar fī Khabar Man Ghabar* (Kuwait: Dā'irat al-Matbū'āt wa 'n-Nashr, 1960–) and the *Ta'rīkh as-Saghīr,* called *K. Duwal al-Islām* (Hyderabad: Dā'irat al-Ma'ārif al-'Uthmānīya, 1364–65/1944–45), contain anything on Ibn al-Qayyim, both ending their historical coverage at a time earlier than his death.

literature also have information, but it is derived from these primary sources.[105]

In 712/1312, at about the age of twenty-one, Ibn al-Qayyim attached himself to the great Ḥanbalī scholar Ibn Taimīya and eventually became his leading disciple. Ibn Taimīya was most influential in shaping his thought, and Ibn al-Qayyim in turn spread Ibn Taimīya's influence in his own teaching and writing. The consequences of his loyalty were many persecutions, several stays in prison, and even torture. To understand some of the personal qualities in Ibn Taimīya that inspired such loyalty, one need only read Ibn al-Qayyim's description of his steadfast, contagious good humor and his personal courage and boldness.[106] Ibn al-Qayyim himself was reported to have been a man with an outgoing personality, good-natured, and free of envy or contempt for anyone, a man who loved people and was himself beloved by many.

In prison, the two men used to keep up their courage by passing the time in long hours of devotions and by writing books and letters. When Ibn Taimīya's jailers in the citadel of Damascus in 728, pressed by his enemies to stop his polemics, refused to let his sons bring him any more paper and ink, this ultimate in privations was too much for the old man, and he fell ill and died. Perhaps there are echoes of this event in Ibn al-Qayyim's description of the psychology of the love of learning and books and the anecdote he tells about the scholar whom a physician deprived of his beloved books during his illness on the grounds that they tired him excessively. The patient argued the contrary and reacted in much the same way as if he were about to be deprived of the one beloved person who made his life worth living.[107]

It is possible that Ibn Qayyim al-Jauzīya wrote the *Rauḍa* in prison. At least it seems to have been written in Egypt, for he refers

105. Ibn Ḥajar al-ʿAsqalānī (d. 852/1449) in *Ad-Durar al-Kāmina* draws on Dhahabī, Ibn Kathīr, and apparently Ṣafadī. Ibn Taghrībirdī (d. 874/1469) in *An-Nujūm az-Ẓāhira* and as-Suyūṭī (d. 911/1505) in *Bughyat al-Wuʿāt* both appear to derive from Ṣafadī. Ibn al-ʿImād (d. 1250/1832) in *Badr aṭ-Ṭāliʿ* mostly copies out Ibn Ḥajar, including that author's quotations from Dhahabī and Ibn Kathīr.

106. See Ibn Rajab, II, 402–403.

107. *Rauḍa* 68–69. The man about whom the anecdote was told was Ibn Taimīya's grandfather.

in the introduction to the fact that he is far from his homeland and without his books. The editor has noted that he sometimes quotes traditions inexactly, apparently not having copies of the collections with which to check the accuracy of his memory. Normally, a man like Ibn al-Qayyim would have been meticulous about such things. However, there is so much material which *is* accurately quoted—passages from other books on love, for example—that he must have had copies of them to study.

The *Rauḍat al-Muḥibbīn* appears to be the fruit of his mature experience, composed with care and much thought. It is written out of a good muftī's concern for both the temporal and eternal happiness of his readers. Possessing a proper appreciation of the good things in life that God has given and a respect for the beauty and joy of human love, nevertheless he looks with concern upon those who would risk falling into sin.[108]

Toward the end of his book, without denying the value of human love or stinting his thorough discussion of it, he writes of the priority that love of God should have.[109] Ibn al-Qayyim's love of God was not that of a Ṣūfī, however. He taught a love of God based on the principle that to love God is to live according to the *Sharī'a* (Sacred Law). Like Ibn Taimīya, he rejected anything resembling "union with God." For him, the highest aim was the worship or service of God, *'ibāda*, whose basis was the observance of the *Sharī'a*. Ibn Taimīya had redefined, as it were, in his own terms many of the Ṣūfī expressions—fear of God, confidence in him, humility, love for him, even *fanā'*, annihilation in God.[110] Ibn Rajab says quite explicitly, however, that Ibn al-Qayyim was thoroughly versed in the system, methods, and theory of Sufism.[111] He says that this interest in mysticism sprang from his prison days, where his turning

108. Since the *Rauḍat al-Muḥibbīn* will be discussed in some detail in later chapters, I will not sketch the contents here.
109. Especially in Chapters 21, 22, and 26.
110. W. Montgomery Watt, *Islamic Philosophy and Theology* ("Islamic Surveys," I; Edinburgh: Edinburgh University Press, 1962), 162, and Henri Laoust, *Essai sur les doctrines sociales et politiques de Taḳī-d-Dīn Aḥmad b. Taimīya* ("Recherches d'archéologie, de philologie, et d'histoire," t. X; Cairo: Institut Français d'archéologie orientale 1939), 89–93, 469–473.
111. Ibn Rajab, II, 448.

to devotions and the practice of love toward God brought him many experiences of true religious ecstasy. With the local organized Ṣūfī communities, however, Ibn Taimīya and Ibn al-Qayyim had some serious friction. They opposed them on some points and in turn gained numerous enemies amongst the *fuqarā'* (mendicant mystics) and *ṣūfīya* (mystics). In view of the large numbers of Ṣūfīs in Damascus in those times, this was hazardous.[112]

IBN ABĪ ḤAJALA'S "DĪWĀN AṢ-ṢABĀBA"

Shihāb ad-Dīn Abu 'l-'Abbās Aḥmad b. Yaḥyā b. Abī Ḥajala (725/1325–776/1375)[113] was born in Tlemcen in the *zāwiya* (hospice) of his grandfather 'Abd al-Wāḥid, a much venerated Ṣūfī. In his youth, he came on a pilgrimage to Mecca and went from there to Damascus, where he stayed to study. Later, he became the director

112. A contemporary source, al-Ḥasan b. Aḥmad b. Zafar al-Irbilī (d. 726), writing in the third decade of the eighth century A.H., says that Damascus had forty-four Ṣūfī communities, or houses, twenty-four for men and twenty for women. (See *Madāris Dimashq wa Rubuṭuhā wa Jawāmi'uhā wa Ḥamāmātuhā*, ed. Muḥammad Aḥmad Duhmān ["An-Nashrāt as-Ṣaghīra," No. 7; Dimashq: Maktabat ad-Dirāsāt al-Islāmīya, 1366/1947], 15–16.) Henri Laoust in "La biographie d'Ibn Taimīya d'après Ibn Kaṯīr," *BEO*, IX (1942–43), 116, calls attention to evidence that Ibn Taimīya had family connections with Sufism. His cousin was a preacher in one of these communities (Ibn Kathīr, XIII, 264) and his father was buried in a Ṣūfī cemetery (Ibn Kathīr, XIII, 303). So also was he, later. See Laoust, "Ibn Taymiyya," *EI*².

Ibn Taimīya once accused a dirty ascetic with long fingernails and untrimmed beard of "sinful innovation," or *bid'a*, and obliged him to get scrubbed and trimmed. (Laoust, *BEO*, IX (1942–43), 133.)

113. *GAL*, G. II, 12–13; S. II, 5–6. *Sh.Dh.*, VI, 240–41; *D.K.*, I, 329, No. 726 (not 331, No. 828 as given in *GAL*). Short autobiography from the author's *K. Maghnāṭīs ad-Durr an-Nafīs*, printed on the title page of *Tazyīn al-Aswāq* and *Dīwān aṣ-Ṣabāba* (margin), (Cairo, 1308). See also the recent article, "Ibn Abī Ḥadjala," in *EI*² by J. Robson and U. Rizzitano.

Also U. Rizzitano, "Il *Dīwān aṣ-ṣabābah* dello scrittore magrebino Ibn Abī Ḥaǵalah," *RSO*, XXVIII (1953), 35–70. He discusses the author and his times, his other works, the sources of the *Dīwān* . . ., and the work itself, providing a translation of the introduction and chapter headings.

of a Ṣūfī community outside the walls of Cairo, but he did not hold the mystical beliefs of the monist type, then very popular. In fact, he was so violently opposed to the teachings of the famous mystic and poet of Cairo, ʿUmar b. al-Fāriḍ (d. 632/1235), and to the Ittiḥādīya[114] movement that he asked to be buried with a book of his own poems (in *qasīda* form) in praise of the Prophet which he had written to counter the mystical *qasīdas* of Ibn al-Fāriḍ.[115]

Ibn Abī Ḥajala was a Ḥanafī in religious law and a Ḥanbalī in creed, being an admirer of Ibn Taimīya. However his friend Abū Zaid al-Maghribī said he used to tell the Shāfiʿīs that he was a Shāfiʿī and the Ḥanafīs that he was a Ḥanafī and the "Muḥaddithūn" that he was one of them. To add another confusing element to the picture of this hard-to-define man, we could note that though he was a Ṣūfī, he wrote one of the most widely read books on the theory of profane love.

His *Dīwān aṣ-Ṣabāba,*[116] The Anthology of Ardent Love, is his most famous work. Its popularity endured at least up to the last century, when it saw several printed editions.[117] Its influence even touched Europe indirectly. Stendahl is reported to have been familiar with extracts of it.[118] The theme is chaste, profane love, and the aim is to please while edifying and informing. In matters of both form and content, Ibn Abī Ḥajala had based himself on his predecessors, though like every such compiler he had added some new material, a few verses, stories, and anecdotes. The book begins with a long introduction filled with dicta and theories about love, its nature and causes, followed by thirty chapters on the *aḥwāl* of love and lovers. These contain stories about certain kinds of lovers: the caliphs and kings, those who fell in love at first sight, chaste lovers, martyrs of

114. See the art. "Taṣawwuf," *EI*[1] or *SEI*, for an explanation of the beliefs of the Ittiḥādīya.

115. Brockelmann gives the wrong impression when he says that as a poet he imitated Ibn al-Fāriḍ.

116. There are four MSS to be added to those listed in *GAL*: (Milan) Ambrosiana Caprotti F 175; (İstanbul) Süleymaniye, Haci Beşir Ağa 527, Haci Mahmud Efendi 5145, and Reisülküttab 970.

117. In addition to the printed editions signaled in *GAL*, there is one printed in 1302 in Cairo. See Süleymaniye, İzmirli İsmail Hakkı 3137/2.

118. *De l'amour,* ed. C. Lory, 177–82, cited by Louis Massignon, *Passion,* I, 173, n. 4.

love, and men of his time sorely tried by love. These chapters also deal with the symptoms and commonplace experiences of love: jealousy, blanching and blushing, dreams, long sleepless nights, the exchanging of notes, and rivals and slanderers. It is not the kind of book that one might expect from the head of a Ṣūfī community, but, viewed in another way, it is not unusual. As Von Grunebaum has put it, in speaking of this period, "Whoever commands the established forms of expression has the means of rearranging the material conveniently prepared by the collector's zeal and the systematic scholarship of centuries. The skilled writer may treat of any subject."[119] If men whose primary field of scholarship was law, theology, history of religion, or tradition had written most of the preceding books on profane love, why should not a Ṣūfī write one? If one assumes that there was no irreconcilable conflict between his attitudes toward love, mystical and profane, then he is a typical example of the scholar of the later Middle Ages who tries his hand in many different fields. Apparently he did not think, as some mystics did, that passionate love of another human person was in every case a vain use of those faculties which ought to be devoted to loving God.

Ibn Abī Ḥajala's contemporary, the *wazīr* Ibn al-Khaṭīb[120] (d. 776/1374) in Andalusia, knew of the reputation of the *Dīwān aṣ-Ṣabāba* and aspired to surpass it with his book *Rauḍat at-Taʿrīf bi 'l-Ḥubb ash-Sharīf,*[121] The Garden of Instruction in Sublime Love, which, however, deals with mystical love. My impression on examining a manuscript of the *Rauḍat at-Taʿrīf* is that Ibn al-Khaṭīb surpassed him only in making the plan of his book more elaborate and in making the prose more recondite with page after page of tiresome *sajʿ*. Even one of the most-used metaphors for love, that of the tree growing in the heart, he has used in an illogical and confusing way by confounding in it two things: love itself and the literature on love. Thus, love is the tree, the soul in which it

119. Von Grunebaum, *Medieval Islam,* 257.
120. *GAL,* G. II, 260–63; S. II, 372–73.
121. See Ibn Khaldūn, *Muqaddimah,* tr. Franz Rosenthal (London: Routledge and Kegan Paul, 1958), III, 98–99, especially the translator's note about a letter Ibn al-Khaṭīb wrote to Ibn Khaldūn mentioning this book.

grows is the earth, love's divisions are the twigs, the stories about love are its leaves, the poetry of love is its flowers, and union with God is its fruit.[122]

AL-BIQĀʿĪ'S "ASWĀQ AL-ASHWĀQ FĪ MAṢĀRIʿ AL-ʿUSHSHĀQ"

Burhān ad-Dīn Abu 'l-Ḥasan Ibrāhīm b. ʿUmar al-Biqāʿī ash-Shāfiʿī (c. 809/1406–885/1480)[123] was born in the village of Khirbat Ruhā in the Biqāʿ between Baʿalbek, Ḥims, and Damascus. He left home after a murderous assault on his family left him gravely wounded and nine of his closest kin, including his father, dead. In time, his wanderings and studies took him to Damascus, Jerusalem, and Cairo. At some point, he took part in raids against Cyprus and Rhodes. As a scholar, he was particularly noted for his opposition to the doctrines of the mystics ʿUmar b. al-Fāriḍ and Ibn al-ʿArabī. His contemporary, as-Suyūṭī, wrote treatises countering the attacks of al-Biqāʿī upon the orthodoxy of these men.

The *Aswāq al-Ashwāq fī Maṣāriʿ al-ʿUshshāq*,[124] The Markets (or Streets) of Yearnings (or Desires) in *The Calamities of Lovers*, was al-Biqāʿī's attempt to improve upon, or make more marketable, as-Sarrāj's *Maṣāriʿ al-ʿUshshāq*, The Calamities of Lovers. He took its contents, shorn of passages which he thought were not up to the quality of the rest, and added some new poetry and anecdotes.

122. Süleymaniye, Esad Efendi 2724, folio 4b. This MS should be added to those listed in *GAL*.

123. *GAL*, G. II, 142–43 (page 142 is incorrectly marked as 141 in the 1949 edition); S. II, 177–78. Suyūṭī, *Naẓm*, 24; Sakhāwī, *Ḍau'*, I, 101–11; b. Ayās, *Ta'r. Miṣr*, IV, 121, 146; *Sh.Dh.*, VII, 339–40 (not 339–42 as in *GAL*).

The fact that Sakhāwī's biography of Biqāʿī amounts to a slander of him can be explained by their bitter personal rivalry. See the biography of Sakhāwī himself inserted at the beginning of Vol. I of the *Ḍau'*.

124. In *GAL* all information on this work is found in the entries for *Maṣāriʿ*, G. I, 351 (not 431 as in G. II, 142, the cross-reference to this entry); S. I, 594. To the MSS listed, Haci Beşir Ağa 552 should be added.

Beyond this he claims to have added the entire contents of Mughulṭāi's *Al-Wāḍiḥ al-Mubīn*, the book on the martyrs of love, and all the stories in Shihāb ad-Dīn Maḥmūd b. Fahd's *Manāzil al-Aḥbāb*. For all its distinguished and comprehensive content, at least two later scholars thought this compilation had faults amenable to improved treatment and arrangement. Al-Biqāʿī would have been displeased had he seen that one of the numerous "improvements" made by Dāʾūd al-Anṭākī was the addition of verses by ʿUmar b. al-Fāriḍ.

DĀʾŪD AL-ANṬĀKĪ'S "TAZYĪN AL-ASWĀQ BI TAFṢĪL ASHWĀQ AL-ʿUSHSHĀQ"[125]

Dāʾūd b. ʿUmar al-Anṭākī aḍ-Ḍarīr (died 1008/1599),[126] born in Anṭākya as his name would indicate, was crippled from very early in life, if not from birth, and could not walk. Some accounts say that he was blind all his life. His father, who was chief of the village of Sayyidī Ḥabīb Najjār, had him carried every day to a nearby *ribāṭ*[127] for instruction. A Persian "scholar" (*shaikh*) who appeared

125. Taken literally, this fulsome, rhyming title is nonsense. The hearer must understand that, just as al-Biqāʿī alluded to the title of as-Sarrāj's book in his own title, al-Anṭākī now alludes to the titles of both men's works in his: The Embellishment of the Markets by Narrating in Full the Yearnings of the Lovers. "The Markets" (*al-Aswāq*) and "the Yearnings" (*al-Ashwāq*) are references to al-Biqāʿī's title and "the Lovers" (*al-ʿUshshāq*) refers to as-Sarrāj's book and secondarily to al-Biqāʿī's. Alternatively, the whole thing can be understood with the "*Aswāq*" in mind as al-Biqāʿī's title and the rest taken literally, with only a sub-liminal hint at the allusions to other authors.

126. *GAL*, G. II, 364; S. II, 491–2; b. Maʿṣūm, *Sulāfat al-ʿAṣr*, 428–30; al-Ifrānī, *Ṣafwa*, 129; al-ʿAyyāshī, *Riḥla*, II, 27; *Sh.Dh.*, VIII, 415–16; al-Qādirī, *N. M.*, II, 123; Shaukānī, I, 246; Muḥibbī, II, 140–49. See also art. "Al-Anṭākī," *EI*², by C. Brockelmann and J. Vernet.

127. In this period, probably a foundation where ascetic disciplines and pious exercises as well as learning were pursued. See art. "Ribāṭ," *EI*¹ or *SEI*.

there to teach treated and healed him and the grateful student became his pupil, studying Greek,[128] medicine, and other subjects under him.

Later, Dā'ūd went to Egypt where he became a leading lecturer in philosophy and medicine and wrote a number of books, many of them medical works. He says that once, when weary of weightier subjects and looking for a new project of the sort that would be a refreshing change, he was looking through literary anthologies and his attention fell on al-Biqā'ī's *Aswāq al-Ashwāq*. That author was a great figure of his time, Dā'ūd said, and the book had great merits, but he felt it could be improved upon. He thought that quoting *isnāds* and the repetition characteristic in relating traditions from the Prophet were necessary to buttress religious opinions but were not called for in a book of this sort. On the other hand, he thought that al-Biqā'ī was too summary at other points where the full text of some poem or anecdote should have been given, and that the whole book needed rearrangement and a different division of content to give it better balance. (Hence the "*tafṣīl*" in the title, a word meaning "narrating in full" or "analyzing" and in its original, concrete meaning "to intercalate [golden beads and pearls] in a necklace," possibly another reference to the necklace in a literary title.) In his introduction al-Anṭākī spelled out the twelve ways in which he "enhanced its good points, rejected what was not to the point, and added what he [al-Biqā'ī] thought [wrongly] that he could dispense with, but without doing anything unprecedented (*farīy*)."[129] He said that the book could be read both by mystics and by those interested only in its more obvious outward and profane meaning. The edifying sayings and erotic verses of 'Umar b. al-

128. Compare this information from Muḥibbī with the remark by al-Anṭākī in *Tazyīn*, III, 195–96. Apparently he could read the Greek of the Septuagint and did so in order to get the correct version of the story of Susanna.

129. Dā'ūd al-Anṭākī, *Tazyīn al-Aswāq bi Tafṣīl Ashwāq al-'Ushshāq* (Beirut: Dār Makshūf, 1957–58, in 6 *juz'*), I, 13–14. I think this is what he meant by "*farīy*" in this context. For other meanings of the term and the Koranic phrase "*laqad ji'ti shai'an farīyan*," alluded to here by al-Anṭākī, see Lane, *s.v. f-r-y*.

Fāriḍ and ʿAfīf ad-Dīn at-Tilimsānī that al-Anṭākī inserted seem calculated to appeal to the mystically inclined.[130]

Beside reworking the *Aswāq al-Ashwāq fī Maṣāriʿ al-ʿUshshāq*, Dāʾūd al-Anṭākī went back to the *Maṣāriʿ* itself, the basis of that book, in order to retrieve some material cast away by al-Biqāʿī. To these he added material from the *Dīwān aṣ-Ṣabāba* and from other sources of that type which he does not name. Without identifying every passage which he took from the above-mentioned three works, one cannot be sure whether he is quoting the material directly from the author or title he names or through one of these three works at second or third hand or even more. One should remember, also, though al-Anṭākī does not mention it, that, according to al-Biqāʿī, some of the *Manāzil al-Aḥbāb* and all of the *Wāḍiḥ al-Mubīn* had already gone into the composition of the *Aswāq al-Ashwāq*. Therefore, al-Anṭākī's work was actually a reshaping of the contents of at least five preceding works on the theory of profane love.

As a literary effort, the *Tazyīn al-Aswāq* is typical of its time. Everything had long ago been said, but not always in the best order or most pleasing manner. For a new generation of readers, it needed reshaping and up-dating with a little new material. The *Tazyīn al-Aswāq* seems to have been very popular, and after the advent of printing, several editions came off the presses of Cairo and Būlāq, at least some of them with the *Dīwān aṣ-Ṣabāba* printed along the margin.[131]

The process of "cannibalizing," as it were, this group of works did not stop with the *Tazyīn*, or with its obscure Maghribī counterpart to be mentioned in a moment. One al-Qannaujī (1248/1832–1307/1890), an Indian Muslim writer, made up a book with the

130. Ṣafadī said that these two poets disguised their mystical views on unity with God (*waḥda*) by expressing them in erotic poetry, using the device of *tawriya*, a kind of double meaning. See Seeger A. Bonebakker, *Some Early Definitions of the Tawriya and Ṣafadī's Faḍḍ al-Xitām ʿan at-Tawriya wa-'l-Istixdām* ("Columbia University Publications in Near and Middle East Studies," Series A, No. VIII; The Hague: Mouton and Co., 1966), pp. 88–89 (= *Faḍḍ al-Khitām*, MS İstanbul, Köprülü 1351, folio 44b).

131. Note that most of the MSS and editions of the *Tazyīn* will be found in *GAL* not under that entry but under that for the *Maṣāriʿ* of as-Sarrāj, since it was somewhat incorrectly described as an "*Auszug*" of that work.

improbable title *Nashwat as-Sakrān min Ṣahbā' Tadhkār al-Ghizlān,* The Intoxication of One Drunk with the Wine of the Remembrance of Gazelles, utilizing the *Dīwān aṣ-Ṣabāba* and the *Tazyīn al-Aswāq.*[132]

THE ANONYMOUS "KITĀB ASʿĀR AL-ASWĀQ FĪ ASHʿĀR AL-ASHWĀQ"

This book, whose title might be translated, "The Prices in the Markets for the Verses about Yearning," appears to have been parallel in content and contemporary with Dā'ūd al-Anṭākī's *Tazyīn al-Aswāq bi Tafṣīl Ashwāq al-ʿUshshāq.* We may assume that the compiler was a Maghribī, since the two manuscripts found so far are both in Tunis and both copied in a Maghribī script but by two very different hands. That in the Bibliothèque Nationale de Tunisie (176 *mim*) gives the impression of being older than that in the Bibliothèque de la Faculté des Lettres (4272) and might easily date from the tenth/sixteenth century. It could not be earlier than the ninth/fifteenth century since the content of the work seems to be taken principally or entirely from al-Biqāʿī's *Aswāq al-Ashwāq* of that century.[133]

Both copies are incomplete, and both end at what is designated Chapter Twenty-Two in the text of the newer manuscript, though its table of contents lists that heading as Chapter Twenty-Three. According to the table, the complete work had thirty-nine chapters. Because they both end at the same point, it might be supposed that the manuscript had been copied from the older at some time before

132. *GAL,* S. I, 595; S. II, 859–60.
133. This *Asʿār al-Aswāq* is not in *GAL* and not yet in a published catalogue. Professor S. A. Bonebakker directed my attention to the two MSS after he had seen them on a research visit to Tunis. I subsequently examined them when I was there in August 1966. Bibliothèque Nationale de Tunisie 176 *mim* has been incorrectly listed there as the *K. Maṣāriʿ al-ʿUshshāq.* Someone wrote that title on the *recto* of the first folio after the loss of the folios from the introductory section in which the correct title had appeared.

the approximately eight folios now missing from the introduction in the older copy had been lost. However, while some chapter headings are carelessly omitted in the texts of both, more chapter headings are omitted in the older one and there are minor differences in the wording of chapter headings. Therefore, perhaps the newer derives from some third copy, also ending at Chapter Twenty-Two (or Twenty-Three) but more carefully done.

Besides al-Biqāʿī's *Aswāq al-Ashwāq*, a number of authors and titles of earlier works on the theory of profane love are mentioned. My impression is that most or all are taken at second or third hand through the *Aswāq al-Ashwāq*, itself the product of cumulative rearrangements of earlier material. Only a tedious attempt to trace every passage to al-Biqāʿī's book would show whether everything in the anonymous Maghribī book was simply a rearrangement of its immediate antecedent or whether the compiler had direct access to some of the other love theory works.

MARʿĪ B. YŪSUF'S "MUNYAT AL-MUḤIBBĪN WA BUGHYAT AL-ʿĀSHIQĪN"

Marʿī b. Yūsuf b. Abī Bakr b. Aḥmad al-Karmī (d. 1033/1624)[134] was born in Ṭūr Karm, near Nablus, studied in Jerusalem, and later in Cairo, where he settled to pursue an academic career. He

134. *GAL*, G. II, 369; S. II, 496–7; Nachträge to S. II, 497, found in S. III, 1292. Muḥibbī, IV, 358–61. Wüstenfeld, *Gesch.*, 355. (Wüstenfeld speaks of "other" biographical sources but actually names only Muḥibbī.)

See García Gómez, "Un precedente y una consecuencia del 'Collar de la Paloma'," *And.* XVI (1951), 324–30. He indicates for the first time that the *Munyat al-Muḥibbīn* belongs to this group of works on profane love and that its author knew and used the *Ṭauq al-Ḥamāma*, possibly directly. [He hopes that it was directly, since if there was a copy of the *Ṭauq* in the Syrian area in the 17th Century, we might yet find another manuscript of the work.]

However, García Gómez thinks the author of *Munyat al-Muḥibbīn* is one Yūsuf b. Yaḥyā b. Marʿī. He knew of two manuscripts of the *Munya*, one in the Maktabat al-Baladīya, Alexandria (*Jim*-4564-*Nun*), of 35 folios, oriental script, and one in the

became a sheikh in the Sulṭān Ḥasan Mosque, but one Ibrāhīm Maimūnī got the office away from him and a sharp rivalry began. Muḥibbī's account makes it sound as though Mar'ī's career as a scholar was a very productive one because he was deeply engrossed in his learned researches. He divided his time between giving *fatwās*, teaching, studying, and writing. His books were reputed to have been composed with great care, so that even his enemies found it difficult to find fault. His *Kawākib ad-Durrīya fī Manāqib al-Mujtahid Ibn Taimīya*[135] is still an important source of information on the life and doctrines of Ibn Taimīya. Though a late work, belonging to the period in which Arabic literature yields very few original productions, Mar'ī b. Yūsuf's *Munyat al-Muḥibbīn* has some merit. It is a kind of précis of the literature on the theory of profane love with a few words on mystical love also. In a concise, clear, and straightforward style, he distills the essence of the subject into ten short chapters. He also injects his own viewpoint into it after

Dār al-Kutub, Cairo (Adab 6252), of 51 folios, 15 by 20 cm., Maghribī script. The first bears the name Yūsuf b. Yaḥyā b. Mara'ī (*sic*) al-Tūrkaramī (*sic*) al-Ḥanbalī, he says. (*And.* XVI [1951], 324) (I do not know whether that is his transliteration or whether the MS is voweled thus. I spell it according to Brockelmann, Wüstenfeld, and others.) The second manuscript he described is listed in the Cairo catalogue as *Al-Muḥibb wa 'l-Maḥabba*, by an anonymous author. García Gómez identified it as the *Munya*. I have found a third manuscript of the work. It bears the full title *Munyat al-Muḥibbīn wa Bughyat al-'Āshiqīn*, attributed to Yūsuf b. Mar'ī al-Ḥanbalī. This last MS also is in Cairo but not in the published catalogue, being listed in a handwritten card file. It is Tal'at (i.e. the collection of the late Tal'at Pasha), Adab 4648, written in a slightly cursive, *naskhī*, 54 folios, 15·5 by 22 cm.

García Gómez cites a biography of Yūsuf b. Yaḥyā b. Mar'ī in Muḥibbī's *Khulāṣat al-Athar*, IV, 508. He died 1078/1667. However, apparently García Gómez did not know that in the same work (IV, 358–61) Muḥibbī gives the biography of Mar'ī b. Yūsuf, of the same town and perhaps the same family, who died 1033/1624, and it is among his works that the titles *Munyat al-Muḥibbīn wa Bughyat al-'Āshiqīn* and *Taskīn al-Ashwāq* are listed. *Taskīn al-Ashwāq* is mentioned in the pages of the *Munya* as another of the writer's books on love. Muḥibbī, a native of Damascus (1061/1651–1111/1699), was a much younger contemporary of that Yūsuf b. Yaḥyā b. Mar'ī to whom he does *not* ascribe the two works. It would seem as though later copyists knew the name of the more recent man better and confused him with the earlier man. Possibly a grandson took the work of his ancestor and attributed it to himself. Lévi-Provençal thought this may have happened in the case of the *K. ar-Rauḍ al-Mi'ṭār* of al-Ḥimyarī but could not prove it. (E. Lévi-Provençal, *La peninsule Ibérique au Moyen Age*, d'après le Kitāb ar-rawḍ al-mi'ṭār fī ḫabar al-akṭār d'ibn 'Abd al-Mun'im al-Ḥimyarī [Leiden: E. J. Brill, 1938], xiii ff.)

135. Cairo, 1329.

quoting from the major predecessors to whom he is indebted, Ibn al-Qayyim, Ibn Ḥazm, Ibn al-Jauzī, Ibn Abī Ḥajala, and Shihāb ad-Dīn Maḥmud b. Fahd. While he was a Ḥanbalī like Ibn al-Jauzī and Ibn al-Qayyim, he seems to have been more friendly than they were towards the Ṣūfīs and their teachings, to judge from the number of times he quotes from them. The whole tone of the treatise is irenical. Frequently his solution after presenting two different, conflicting points of view is to explain that there is some truth in both views.

He begins by establishing the nature of *maḥabba* and the nature of *ʿishq*, their causes, degrees, and names as well as the difference between *ʿishq*, *khulla*, and *maḥabba*. After summarizing the best-known arguments of those who approve of *ʿishq* and those who disapprove of it, and his own answer to them, he goes on to discuss *hawā* separately. Next come the signs of love, the question of whether the union of lovers increases or decreases their longing, the question of whether the concealment of love is possible or not, opposition on the part of the beloved, practical advice for those sick with love, and cautions against transgression. He closes with a long chapter on the virtues of poetry in the course of which he brings up the old arguments about whether poetry is ethical or in conformity with Islamic law. He concludes with selected verses about love, including several folios of his own poetry.

AS-SALAṬĪ'S "ṢABĀBAT AL-MUʿĀNĪ WA ṢABBĀBAT AL-MAʿĀNĪ"[136]

We know very little about the author, Muḥyī ad-Dīn b. Taqī

136. *GAL*, G. II, 276. There are two MSS to be added to the one (Berlin 8431) in *GAL*: Princeton University, Yahuda 5168, folios 76a–101a (fragment); Chester Beatty 4990. The latter actually has *Ṣabābat al-Muʿānī wa Mathābat al-Maʿānī* on the title page. The earliest *ex libris* note on it is from A.H. 1087. Both the Berlin and the Chester Beatty catalogs give the first word of the second half of the title as

ad-Dīn Abū Bakr as-Salaṭī ad-Dimashqī[137] (flourished ca. 1065/1655), beyond what his name tells us. His only surviving works are an anthology of poetry and this book, The Ardent Love of the Afflicted and the Pourer Forth of Meanings. He may have been a grammarian, since the title page of one of the manuscripts of this book calls him the "Sibawayh of his time."[138]

The book begins with an outline of the psychology of the spirit (or self or lower nature, *nafs*) containing extensive unacknowledged borrowing of passages from Ibn al-Qayyim's introduction to his *Rauḍat al-Muḥibbīn*. Chapter One discusses "*ʿishq*: the name, the derivation of the meaning of its name, its definition, causes, and signs . . ."[139] The "*Ṣabbābat al-Maʿānī*" in the title refers to this explanation of the "derivation of the meaning of its name," i.e. the inner meaning to be found in each of the letters *ʿain*, *shīn*, and *qāf*, which, taken together, describe the nature or character of the phenomenon which is called *ʿishq*. This explanation is virtually the only thing which sets off this work from the previous late works on the theory of profane love.

Chapter Two deals with *maḥabba*, its names, signs, and effects, and Chapters Three and Four cover various kinds of lovers and love stories. Stories and theories on the love of the animals, birds, vegetables, and minerals and some discussion of jealousy are thrown together in the Conclusion. In sum, the book is a relatively brief[140] and poorly organized work composed by culling passages from the *Rauḍat al Muḥibbīn*, the *Tazyīn al-Aswāq*, and possibly the *Dīwān*

"Ṣabbābat" (with *ṣād*), a word not in Lane. It would be the noun of intensiveness with the added *tāʾ marbūṭa* to strengthen the idea of intensiveness: "one who (or which) pours forth much or often." There is a slight possibility that the spelling was originally with *sīn* rather than *ṣād*: "the finger [pointing at] the meanings." It can be shown that either word, carelessly rendered, could be seen by a copyist as "*mathā-bat*." Or was the original title word "*mathābat*," meaning "meeting-place?" The Chester Beatty MS (before A.H. 1087) is older than the Berlin MS (A.H. 1106), although Ahlwardt thought at the time he cataloged it that it was likely an autograph. The existence of the Chester Beatty MS was unknown then.

137. I have not yet found biographical sources on him.

138. Chester Beatty 4990, folio 1a.

139. Chester Beatty 4990, folio 7b.

140. Eighty-one folios in Chester Beatty 4990.

aṣ-Ṣabāba and the *Al-Wāḍiḥ al-Mubīn,* or others upon which the *Tazyīn* itself was based. (This very late work has not previously been analyzed in its relationship to this group.)[141]

141. In revising this study, I found that U. Rizzitano had once noted, in discussing Ibn Abī Ḥajala's book, ". . . verso la metà del secolo XVII Muḥyī ad-Dīn . . . as-Salaṭī ad-Dimaśqī compose, sul modello del *Dīwān aṣ-ṣabābah,* un *Ṣabābah al-mu'ānī wa sabbābah al-ma'ānī* . . ." (*RSO,* XXVIII (1953), 57.) Therefore, he was aware of the book of as-Salaṭī, though in view of my findings above—or if he has since examined a manuscript—perhaps he would modify his characterization of it.

PART 2

THE CONTENT AND FORM OF THE WORKS

I

THE ELEMENTS OR RAW MATERIALS OF THE ARABIC THEORY OF PROFANE LOVE

A wide variety of elements went into the making of the writings on the theory of profane love. These raw materials, as it were, are quite different in scope and origin. They exemplify many of those strands of culture and tradition which contributed to Arab Islamic civilization, as well as several of the branches of learning which developed within it. Here are the Arab poets and masters of prose, the Greek philosophers and physicians, the scholars of Tradition (Ḥadīth), the storytellers and popular preachers, the Muslim theologians, philosophers, and mystics, and the Arab lexicographers and philologists. In an attempt to examine what might be known about love—love as a state of the heart, mind, or soul—our writers, as a group, drew upon them all. Their more comprehensive works contain elements out of every one of these sources.

The factor which most determines the character of these books is the religious one. Both the orientation of a particular book and the character of its composition, as well as certain minor details, are strongly determined by the author's ethical and religious attitudes. Their effect will be perceived in the discussion (Part 2, Chapter II) of the formal structure of the works and the major divisions of opinion which appear (Part 3, both chapters). We shall see how these attitudes affect the author's treatment or use of the elements of profane love theory—Ḥadīth, Koran verses, anecdotes, stories, poetry, philosophy, and so forth—as well as the general argument and plan of the works. In some cases, the writer may not have enunciated his viewpoint clearly in the text, indeed he may have refrained from expressing it, but when his work is compared with others on the subject, many of his assumptions become clear.

KORAN VERSES AND TRADITIONS

Because of the authority they possessed, the Koran and the formal traditions, the Ḥadīth, reporting the sayings and acts of the Prophet, played a large part in the formation of Islamic standards of ethical conduct. Thus, it was natural that these two sources should be quoted in the books on love for guidance upon questions of what is right or wrong, blameworthy or praiseworthy, and becoming or unbecoming to the Muslim. The author's concern in such instances was usually with what is polite, ethical, virtuous, or pleasing to God, rather than with whether a certain action falls into such categories as "forbidden (*ḥarām*)" or "not forbidden (*ḥalāl*)." This is well illustrated in the tradition "Of those things which are not forbidden by Sacred Law, the most hateful to God is divorce."[1]

Traditions having to do with ethical, pious, or polite conduct are quoted most copiously in the *I'tilāl al-Qulūb, Dhamm al-Hawā,* and *Rauḍat al-Muḥibbīn,* works which form a distinct, ethically oriented subtype of this literature and will be discussed as such in the next chapter. The authors of these books were careful to take the priorities of the Muslim's relationship and responsibility to Allāh into account in all aspects of the theory of profane love. Because of this, certain traditions by their nature figure prominently in their works but find no place in other works written in the more secular spirit of Arabic

1. *Rauḍa,* 217.

adab literature. An example of this is the tradition enjoining the Muslim to avert his gaze from all those who are not "lawful" to him, i.e. from all women that are not his wives or concubines and from all youths. Other traditions akin to it are the injunction to avoid being alone with such women or youths and to avoid having them sit in the range of one's view at social gatherings and, in a similar spirit, warnings about the threat that women pose to moral life in general: "I left behind me no source of temptation to men more detrimental than women." "Be wary of the world and be wary of women." "The things I fear most for my community are women and wine."[2]

The Ḥadīth and verses from the Koran not only provided guidance on ethics, piety, and good manners, but they were consulted for their insights on man, the world, and God. A typical tradition of this kind found in almost every book on love or friendship is the famous one explaining the attraction of one personality to another as an affinity of like for like. 'Ā'isha is reported to have told the following story about the Prophet's words on this subject:

> *A woman used to visit the Quraish and make them laugh. She once came to Madīna and stayed at the house of a woman who had the gift of making people laugh. The Prophet said, "At whose house did the lady So-and-so stay?" and she* ['Ā'isha] *replied, "With So-and-so, who makes everyone laugh." So he said, "Souls are troops and those who recognize one another seek each other's company and those which do not, clash."*[3]

The most important and fundamental divisions of opinion in the Arabic theory of profane love, and a good many trivial ones as well, arise directly or indirectly out of differences over the use or interpretation of certain verses of the Koran and certain Ḥadīth. Those differences of opinion which have broader theological or ethical implications give rise to the most heated discussion. On topics less emotionally charged, the writers are sometimes content to quote a

2. *Rauḍa*, 94.
3. *Rauḍa*, 71.

dozen different opinions or theories without expressing any preference for one or another.

There are many ideas which are a part of love theory which are based on sacred texts and are completely non-controversial, finding universal acceptance, in fact. Thus, for example, everyone agrees that it is a good thing to do all one can to bring about the lawful union of a lover with his beloved, even if, under some circumstances, it should involve considerable emotional or financial sacrifice to oneself. Proofs and illustrations of this begin with a tradition which tells of a case where the Prophet tried to reunite an estranged wife with her grief-stricken husband.[4] Such deeds are seen as an expression of the virtues of compassion, magnanimity, kindness, and, sometimes, self-restraint. Islamic tradition adds that God will richly reward such actions.

Traditions from the Prophet are, of course, not the only traditions put to good use in these books. Large numbers of traditions about the sayings or doings of respected religious or political leaders, including pre-Islamic and foreign personages, are used for evidence and illustration, edification and entertainment.[5] Often these other traditions touch on themes for which no authoritative tradition from the Prophet exists, or they serve as corroborative testimony and give additional detail on a subject. Actually, as in the case of some legal and other traditions, it is highly probable that some of the sayings of Companions or other early Muslims are the earlier traditions, while those purporting to be from the Prophet were put into circulation at a later date.

Another, albeit less important, use of the Ḥadīth in these books is in quotations for textual evidence (*shawāhid*) of the meaning or

4. *Rauḍa*, 375.

5. It is sometimes impractical to draw a distinction between the function of the anecdotes, discussed later in this chapter, and traditions. We may have an anecdote or a proverb which is also a tradition by virtue of the manner in which it was transmitted. Thus Suwaid b. Saʿīd, who, as we shall see (Part 3, Chapter 1), transmitted, if he did not invent, the tradition on the martyrs of love, is reported to have transmitted as a tradition the words "*Zur ghibban tazdad ḥubban*," "Visit infrequently (or "every other day") and be loved more," which are quoted elsewhere as a proverb. See G. W. Freytag, *Arabum Proverbia* (Bonn: A. Marcum, 1838), I, 587–88, and Lane, *s.v. gh-b-b*.

usage of a word or term. In the first centuries of Arabic philology, the Ḥadīth were thought unfit for grammatical investigation, because it was agreed that they contained not the original words of the Prophet or the Companions but only the sense. Their expression was thought to be influenced by later traditionists whose knowledge of the subtleties of pure Arabic expression was in doubt. The lexicographers, on the other hand, from the very beginning seem to have had no scruples against using the Ḥadīth as *shawāhid* for semantics, and eventually the religious prestige of the Ḥadīth seems to have led to their more general use as an example of pure Arabic.[6]

POETRY

Poetry is quoted in all the works on the theory of love. Some are largely anthologies of poetry. The best discussions of love turn frequently to verse to illustrate aptly the ideas under discussion, to reinforce the author's statements, or to express his thought more subtly. The poets quoted are taken from every century, though the classical poets (pre-Islamic, Umayyad, and early ʿAbbāsid) are strongly favored. Frequently, the authors themselves compose verses to express a particular emotion, thought, or experience. At first glance, it might seem as though such extensive use of poetry was merely a manifestation of the Arabs' insatiable appetite for it. It seems to weave such a spell over them that even those authors who wrote serious, dogmatic polemics against passionate love could not resist quoting many pages of verse whose appealing portrayal of the thought and feelings of the lover would seem to work against the author's expressed ends.

Poetry, then, might seem incidental to the burden of the author's discussion, just so much decoration or elaboration of the essential

6. See L. Kopf, "Religious Influences on Medieval Arabic Philology," *Studia Islamica, V* (1956), 50–51.

ideas. The striking aptness of some of the verse that he uses might be purely fortuitous or attributable to the fact that on the subject of love there was a large fund of poetry to draw upon.[7] Though this very often *is* the case, one cannot escape the conclusion that in some instances the prose discussion of theory is secondary to the poetry (rather than the reverse) in the sense that the themes and images of Arabic poetry were the raw material for the theoretical formulations.

The development of an original body of theoretical concepts about the psychological, emotional, or spiritual mechanisms of love appears to spring from a systematic anthologizing of the best in Arabic poetry on these themes. In the ʿAbbāsid period, men like Muḥammad b. Dā'ūd began to collect verses on a subject or idea, comparing different ways of expressing the same idea. This critical activity lent itself to a refined awareness of the whole spectrum of emotions, situations, and experiences of love. Though the collector or critic was aware of the fact that the poet might be portraying only his own immediate feelings and perceptions, he was also aware that the effect of the poet's activity was to articulate the universal experience of his listeners. Certainly, no theme is more universal than love, but the poet must make the listener feel that he has touched the pulse of reality.

As the Arab poets, beginning with the period of the early ʿAbbāsid caliphs, tried to outdo one another, they extended through allusion and metaphor the possibilities for the refined expression of the experiences of one in love. The struggle to say something clever or fresh, to win applause and patronage, and the tendency to experiment with new poetic themes, added both to the quantity and the originality of poetry. Some of it, however, became hopelessly recondite and strained and lost the ring of truth. Such poetry would, of course, be useless as a source for love theory. Muḥammad b. Dā'ūd al-Iṣbahānī, who not only composed an anthology on love,

7. Love poetry, both in the form of *ghazal* and in the form of *nasīb*, enjoyed great popularity in pre-Islamic and Umayyad literature. Whether one thinks with Blachère that the two forms were aspects of one tradition or holds with H. A. R. Gibb that the two forms had no demonstrable connection does not matter much here. See R. Blachère and A. Bausani, *EI²*, art. "Ghazal," and H. A. R. Gibb, *Arabic Literature* (2nd ed. rev.; Oxford: Clarendon Press, 1963), p. 44.

the *Kitāb az-Zahra*, but commented on some of the verses, was very harsh on unrealistic conceits.

Although verses alluding to the physical beauty of the beloved occur in love theory works, these writers as a rule are not much concerned with the analyzing or describing of the fine points of manly or womanly beauty and the sensual appeal of particular features.[8] In principle, beauty is recognized as liable to attract love, but it is also recognized that what is beauty in one man's eyes is not beauty in another's. This is an axiom of love and one of its mysteries. The writers therefore look deeper for the causes of love. A favorite illustration of this is the often-repeated anecdote about ʿAzza and Kuthayyir.

> *It is related that ʿAzza paid a call on al-Ḥajjāj. On seeing her* [for the first time, evidently], *he exclaimed, "O, ʿAzza! You are not as Kuthayyir has described you, by Allāh!" To that she replied, "O, Commander! He does not see me with the same eye with which you see me."*[9]

Jāḥiẓ, too, speaks of the woman who would not seem to have anything to commend her but some unrecognized womanly quality which makes her dear to her husband's heart.[10] For this reason, the writers on the theory of love show more interest in the verses describing the psychological or spiritual phenomena of love, for example the poetic descriptions of the role of the eye, the heart, and the will in the process of falling in love. Poetry furnishes plenty of material for the theoretical analysis of this phenomenon. Ibn Qayyim al-Jauzīya devoted two chapters[11] of his book to an imaginary dispute between the eye and the heart over the measure of responsibility of each for the catastrophe of *ʿishq*. Here Ibn al-Qayyim articulated in prose dialogue and discussion interspersed with verses the whole psychology of the wandering gaze that smites with love

8. Another difference between books like *K. Akhbār an-Nisā'*, with its more superficial concern over what pleases men, and the works on love theory, which are largely concerned with what makes people soul-mates.
9. *Rauḍa*, 65.
10. "R. fi 'l-ʿIshq wa 'n-Nisā'," *Majmūʿat Rasā'il*, 165.
11. Chapters 6 and 7.

or is smitten. He exhibits at its best that process whereby the scholarly and reflective mind, working on the poets and other sources, extracts the lessons and principles to be perceived there, producing what we may call theory of love.

The terseness of style which is typical of Arabic poetry and the fact that, especially in older poems, the logical connection between one line and the next is not always immediately apparent and may even be nonexistent, offer some peculiar problems to authors who use poetry for proof texts or illustration. A particularly terse line may express a whole complex of ideas and therefore appears several times in the same work to illustrate these ideas. Where a theme does not continue from one line to the next, the writer may be forced to quote intervening lines before he arrives at a second line which picks it up. On the other hand, there are many instances where a single line or even a single hemistich would suffice to illustrate the point under discussion, but the author, conscious of the anthological tradition which is part of this literature, cannot forego quoting some additional lines or even the complete poem.

Discoveries or perceptions about the psychology of love are, of course, not unique to the Arabs or to the medieval Islamic world. Every nation and, indeed, every generation wrestles in its own way with its unsolved mysteries. Whether the medieval Arabs excelled other peoples in their perceptions on this subject is not for us to decide here. However, it seems evident that the qualities of Arabic poetry and the popularity of love as a theme for the poets contributed much to the development of the Arabic theory of profane love.

ANECDOTES AND STORIES

As becomes Arabic books of erudition such as these, the anecdotes and stories appearing there are all assumed to be at least partially historical. In some cases they are accompanied by chains of transmitters and, if not, are usually attributed to some reputable authority. Medieval Arabic scholarship had little use for unauthenticated fiction. Anonymous stories of free invention such as are found interwoven with those purporting to be historical in the *Thousand and One Nights* were seldom thought sufficiently dignified for the attention of reputable littérateurs and scholars.[12]

In a sense, stories and anecdotes often serve the same function as poetry in the books on the theory of love, for they are both the source of theoretical formulations and the illustrative material for them. The great majority are quite short, a few lines or one or two paragraphs. Therefore, the reason for their inclusion at a particular point is readily grasped by the reader. As with poetry, if the quotation is famous and particularly appropriate in the context, it would appear in some cases that the theoretical generalizations were arrived at by reflection upon this evidence. Sometimes, though, however old the anecdote may be or however clearly it makes a point, it is apparent that it is merely given as confirming evidence or illustration of some dictum enunciated already by an authority which carries greater weight.

The function of the anecdote or story in a book on the theory of love depends somewhat on the character of the individual book. The authors of the most systematic and analytic works on the subject often use the stories and anecdotes as proofs or examples for the ideas discussed. Where the book has more the nature of a structured anthology on love and love theory, they may simply be recited as illustrating a particular phenomenon or category of love. Many of the stories are so well known that one cannot escape the conclusion that in some cases the author's classifications of types of love (or his chapter headings) are just an excuse to retell these stories of which the public apparently never grew tired.[13] In such cases, there

12. As a consequence of this attitude, the production of books of fantastic or fictional stories fell increasingly after the 3rd/9th century to anonymous or obscure men. Reputable scholars disdained to compose or collect tales thought to be fit only for frivolous or ignorant persons and women and children. See Nabia Abbott, "A Ninth Century Fragment of the *Thousand Nights*," *JNES*, VIII (1949), 158.

On the place of the two types of story, fictional and historical, in the *Thousand and One Nights*, see Mia I. Gerhardt, *The Art of Story-Telling* (Leiden: E. J. Brill, 1963), 377 ff.

13. Just as some late works on *badīʿ* (figures of speech) appear to be an excuse for the quoting of isolated favorite lines of poetry.

is often no real discussion after the introductory part of the book. The writer has pleased himself and, presumably, the reader by pigeon-holing the mass of stories about lovers. "Love, dear reader, comes in these varieties. . . ."

Though most of the anecdotes and stories are about Muslims, both city Arabs and bedouins, there are some which are about non-Islamic and non-Arab peoples—Israelites and ancient Greeks, Indians, and pre-Islamic Persians, as well as members of non-Muslim minorities living in Muslim society. Not surprisingly, stories of foreign origin are often quite altered by the time they are retold in these books. The story of Susanna and the Elders, for example, from the Apocryphal book of Daniel appears and reappears for centuries in various altered and abbreviated versions before Dā'ūd al-Anṭākī presents the correct version taken directly from the book of Daniel and calls attention to this fact.[14]

INFORMATION FROM THE ARABIC LEXICOGRAPHERS AND PHILOLOGISTS

The two general categories of raw material just mentioned, poetry and anecdotes or stories on love, are the most constantly employed and contribute to every aspect of love theory. A much more limited and specific but nevertheless essential element was the information drawn from lexicographers and philologists on the etymology of words used for love, their exact meaning, and proper usage. These were matters which, logically, called for treatment early in the book, though some authors evidently did not see this need.[15] Generally, just the name of the scholar is given, though sometimes the name of the work, usually a dictionary, is mentioned. We can

14. *Tazyīn*, III, 195–98. Earlier, incorrect versions are in *Maṣāri'*, I, 74, and *Rauḍa*, 196. Cf. Daniel 13 (in the editions of the Bible with separate Apocrypha: The History of Susanna).
15. See Part 3, Chap. II.

take a passage from Ibn Qayyim al-Jauzīya's *Rauḍat al-Muḥibbīn* as an example, since this aspect of love received its fullest treatment there. After holding forth for a page on the theories about the etymology of the word *ḥubb,* how from the root *ḥ-b-b* it came to mean "love," he moves on to a discussion of the morphological patterns and meanings of other words having to do with love derived from the same root:

> *He [al-Jauharī] says in* aṣ-Ṣaḥāḥ, "Ḥubb *is* maḥabba *[both meaning love] and likewise* ḥibb, *voweled with* i. *And* ḥibb *is also synonymous with* ḥabīb *[beloved] just as in the case of* khidn *and* khadīn *[both meaning intimate friend]." I say: One may compare this to* dhibḥ *[sacrificial victim] which also has the meaning* madhbūḥ *[one sacrificed].*[16]

Discussing the meaning and etymology of the word *ʿishq,* he says:

> *Ibn Sīda said, "*ʿIshq *is the lover's admiration for the beloved. It may occur in chaste love or in immoral love." . . . Farrā' said, "*ʿIshq *is a sticky plant and the name* ʿishq *is applied to that well-known phenomenon in man because of its clinging to the heart." Ibn al-ʿArābī said, "*ʿAshaqa *is synonymous with* lablāba *[a type of ivy-like vine,* Dolichos lablab], *which is green or yellow and clings to the trees which are close to it."*[17]

These are plain matters of etymology, usage, and meaning, but one often finds quite another kind of discussion of terminology, which is not always clearly kept apart from the matters just illustrated above, and which also comes from the philologists. In these instances, the question asked or implied is: "What is *ʿishq* (or *hawā,* etc.)?", not "What is the etymology of the word and its synonyms?". The information elicited is as much philosophical or cultural as linguistic. Though the original sources of such statements are often not named,

16. *Rauḍa,* 17.

17. *Rauḍa,* 25–26. Articles on the lexicographers mentioned in the quotations may be found (*s.v.*) in *EI*². See also John A. Haywood, *Arabic Lexicography* (2nd ed.; Leiden: E. J. Brill, 1965), *passim.* See the index, *s.v.*, except for Farrā', who was primarily a grammarian of the "School of Kūfa," and is not mentioned there.

one scholar whose name does appear often is al-Aṣmaʿī (123/739–217/831), the early philologist and lexicographer.[18] He traveled about among the bedouin Arabs, it is reported, in order to take down verses or other philological material from their lips. He passed on many sayings which he heard from simple men and women of the desert, illustrating true Arabic eloquence, the piety of plain-living people, and sometimes their profound grasp of the deeper things of life. One of these has already been quoted to illustrate two different interpretations of what love is.[19] In another interview, al-Aṣmaʿī reports that he heard another opinion about the nature of *ʿishq*:

> *I asked a bedouin Arab about* ʿishq *and he said, "It is too sublime to be seen and it is hidden from the eyes of mortals, for it is concealed in the breast like the latent fire in a flint, which when struck produces fire, this fire remaining hidden as long as it is left alone." Some of the Arabs say, "*ʿIshq *is a kind of madness. Madness has its varieties and* ʿishq *is one of them."*[20]

OPINIONS OF PHILOSOPHERS AND PHYSICIANS

A number of passages in these writings dealing with the theoretical questions of what love is, its causes, the mechanism of its onset and development, and its signs and symptoms, are drawn from the *falāsifa* (philosophers), *ḥukamāʾ* (philosophers or physicians), and *aṭibbāʾ* (physicians), be they Greek, Hellenistic, or their oriental Christian and Muslim heirs. The quoted authorities are not always actually named, phrases such as "the ancient philosophers" being used. These opinions seemed to have a special fascination for the Arabs because they offered satisfying explanations, sometimes quite detailed, for phenomena otherwise mysterious and inexplicable.

18. See Haywood, 42–44, and B. Lewin, *EI*², art. "Al-Aṣmaʿī."
19. See Introduction, n. 6.
20. *Rauḍa*, 139.

The variety of theories available offered an explanation to please every turn of mind. Those writers who wished to discredit *ʿishq* and *hawā* made good use of the authority of negative opinions such as those explaining love as a blind, unreasoning delusion serving no good purpose, the vain preoccupation of a heart empty of something worthwhile, or the result of some physiological imbalance. Those writers whose only concern is to instruct and entertain the reader by presenting every interesting and authoritative opinion take a more detached view and do not emphasize one type of scientific or philosophical theory at the expense of another.

Some opinions sound like accurate quotations from Greek works on ethics or medicine (where love is regarded as a disease). Some of the early authors on love appear to have taken them from Arabic translations of Greek works, if not from the Greek texts themselves, or from some work in Arabic containing extracts and summaries from Greek works. It is worth noting that the lifetime of Ibn Dāʾūd, author of the *K. az-Zahra*, coincided with the period of greatest translation activity. We know that he was a relator of scholarly traditions from al-Kindī,[21] and we might therefore conclude that he studied under that scholar, whose work encompassed the whole field of Greek science and philosophy. If he did not study such subjects under al-Kindī, he at least would have had access to correct information from texts and through expert friends. It is evident, however, that most writers after the first few to write on the theory of love simply took over the sayings of physicians and philosophers as found in earlier works on the same topic.

There were theories about love which had their origins in various dualist philosophies of the East and were known in learned circles in the Islamic world. Masʿūdī claims to have known about them, but unfortunately the work in which he says he gave these theories is not thus far available to us.[22] In his *Murūj adh-Dhahab*, he does give an explanation of the nature of love by a Zoroastrian.[23] References

21. See above, page 7.
22. See Appendix.
23. In *Tazyīn*, I, 56, there is a quotation attributed to some dualists. I believe I have seen one or two other references to them in other works, but I am not certain.

to the opinions of such persons or groups are not common in the works on love theory, probably because of the strong prejudices against them in the Islamic world.[24]

An attempt to trace some of these fragments attributed to Greek philosophers and physicians would seem worthwhile. However, in most cases, the task calls for the experience of one who has dealt with the Greek works known in the Islamic world. Some idea of the possible discoveries which might issue from such inquiries can be gained from Richard Walzer's analysis of one such quotation in the *Kitāb 'Atf al-Alif al-Ma'lūf 'alā al-Lām al-Ma'ṭūf* by ad-Dailamī (fourth/tenth century), the oldest complete and extant mystical book on love. Walzer concluded that the passage might well represent a fragment of a lost dialogue of Aristotle.[25] One difficulty which complicates the tracing of such fragments is that some quotations have been attributed by Arab authors to more than one authority. This turned out to be the case with the fragment from ad-Dailamī.[26]

24. *Murūj*, VI, 375–76.
25. *Greek into Arabic*, 48–49.
26. Walzer adds in a footnote that S. M. Stern informed him that the definition of love (given in the fragment of dialogue) attributed to Aristotle is also found under the name of Hippocrates in Ḥunain b. Isḥāq's *Nawādir al-Falāsifa* (Hebrew version, *Musre ha-Pilosofim*, ed. Löwenthal, 35), as well as in three books with which we are concerned here, namely, the *K. az-Zahra*, p. 17; the *Murūj*, VI, 377–79, where the definition is attributed to "a physician"; and the *Dīwān aṣ-Ṣabāba*, p. 11, where it is attributed to Pythagoras. It may be added that it also appears in a similar form in the *K. al-Maṣūn* (Leiden Or. 1951), folio 27b–28a; *Tazyīn*, I, 59–60; and *Ṣabābat al-Mu'ānī* (Chester Beatty 4990), folio 17b. It should be noted, however, that there are considerable differences between versions and that the versions in the *K. az-Zahra* and the *Murūj*, the longest and most detailed, read like a passage from a medical text rather than an Aristotelian dialogue. They describe love as a serious pathological syndrome affecting the brain, the emotions, and the digestive and circulatory systems.

II

THE EVOLUTION OF FORM AND CONTENT IN THESE WORKS

As one examines the development of this group of works over nearly a millennium, there are certain aspects of content and form which lend themselves to analysis and description and which reveal an essential unity as well as some variety. The unity is in the evolution of traditional and typical features of form and content; the variety consists in minor variations of form or content or differences in the spirit or motive that dominated the authors. Some wrote in the more secular spirit of *adab* literature and some were ruled by religious and ethical considerations, but, in fact, the spirit in which they wrote was seldom purely that of *adab* nor yet entirely religious, though in any one work the balance usually tipped heavily in one direction or the other.

In the structure or content of the twenty works in this group being studied here, the frequency of certain features strikes the attention. The most obvious of these, alluded to already in the introduction and survey of authors and works, is the twofold division of content into (1) a discussion of the essence, nature, causes, names, and kinds of love and the differences between these kinds, and (2) the "circumstances" (*aḥwāl*) of the lovers, a term which covers many kinds of theorizing about the conduct of lovers and schemes for classifying lovers and their love affairs. The rudiments of these two types of subject matter are even to be seen in

Jāḥiẓ's two short essays as well as in the anonymous essay on love containing the fragment from Aḥmad b. aṭ-Ṭayyib as-Sarakhsī, discussed earlier.

I have said that this twofold division of subject matter is an obvious one, though, in fact, it was not at first always quite so obvious to me, and I have not seen these works discussed in these terms by Western scholars. The full significance of the term "*ḥāl*" (pl. *aḥwāl*) in the designation of the content of these works first came to my attention when I read the introduction to Kisā'ī's *Rauḍat al-'Āshiq* (seventh/thirteenth century). Kisā'ī speaks about the earlier works on love, unfortunately not named, as though the normal division of their content was, or ought to have been, the twofold one just described.[1] He criticized them all for their failure to strike a balance between the two parts, and possibly he means to indicate that some authors even neglected to include one of the two aspects of the subject matter on love. His remarks led me to look for this logical division of content in other works. It had already become clear to me that the later, more systematic books on the theory of profane love typically began with a discussion of its nature, names, causes, and so forth, but after that familiar beginning, one finds more variety in the content of the main part of the work, though certain subjects repeat themselves from book to book and seem to become traditional to the repertory. The common factor that underlies the several kinds of subject matter was not very clear to me. I did not know in what broad terms the Arab authors themselves might conceive this group of subjects since in many books, if there is an introduction or statement on the content about to be presented, it designates the topics to be treated one by one without taking notice of the content in broader terms. The "*aḥwāl* of the lovers" as used

1. See above, also, pages 30–31. The kinds of subject matter which Kisā'ī meant to include under the "*aḥwāl* of the lovers" may be inferred from the content of his own work, very typical of books of this group: (1) Kinds of lovers (prophets, caliphs, bosom friends, refined people [*ẓurafā'*], virtuous men, nobles) or rather, men of these categories whose love stories are known and are related under these headings; (2) Stories of love classified by the fate of the lover (those killed by love, those driven mad); (3) Conduct of lovers and those around them (the humility of lovers and the pride of the beloved, fidelity in promises, manly honor and integrity, treachery, suspicion, gentility, bringing lovers together, aiding them, carrying their messages).

by Kisā'ī fills the need for a concept that explains historically the presence of so much seemingly divergent material. As an organizing concept it is broad and sufficiently flexible to cover the subject matter, yet it sets it apart from the sections dealing with the nature, causes, names, and so on, of love.[2]

Kisā'ī's use of this term lends significance to Ibn Dā'ūd's declaration that he intends his book to contain a discussion of the essence (*kaun*) of *hawā* and its causes (*asbāb*) and the conditions that occur in it (*al-aḥwāl al-ʿāriḍa fīhi*) and that he will present the poetic themes portraying each *ḥāl* in the order that these *aḥwāl* befall the lover, one after the other (*tartīb al-wuqūʿ ḥālan fa-ḥālan*).[3] In Ibn Dā'ūd's book the *aḥwāl* consist of fifty phenomena or symptoms of love, expressed in aphorisms or axioms which are given in the form of chapter headings.[4] Nykl and García Gómez have emphasized how very different the *Kitāb az-Zahra* is in content and spirit from the *Ṭauq al-Ḥamāma* of Ibn Ḥazm, though both authors were Ẓāhirīs and both books are on love.[5] While there are differences, some already mentioned in the survey and some soon to be discussed here, there are two common features which to the best of my knowledge have been overlooked so far: First, the two books have the same basic structure and, furthermore, are the only two clear examples of it in the third to fifth centuries A.H., though this structure becomes the standard one and reaches a fuller development in the works of the centuries following. Thus, both books treat the essence, nature, and causes of love in the first chapter, the *Kitāb az-Zahra* providing more on this than the *Ṭauq al-Ḥamāma*, and then both books proceed to their main subject, the *aḥwāl* of the

2. The writers on profane love may have borrowed this usage of "*ḥāl*" from the technical vocabulary of medicine as the mystics are thought to have done. See L. Gardet, art. "*Ḥāl*," *EI*², and Massignon, *Passion*, II, 554.

3. *Zahra*, 5.

4. These chapter headings (*Zahra*, pp. *alif-jīm*) may be found in French translation in Massignon, *Passion*, I, 171–72, though, as Nykl (*Zahra*, foreword, 6) has pointed out, they are in some cases not very accurate renderings.

5. *Zahra*, foreword, 7. García Gómez (*al-Andalus*, XVI [1951], 312) says: ". . . la realidad es que ambas obras tienen poquísimo de común: la oriental es sobre todo una antología de versos ajenos sobre el amor, mientras la andaluza es un tratado psicológico, con sus ribetes de filosofía; aquélla está llena de exquisita afectación y de afeminada pedantería, mientras ésta resulta natural y humana, directa y caliente."

lovers in the order of their occurrence. The second feature which these two books have in common is the fact that the *aḥwāl* with which they both are primarily concerned are the psychological phenomena of love. In the *Kitāb az-Zahra* these are discussed and illustrated in poetry, with the emphasis most on the illustration in poetry, while in the *Ṭauq al-Ḥamāma* these phenomena are mainly a subject for discussion in prose, the poetry—mostly the author's own—taking second place. Therefore, it is not being very accurate to observe, as García Gómez does, that the *Kitāb az-Zahra* is above all an anthology of verses, while the *Ṭauq al-Ḥamāma* is a psychological treatise.[6]

The similarities do not end there, however, for a comparison of the two books shows evidence—in themes, Ḥadīth, and phraseology common to both—of the possible influence of the *Kitāb az-Zahra* upon the author of the *Ṭauq al-Ḥamāma.* Such evidence has been presented to demonstrate the possible influence of the *Kitāb al-Muwashshā* upon the *Ṭauq,* while the *Kitāb az-Zahra* has been dismissed as a most improbable source of influence.[7] The fact is, however, that a careful comparison of the themes and phraseology of the *Kitāb az-Zahra,* the *Kitāb al-Muwashshā,* and the *Ṭauq al-Ḥamāma* shows a certain number of parallels which could be used to show an affinity between any two books or between all three. Some of the parallels that have been presented as evidence of the possible influence of *Kitāb al-Muwashshā* upon the *Ṭauq al-Ḥamāma* would serve equally well to demonstrate the possible connection of the *Kitāb az-Zahra* with the *Ṭauq* or with both books, because they occur in the *Kitāb az-Zahra* also.[8] Other parallels could be found between

6. See n. 5, above.

7. García Gómez, *al-Andalus,* XVI (1951), 309–323.

8. For example, the following citations from the *K. az-Zahra* correspond with the parallels (cited here by page and item number) between the *K. al-Muwashshā* and the *Ṭauq* quoted by García Gómez in the article in *al-Andalus* just mentioned: The themes of two chapters in the *K. az-Zahra* (43 and 44) on the inability to keep love a secret = p. 315, No. 2; the martyrs-of-love tradition (*Zahra,* 66) = p. 318, No. 16; the tradition on people who have a natural affinity for each other (*Zahra,* 14) = p. 315, No. 7 and 317–18, No. 15.

As to parallels between the *K. az-Zahra* and the *K. al-Muwashshā,* García Gómez has pointed out that some of the axioms or epigrams that appear as chapter headings in *K. az-Zahra* appear also in the *K. al-Muwashshā* as sayings which the

the *Kitāb az-Zahra* and the *Ṭauq* which do not exist between that work and the *Kitāb al-Muwashshā*.[9] All these works might be best conceived of as based on a common fund of knowledge or theory about love and lovers, circulating orally and in written form. Thus, parallels could be found also between the *Ṭauq al-Ḥamāma* and the *Maṣāriʿ al-ʿUshshāq*, which was committed to writing in the East about thirty-five years after the *Ṭauq* was written in Spain, but these similarities would not, of course, represent borrowings from the

ẓurafā' inscribe on seal rings. He questions which book was the original source. (See *al-Andalus*, XVI [1951], 322–23; *K. al-Muwashshā*, ed. Brünnow, 164.) It would appear to me that Ibn Dā'ūd invented them (or some of them), because he was asked about one of them in a conversation reported in the *K. al-Maṣūn* (Leiden Or. 1951, folio 50b.). The two men were probably acquainted, for Ibn Dā'ūd's friend Nifṭawayh is quoted frequently in the *K. al-Muwashshā*. They seem to have been members of the "in-group" who thought of themselves as the *ẓurafā'*, "refined people." M. F. Ghazi ("Un group social: 'les Raffinés [Ẓurafā']'," *Studia Islamica*, XI [1959], 39–71) characterized the ideals of the *ẓurafā'* (pp. 45 and 63, especially), in such a way that it would be impossible to exclude Ibn Dā'ūd from their number. Add to this the fact that he expresses the *ẓarf* ideal in the *Kitāb az-Zahra*, especially in his discussion in the introduction of the type of person who has an affinity for *hawā*, in the sense of *ḥubb ʿUdhrī* and in the chapter title (Chap. 8) "He Who Would Be a *Ẓarīf* Must Be Chaste." Yet Ghazi seems to go out of his way to avoid mentioning Ibn Dā'ūd, making it appear that he follows García Gómez in regarding Ibn Dā'ūd as a man wholly different in outlook and temperament from al-Washshā' and the *ẓurafā'*. This interpretation seems to stem from the uncritical acceptance of Massignon's portrayal of Ibn Dā'ūd (*Passion*, 160–82), which is unbalanced. Massignon was searching for clues to the motivation for Ibn Dā'ūd's opposition to the mystic al-Ḥallāj and seems not to have been at all certain whether it was for doctrinal reasons, because of his own ideal of human love, or because of a clash of personalities. In an attempt to show how their personalities were very different, Massignon presents a picture of Ibn Dā'ūd that is overdrawn, making him a peevish, effeminate, ennervated esthete. He selects only two anecdotes about him to portray his character, one from his early childhood, interpreted as a forecast of his adult character, and one (of doubtful credibility) probably from his adolescence, which tells more about the foolish narcissism of the teller of the tale, his friend Ibn Jāmiʿ, than about Ibn Dā'ūd. A reading of the entire account of Ibn Dā'ūd in the *Ta'rīkh Baghdād* and the anecdotes about him scattered in the *Maṣāriʿ* and the *Kitāb al-Maṣūn* gives a more balanced picture of him as a respected man-among-men as well as a popular public figure and scholar-*ẓarīf*.

9. For instance, the idea that in some instances of betrayal by the beloved "consolation" or "forgetting" the beloved is *not* to be considered the only honorable course of action by the lover (as in the parallel between the *Ṭauq* and the *K. al-Muwashshā* [*al-Andalus*, XVI (1951), 319], item No. 20) but on the contrary are merely "allowable" or "not to be blamed." Here the *K. az-Zahra* (p. 155) better parallels the opening paragraphs of the chapter on *sulūw* (forgetting, consolation) in the *Ṭauq* where this type of case is discussed.

Ṭauq, for the *Maṣāri'* consists of literary and psuedo-historical traditions bearing *isnāds* and circulating in the East since long before the *Ṭauq al-Ḥamāma* was written. Ibn Ḥazm must have been familiar with at least part of this material from traditions transmitted orally and from written collections in Spain. The Islamic West also shared with the East an ideological stock-in-trade that can be traced as far back as the catalogue of ideas about passionate love to be found in the *Dīwān* of Al-'Abbās b. al-Aḥnaf (d. 190/806), known in the West as well as the East.[10]

After the *Kitāb az-Zahra,* the next book which fits clearly the typical twofold division of subject matter is the lost *Kitāb ar-Riyāḍ* of Marzubānī, except that the evidence leaves us uninformed as to whether the sections on the nature, kinds, and names of love formed the introduction to the book or came later. The fact that the authors of the majority of the works which included such a discussion *did* use these subjects as an introduction would lead one to think so, as would the fact that the book appears from Ibn an-Nadīm's detailed and specific description of it in the *Fihrist* to be a systematic, well-organized treatise, not simply an anthology. Furthermore, the great length of the *Kitāb ar-Riyāḍ* and the fact that it "discussed love and its ramifications, and discussed its beginning and its end, what the philologists and lexicographers said about its names, its kinds, and the derivations of these names, with quotations from pre-Islamic poetry, the poetry of the poets living partly in the pre-Islamic era, the early Islamic poets, and the Moderns as textual evidence"[11]

10. See Von Grunebaum, "Avicenna's *Risâla fî 'l-Išq* and Courtly Love," *JNES,* XI (1952), 233–38. As further evidence of literary material on love which passed from the Islamic East and North Africa to Spain, I note that Ibn Khair al-Ishbīlī (502/1108–575/1179) recorded studying with Spanish Muslim teachers the following books: (1) Al-Kharā'iṭī's *I'tilāl al-Qulūb,* (2) *Akhbār Nifṭawayh* (Nifṭawayh, the friend of Ibn Dā'ūd, al-Washshā', and al-Marzubānī), and (3) Huṣrī's *K. al-Ādāb* (he does not mention *K. al-Maṣūn*). The second and third contained only *some* material on love—I only speculate about the second, of which we have no extant copy as far as I know. If Ibn Khair studied such books 50–60 years after the death of Ibn Ḥazm and with Spanish teachers, then there is some likelihood that they were known there in Ibn Ḥazm's time. (Ibn Khair, *Fihrist,* ed. F. Codera and J. Ribera Tarrago ["Biblioteca arabico-hispana," Vol. IX–X; Saragossa, 1893–95], pp. 408, 398, and 380, respectively.)

11. *Fihrist,* 133.

appears to qualify it as containing a substantial introduction to the subject of love, more substantial in this respect than its predecessors. The *Kitāb az-Zahra*, for example, did not deal with the names and kinds of love or the opinions of philologists and lexicographers on these names, and the information or theories about love's essence, nature, and causes, though they are announced beforehand in the introduction to the book, are slipped in under Chapter One, whose heading is "He Whose Glances Are Many Will Have Continuing Distress."

I have demonstrated in the survey of the authors and works in the first part of this study while establishing the fact that the *Kitāb ar-Riyāḍ* belongs to this group of works, that it contained also the second category of subject matter typical of love theory, the *aḥwāl* of lovers. We have noted already the prominence of Marzubānī as a *rāwī* of anecdotes, theories, and pseudo-historical traditions on love such as make up the contents of works on profane love and the fact that his own book is actually quoted in a few places. Given the general tendency of the authors of these works to borrow heavily from their predecessors, it would appear that the *Kitāb ar-Riyāḍ* had a substantial influence upon the form and content of later works. The extant examples containing all the features of form and content said to have existed in Marzubānī's book appear for the first time in Kisā'ī's book about three hundred years later, though, as I have said, Kisā'ī takes it for granted then that such features would be normal to a book on this subject. Besides the evidence just given for envisioning the *Kitāb ar-Riyāḍ* as having an orderly introduction to the names and kinds of love, and so on, there is an example of a book on a parallel subject organized in this fashion which still survives. It is the *Kitāb ʿUqalāʾ al-Majānīn* (The Wise Madmen) of Abu 'l-Qāsim al-Ḥasan b. Muḥammad b. Ḥabīb an-Nīsābūrī (d. 406/1015),[12] who collected traditions and tales from the same group of scholars responsible for the transmission of the material on love. The book is arranged on such a rational plan with a substantial and orderly introduction to the names for madness and their

12. See above, page 26.

etymologies and the varieties of madness—even madness in animals—and proceeding to what we might call the *aḥwāl* of persons afflicted with madness, such as "Persons who were called mad but actually were not (drunkards, childish persons, etc.) . . . Those who became mad from the fear of God . . . Those who were mad and foolish, yet were actually of sound mind . . . Those who acted like fools in order to gain wealth . . . Those who acted foolish in order to be delivered from tribulation or calamity . . ." and so on through nine categories.[13]

Among book-length works on the theory of profane love, the two notable exceptions to the typical form are both in the third to the fifth Islamic centuries, the first phase of this literature. Two of them, the *Kitāb al-Maṣūn* and the *Maṣāri' al-'Ushshāq*, are unstructured anthologies, but even the *Kitāb al-Maṣūn*, though it has no headings or chapters, shows some rudiments of arrangement, beginning as it does with quotations on the nature of love. We would hardly be justified in refusing to include these works in the group because of this structural difference, or, rather, lack of structure; their content is clearly identifiable with that of the more systematically presented writings. To use the Arabic literary simile of the necklace once again, the difference is partly that between a necklace in which the beads are arranged in a pattern and one in which the same kinds of beads are strung at random.

The *Manāzil al-Aḥbāb* (early eighth/fourteenth century) is also not organized like the typical work and yet is not a simple anthology. Its contents are arranged under eighteen subject headings whose order does not seem entirely rational. These headings are not numbered as chapters and the author does not give an introduction outlining his scheme of presentation as the authors of the more systematic books did. His presentation of the names, kinds, nature, and causes of love comes after the first quarter of the work, not at the beginning as in the more typical work.

The *I'tilāl al-Qulūb*, The Malady of Hearts, by Kharā'iṭī, marks the beginning of a subtype of the work on the theory of profane love, one which has as its dominant theme an ethical or religious concern

13. *K. 'Uqalā' al-Majānīn*, pp. 16–37.

lest the soul be overpowered by *hawā* (understood there usually in the sense of "evil desires" or "lust") or *ʿishq*, passionate love. This lust/love division of the subject matter will be further explored from the semantic and doctrinal points of view later. The Ḥadīth and anecdotal material having to do with *hawā* and how the latter is to be combated are the subject of the first twenty-one chapters. Abruptly, the author turns in a new direction in Chapter Twenty-Two, on "The Excellence of Beauty, the Privileges Which God Has Accorded to Those Who Are Provided with It and the Duties He Has Imposed on Them."[14] Next come chapters on *maḥabba* and *hawā*, now seemingly used in the sense of "passionate love." These chapters seem imbued with a quasi-mystical character in the sense that a mystique of love connected with ʿUdhrī ideals suffuses them and the code of love which they contain seems influenced by both

14. The chapter headings of the *Iʿtilāl al-Qulūb* as they appear in the Bursa MS Ulu Cami 1535 are given by J.-C. Vadet in "Littérature courtoise et transmission du *ḥadīt*," *Arabica*, VII (1960), 157–59. However, some chapter headings have been omitted and one chapter heading erroneously split up. There are actually 57 chapters in the manuscript. Vadet also does not give the full chapter heading in all cases, but I shall not attempt to supply those here. The titles listed there as Chapters 8 and 9 should be one chapter, Chapter 8. Between Chapters 48 and 49 there should be inserted a chapter entitled, "About Jealousy over Women" ("Fī Dhikr al-Ghaira ʿala ʾn-Nisāʾ"), between Chapters 52 and 53 a chapter entitled "The Dreams of Those Afflicted by Passion Who Feel Sorry for Themselves" ("Fī Dhikr Aḥlām Ahl al-Hawā al-Mushrifīn ʿalā Anfusihim"), and between Chapters 55 and 56 a chapter entitled, "Those Who Say There Is No Recovery from *Hawā* after It Has Gained a Foothold" ("Man Qāla Lā Burūʾ li ʾl-Hawā baʿda Tamakkunih"). After these additions and corrections are made, the chapters must be renumbered.

Chapter 44 in Vadet's list (43 in the MS), given as "Un titre peu lisable," seems on inspection of both the MS and the microfilm in my possession to read quite plainly "At-Taḥaffuẓ min Sabab Yūjib al-Ghadr" ("Guarding Against Anything That Would Necessarily Lead to Betrayal"). Chapter 52, which is correctly numbered but again listed as illegible, reads clearly, "Fī Dhikr Amānī Ahl al-Hawā al-Mushrifīn ʿalā Anfusihim" ("The Longings of Those Tortured by *Hawā* Who Feel Sorry for Themselves"). (See *Wāḍiḥ*, 27, line 1, for a similar use of "*amānī*.")

Chapter 4 (correctly numbered) is erroneously read by Vadet as "Fī dhikr man ǧaʿala Allāh fī qalbih wa-aʿṭā" ("De ceux aux cœurs desquels Dieu a prodigué ses faveurs"), which he finds makes no sense (159, note 1) in terms of the content of the chapter, and which he therefore takes as evidence for his opinion that the Bursa MS has been badly maltreated by a copyist. Actually the word after "qalbih" is plainly "wāʿiẓan", which fits the context. This same chapter may be found, taken over almost unchanged, in *Dhamm al-Hawā* as Chapter Nine, "Fī Dhikr al-Wāʿiẓ min al-Qalb."

the *adab* and *murū'a* (manly honor) concepts and the wish to please Allāh.[15]

It is clear that the *I'tilāl al-Qulūb* was the ancestor to Ibn al-Jauzī's *Dhamm al-Hawā*. The similarity in the overall structure of the two books and the fact that a number of chapters in the first book reappear with or without additions in the second are the most obvious evidence of this. A closer examination of the *Dhamm al-Hawā* confirms this impression, for the name of Muḥammad b. Ja'far or Muḥammad b. Ja'far al-Kharā'iṭī occurs with moderate frequency in *isnāds* there. However, as a source of content the *Maṣāri' al-'Ushshāq* is at least as important, judging from the frequency with which the name of Abū Muḥammad Ja'far b. Aḥmad as-Sarrāj, or identifiable elements of that name, appear in *isnāds*. A detailed study of the dependence of the *Dhamm al-Hawā* on these two earlier books remains to be done and, among other things, may cast light on whether or not the text we have of the *I'tilāl al-Qulūb* is an abridgment. One of the difficulties in any attempt to assess how much of the two earlier books has been taken over in the *Dhamm* is that Ibn al-Jauzī, in dealing with traditions which he obviously took from these two books, sometimes quoted alternative versions taken from other sources. Thus a tradition which occurs in a chapter in the *I'tilāl* will be given in the corresponding chapter in the *Dhamm* with an *isnād* which in some cases does not contain the name of al-Kharā'iṭī.[16] What Ibn al-Jauzī's motives for this may have been is not clear.

15. It is difficult at this time to be more precise than this. The *I'tilāl* is not a long work and it contains an extremely heterogeneous collection of material simply put down under chapter headings. Therefore, it is very difficult to discern its tendencies, and especially since we know rather little about the author and the circles he moved in. Vadet, in *Arabica*, VII (1960), 140–66, is unable to be precise, either, in his characterization of the book. He calls attention to, among other things, the ambiguities between "la mystique de l'amour" and "l'amour mystique" sometimes apparent in works such as the *I'tilāl* which tend towards a Ḥanbalī type of moral rigorism and religious devotion. (See Vadet, pp. 160–61.)

16. On the other hand, traditions can be found in the *Dhamm* which bear the name of one of these two men, Kharā'iṭī or as-Sarrāj, but which do not appear in their books. This does not necessarily mean that our present versions of their two books are incomplete; it could just as well mean that Ibn al-Jauzī had additional anecdotes, Ḥadīth, etc., from other sources depending on these two authors, either oral or written.

One of the reasons given by Vadet for thinking that the *I'tilāl al-Qulūb* as we have it now in the Bursa manuscript has been abbreviated is that four chapters he mentions are very short, not more than a folio in length.[17] A careful check of this manuscript will show, in fact, that sixteen chapters, nearly one-fourth of those in the book, are less than a folio in length, but this brevity cannot be taken as a necessary indication of missing contents, eliminated, as he suggests, by a copyist who may have had a bias against traditions having to do with the spiritual perils of *hawā*. The length of chapters in such books is often determined, quite simply, by the available supply of traditions on that particular subject or theme. For this reason, many chapters of the *Dhamm al-Hawā* and other books on love are equally short. Chapter Four of the *I'tilāl al-Qulūb*, one of those named by Vadet as abnormally short, is entitled, according to my reading of the manuscript, "He in Whose Heart God Has Placed an Admonisher, or Warner." It reappears in the *Dhamm al-Hawā* essentially unchanged as Chapter Nine, "The Warner of the Heart." If there had existed other traditions on this subject, surely Ibn al-Jauzī, who without doubt had very complete written and oral sources, would have included them, but the chapter in the *Dhamm* is every bit as brief as that in the *I'tilāl al-Qulūb*.

It may well be, as Vadet has suggested, that the absence of *isnāds* in the *I'tilāl al-Qulūb* is the work of an abbreviator, though it is not unthinkable that Kharā'iṭī himself omitted them. He makes it clear in his introduction that he conceived of the book as a venture in pious *adab* in the sense that it was his intent to make the book as appealing as possible while at the same time maintaining its integrity as a book with a moral or ethical concern. Many later writers on love dispensed with *isnāds* or gave only abbreviated indications of the source of a tradition or anecdote. In fact, only three of the twenty treatises on love examined in this study are characterized by full *isnāds*, consistently used and linking the writer with the supposed original source. These are the *Maṣāri' al-'Ushshāq*, the *Dhamm al-Hawā*, and the *Aswāq al-Ashwāq*. To argue that Kharā'iṭī

17. Vadet, *Arabica*, VII (1960), 159.

probably was very careful in observing the formalities of *isnāds* does not seem to me to help us in deciding whether he used them in the *I'tilāl al-Qulūb*.[18] Most of these authors who did not use *isnāds* in their works on love did use them elsewhere when they saw a need for them.

One of the noticeable changes in emphasis between the *I'tilāl* and the *Dhamm al-Hawā* is the emphasis in the later book on the *'aql* (intellect or rational soul) as a defense against evil desires.[19] An emphasis on the importance of devotional practice, "taking refuge in God," and avoiding the corruption of the heart by concerns other than love of and obedience to God is found in both books. The two books are alike in shifting rather suddenly at midpoint from a discussion of *hawā* (evil desire) to the largely secular and profane concept of passionate love, but the nature of the treatment given to the second subject by the two authors is quite different. Kharā'iṭī is interested in the mystique of love and a code of conduct for lovers that demands honor, discretion, fidelity, and chastity. His book discusses how one ought to bear up under the onslaught of love and how the friends of the lover ought to help him in his distress. (If worse comes to worst, one can find rest for one's heart in weeping, according to Chapter Thirty-Nine.)[20] Ibn al-Jauzī, by contrast, does not advise lovers how to conduct themselves with pious gentility; his approach is very negative, as will be remembered from the description of the *Dhamm al-Hawā* given earlier. His purpose is to frighten believers away from passionate love. Beginning with Chapter Thirty-Nine, on the nature of *'ishq*, he steps into the shoes of the writer of an *adab* book on the subject, as it were, introducing the reader to the nature, causes, names, kinds, and degrees of love. He follows with chapters on the *aḥwāl* of the lovers, telling stories which emphasize the helplessness of those who let *'ishq* get a hold on them, the fatalities it brings, and the most horrendous *aḥwāl*,

18. See Vadet, *Arabica*, VII (1960), 158. I note that Kharā'iṭī used full *isnāds* in his *Makārim al-Akhlāq* (Cairo: Maṭba'at as-Salafīya, 1350/1931) and his *Masāwī al-Akhlāq* (Damascus, MS Ẓāhirīya, 79).
19. Further discussion of the "battle against *hawā*" will be found in Part 3, Chap. 1.
20. *I'tilāl al-Qulūb* (MS Bursa, Ulu Cami 1535), folios 85b–87b.

love that ends in suicide, murder, and incest. Structurally, therefore, the second half of the *Dhamm al-Hawā* conforms to the general plan of the typical book of this group, except that its contents are given a strong moral.

Ibn Ḥazm's *Ṭauq al-Ḥamāma* comes as a startling development when viewed in the context of the preceding works. Though it is not original in its over-all structure or in the themes it treats, being in that respect influenced to some degree by its predecessors and fed with ideas from the common fund of *akhbār* (stories, anecdotes, traditions) on love, it differs radically in content from its oriental predecessors. The use of the author's own poetry and of stories about himself and his contemporaries[21] and a style of writing that is direct, brisk, and personal makes Ibn Ḥazm's book something new among Arabic works on profane love. García Gómez explains that the *Ṭauq*, together with the writings of Abū ʿĀmir b. Shuhaid (A.D. 992–1035) constitute the major representatives of a school of literature in Andalusia which was aristocratic, Arabophile, nationalist, personal, and independent in character. It sought to give full expression to the temperament and personality of the author. It scorned to indulge in the oriental vice of endless citations and quotations from earlier works or the conscious display of the author's polish in grammar and rhetoric.[22] The resulting freshness and individuality of style make the *Ṭauq al-Ḥamāma* unique among its kind.

The fact that in the *Ṭauq* Ibn Ḥazm has stripped the oriental Arab tradition of literature on love of its bedouin and Baghdādī attire and reclothed it in the Cordovan style,[23] makes it less easy to see what previous works might have contributed to its formation. Ibn Ḥazm mentions the name of only one earlier author on the

21. Though the stories in the *Ṭauq* are supposed to represent actual events, except for alterations in names in some cases, some actually may be old stories remodeled and set in Ibn Ḥazm's Andalusia. Compare the story in the *Rauḍa*, 455–56, about a devout Israelite with the very similar story in the last chapter (Bercher ed., 374–77) of the *Ṭauq* about the young man who burned his finger off rather than give in to temptation.

22. García Gómez, *al-Andalus*, XVI (1951), 310–11.

23. The metaphor is that of García Gómez, *al-Andalus*, XVI (1951), 312.

subject, Muḥammad b. Dā'ūd, and he does so only to disagree with his view that the spirits of those who fall in love are segmented spheres that were divided by the Creator before being joined to their bodies and which ever seek to be reunited on earth and become one again.[24] The influence of the *Ṭauq al-Ḥamāma* on later works is, on the other hand, not difficult to detect. Since their authors, all orientals in their writing habits and views on literature, continued in the old habit of quoting and collecting material from earlier works, it can be seen from an analysis of their content and from occasional references to Ibn Ḥazm and his book what a wide circulation and influence the *Ṭauq al-Ḥamāma* had in later centuries.

Among the books on love, Mughulṭāi's *Wāḍiḥ al-Mubīn* was unique for its dictionary format and the fact that it specialized in martyrs of love. One might say, therefore, that he specialized in one of the *aḥwāl* of the lovers. In doing so, he may have been inspired by Marzubānī, whose work he knew. (He is one of the few who quoted it by name.) Both men's books are introductions to the names, kinds, causes, and nature of love and stories of one category of lovers, the *mutayyamīn* among the poets in the first case and the martyrs in the second. In fact, some of the *mutayyamīn* were martyrs of love, and, as has already been indicated, it appears that Marzubānī touched upon the martyrs of love in his book on the *mutayyamīn*.

Ibn Qayyim al-Jauzīya's *Rauḍat al-Muḥibbīn* represents the full fruition of both the *adab* and the religious or ethical tendencies in this group of works, in so far as these two are not at odds with one another. It shows a great investment of labor, reflection, and personal thought. Continuing in that oriental tradition which Ibn Ḥazm professed to scorn but actually built upon, Ibn al-Qayyim based himself completely on the now well-established tradition of works on the theory of profane love. He quotes verses, anecdotes, and Ḥadīth which have been used in previous works on love, and many of his

24. Actually, this was not Ibn Dā'ūd's view. He merely reports this opinion along with many others, saying, "One of the philosophers alleges that . . ." Compare *Ṭauq*, Bercher ed., 14–15, with *Zahra*, 15. This quotation in the *K. az-Zahra* seems to be a reflection of the speech of Aristophanes in the *Symposium*. See W. R. M. Lamb (tr.), *Plato: Lysis, Symposium, Gorgias* ("Loeb Classical Library," No. 166; Cambridge: Harvard University Press, reprinted 1961), 133–45.

chapter subjects are those traditionally a part of Arabic love theory. Yet, in so far as the *adab* tradition allowed, Ibn al-Qayyim was an author, not a compiler. Compared with Ibn al-Jauzī, the predecessor whose work is nearest to the *Rauḍat al-Muḥibbīn* in spirit, Ibn al-Qayyim was much more of a thinker and theorizer. Ibn al-Jauzī marshaled masses of traditional material under subject headings along with an introductory and concluding sentence or two; his personal contribution amounts mainly to the first paragraphs of the book, in which he set the over-all theme of the book by addressing it to the young man in distress from the assaults of *hawā*, and to the concluding two chapters on remedies for *ʿishq* and general advice on preserving oneself from *hawā* and *ʿishq*. He seems under a compulsion to quote everything in existence on the chapter topics. As long as it has a good chain of transmitters, he evidently feels it will strengthen his case. He is mastered by his material, while Ibn al-Qayyim masters the traditional material to his own ends. He has surveyed the subject of profane love with the analytic eye of a competent religious scholar and he is able to elucidate fully a number of theoretical issues left unclarified in previous books on love, then offer his solutions in some instances, solutions which fit neatly into his comprehensive theory. For the first time in some cases, we are shown clearly some of the major issues in the theory of profane love, both those which arouse the concern of the scholar of religious law or the theologian and those which seem to be only subjects for speculation and whose discussion is more entertaining than controversial. We see that the question of whether there are martyrs of love or not, whether or not it is lawful to look at certain persons, whether or not falling in love is voluntary or involuntary, and whether or not the sexual relationship spoils love and ends it—and other like questions—are sensitive issues upon which more is at stake than one might at first suspect. It is in dealing with these questions and others that Ibn al-Qayyim rejects certain widespread theories and formulates a coherent over-all theory, or theoretical structure, in which every piece of traditional material has to support his conclusions about the nature of love and how to deal with it.

The tendency on the part of writers on this subject to be mere anthologizers at bottom was very strong; it seems as though it was necessary for a man like Ibn al-Qayyim to come along with both a keen interest in the subject and an ax to grind before the potentialities of the topic are well exploited. Compared to other books before and afterward, his says something; every chapter moves logically into the next and the whole book has a persuasive message: that there is a true Islamic theory of love, profane love and also sacred, which is not only right but works out far more happily than the misguided theories of various mystics, sectarians, heretics, and essentially pagan poets.

The process by which the late works of the ninth/fifteenth to the eleventh/seventeenth centuries were composed out of their predecessors has already been partially described in the introductory survey of the authors and works. They conform to the typical pattern of the *adab* work on this subject and represent mainly an attempt to update their predecessors with later poetry and stories and to rearrange the content in a way that the author considers more logical and esthetically pleasing. "Superanthology" seems a good label for them because, unlike at least some of their predecessors, they really do not have a message. In spite of their logical order and comprehensiveness, they are typical of many Arabic anthologies in that the relation of one part to the other is not clear, except for the fact that each part bears a relationship to the over-all theme. Thus, the larger part of the *Tazyīn al-Aswāq* is devoted to stories about lovers: lovers of Allāh, lovers of slave-girls, lovers of youths, and non-human lovers—animal, vegetable, mineral, and celestial.

III

THE DISCUSSION OF TERMS AND THEIR USE

Early in the history of Arabic prose writing, it became the practice of some scholars to begin a monograph by discoursing at length on the names and terms involved. The reasons for this would seem to be the same that motivated scholars to compile specialized and general vocabularies and lexicons. In the words of John Haywood:

> *The Arabs were proud of their language—and in this respect some non-Arabs were 'more Arab than the Arabs'! They were proud of its copiousness, proud of its many features which they fancied were peculiar to it, but chiefly proud because it was God's language. This language must be kept pure, free from foreign pollutions, and from the corruptions due to ignorance and laziness.*[1]

The authors of some of these early monographs were, in fact, philologists and lexicographers. Al-Aṣmaʿī, one of the earliest such authors, has a *Kitāb al-Ibil* (The Book of the Camel), which begins with a vocabulary concerning the camel and includes the names given to it at every stage of its life.[2] Two similar treatises on the horse, both

1. Haywood, 10.
2. In *Texte zur arabischen Lexicographie*, ed. August Haffner (Leipzig: Otto Harrassowitz, 1905), 66–157.

entitled *Kitāb al-Khail*, were written by al-Aṣma'ī and by his rival Abū 'Ubaida.[3]

Particularly for city Arabs and non-Arab converts to Islam, such introductions and vocabularies for subjects long familiar to the bedouin Arab were almost essential. The vocabulary relating to those things with which the Arab was most conversant was exceedingly rich. He tended to give distinctive names to slightly differing varieties and conditions of the same thing.[4] Since poetry was so universally recited and appreciated, the Arabic poets certainly added to the wealth of the language through their habit of searching out and using (and thus preserving or putting into greater currency) rare and unusual words and dialectal forms.

The fact that love is an intangible and subjective topic rather than a material and objective one increases the need for precision of expression while at the same time making it more difficult of achievement. However, in much the same manner as in the instances just cited, the popularity of the subject and the preoccupation of the poets with it assured the development of a copious vocabulary. As noted in the previous chapter, a section on the names and kinds of love and the etymologies and meanings of the names for love became a traditional part of the more systematic and logically arranged books on the theory of love. Though the treatment accorded this part of the works is rather uneven, there are certain vocabulary lists and discussions of words which are worthy of special attention in a brief chronological survey of the development of this aspect of the theory of love.

At a time when Arabic lexicography and philology were still in relative infancy, Jāḥiẓ made an enduring contribution to the

3. Al-Aṣma'ī, *Das Kitâb al-Chail*, ed. August Haffner, *Sitzungsberichte der Akademie der Wissenschaften zu Wien*, Phil.-hist. classe, Vol. 132 (1895), No. 10. Abū 'Ubaida, *Kitāb al-Khail* (Hyderabad: Dā'irat al-Ma'ārif al-'Uthmānīya, 1358/1939. On Abū 'Ubaida see the article (*s.v.*) by H. A. R. Gibb in *EI*² and Haywood, index. *Les livres des chevaux*, ed. Giorgio Levi della Vida (Leiden: E. J. Brill, 1928).

4. Sometimes this is explained as due to his atomistic *Weltanschauung*, his habit of seeing each thing on his horizon as primarily an individual entity, rather than as a representative of a class of things. Chaim Rabin (*EI*², art. "'Arabiyya") credits this rich vocabulary to the bedouin's power of observation, poetic exuberance, and, possibly, dialect mixture.

understanding of the terminology for love. In his "Risāla fi 'l-'Ishq wa 'n-Nisā'," he made this statement:

> 'Ishq *is the name for what exceeds that which is called* ḥubb *and every* ḥubb *is not called* 'ishq, *for* 'ishq *is the name for what exceeds that degree, just as* saraf [*prodigality*] *is the name for that degree which is more than that which is called* jūd [*liberality*] *and* bukhl [*stinginess*] *is the name for what falls short of the level which is called* iqtiṣād [*economy*] *and* jubn [*cowardice*] *is the name for what falls short of the quality which is termed* shajā'a [*courage*].[5]

These words of Jāḥiẓ recur often in the later works on love. Usually his name is given, but none name the work in which he wrote this definition. Ibn al-Jauzī in his *Dhamm al-Hawā* gives it in the form of a tradition with an *isnād* finishing with the name of Jāḥiẓ. We do not know whether he or any other writer had read the "Risāla fi 'l-'Ishq."[6] Even when written texts were available, those who were careful to verify the source and accuracy of what they quoted preferred to rely on the pedigree provided by the *isnād* of a quotation or the reading certificate of a book. Consequently, they named the transmitters and not the title of the work where the quotation occurred. This quote from Jāḥiẓ contains among its transmitters two names of special interest, al-Mubarrad, the philologist, and al-Marzubānī, author of the *Kitāb ar-Riyāḍ* and prominent *rāwī* of information on profane love. Jāḥiẓ also wrote a much more detailed and thoughtful discussion of the meanings and usage of the terms *ḥubb, hawā,* and *'ishq* and the relationship between these states and how they differ from one another. As far as I know, nothing from this discussion, found in the "Risālat al-Qiyān,"[7] ever appeared in the later works on love and so it would seem not have been known. It is possible that the essay was not widely circulated

5. "R. fi 'l-'Ishq wa 'n-Nisā'," *Majmū'at Rasā'il*, 161–62.
6. Ibn al-Jauzī's version (*Dhamm*, 295) of Jāḥiẓ's definition is worded a little differently from that in the *risāla*. Ibn al-Qayyim's version and that of Maḥmūd b. Salmān b. Fahd are quite close to the text of the *risāla*. (See *Rauḍa*, 138, and *Manāzil* [Aya Sofya 4307], folio 8b.) It seems that Ibn al-Jauzī's version was orally transmitted on some occasion when Mubarrad, the first transmitter in the *isnād*, was present.
7. "R. al-Qiyān," *Thalāth Rasā'il*, 67–70. French translation by Pellat, *Arabica*, X (1963), 138–41.

or that it was viewed with disfavor because of the attacks upon the conservative Sunnī scholars contained in it.[8]

It is also curious that the view expressed by Jāḥiẓ in his "Risāla fi 'l-'Ishq wa 'n-Nisā'," that the term *'ishq* can be correctly used only to refer to the passionate love that a person feels for another person of the opposite sex, does not find any place in the discussions in later works on the theory of profane love.[9] This may argue that the "Risāla fi 'l-'Ishq wa 'n-Nisā'" was unknown to those later authors or that Jāḥiẓ's view was ignored because the use of that word in other senses had become so well established that his view had only historical interest, having lost out almost as soon as he wrote it. The use of the word *'ishq* to refer to either heterosexual or homosexual affections became established about that time.[10] Its use in the mystical sense had also been introduced by 'Abd al-Wāḥid b. Zaid, who died (793) when Jāḥiẓ was a young man, and by the mystical school of Basra. They deliberately used the word *'ishq* rather than the Koranic "*maḥabba*" to mean the "réciprocité vitale d'amour," or "une attraction entre Dieu et l'âme."[11] It may be that it was these new uses of the word which prompted Jāḥiẓ to write the essay, though he makes no allusion to them. He says that one does not use the word with reference to parents, children, mounts, houses, or such abstract concepts as honor.[12]

8. See Part 3, Chap. 11.

9. So far I have seen just the passing reference (*Wāḍiḥ*, 52) to the fact that Abū Hilāl al-'Askarī (d. 395/1005; *GAL*, G. I, 126; S. I, 193–94) in his *K. al-Talkhīṣ* says that "*al-'ishq lā yakūn illā li 'n-nisā' khaṣṣatan.*" (*'Ishq* refers only to women alone.) This book was a lexicon, not a book on love, and Mughulṭāi does not further discuss this idea.

10. At least the story of Ibn Dā'ūd's "martyrdom" (above, pages 10–11) implies that the word was used thus in the generation after Jāḥiẓ, for the verb *'ashiqa* is used in the alleged Ḥadīth of the Prophet ("He who loves passionately . . . [*Man 'ashiqa* . . .]) that Ibn Dā'ūd was reported to have quoted with reference to his intense feeling for a man, his friend Jāmi'. I have not yet made a special effort to trace back such a usage to an earlier date.

11. Massignon, *Opera Minora*, II, 246–47.

12. In the "R. al-Qiyān," 69 (= Pellat, *Arabica*, X [1963], 140), he seems to have changed his mind a little and allows that *'ishq* may be used with reference to the feeling of a male toward a male, providing the element of lust is present. He specifically says that one must use the word *ḥubb* with reference to the believer's love for God or God's love for the believer.

The first attempt at a comprehensive discussion of terminology for which we have evidence to date is that in the *Kitāb ar-Riyāḍ* by Abū ʿAbd Allāh al-Marzubānī. Its importance for this part of love theory first came to my attention while reading a remark made by Ḥuṣrī in his *Kitāb al-Maṣūn*. After giving a list of no less than eighty words which denote the characteristics (*awṣāf*) of love and its kinds (*ḍurūb*), he concludes with the observation that these terms were given by Marzubānī and that they represent a selection and not an exhaustive list.[13]

In Ibn an-Nadīm's *Fihrist*, we read that Marzubānī's *Kitāb ar-Riyāḍ* included a discussion of what the philologists and lexicographers said about the names for love (*ḥubb*) and its kinds (*ajnās*) as well as the derivations of these words with examples of usage taken from the poetry of every period.[14] It would seem that this discussion was the first of its kind in a book on the theory of profane love and that it became a model for similar discussions which we find at a much later date.

Though Ḥuṣrī apparently reproduces Marzubānī's entire list, he does not make it a part of any well-organized discussion. Ḥuṣrī simply gives it as part of an anthology on the nature of love and on the question of whether or not the lover can conceal his affliction. It would appear that the list of eighty words represents an isolated fragment which was once part of the discussion of terminology in the *Kitāb ar-Riyāḍ*, the only book Marzubānī wrote on love listed in the *Fihrist*.

Kisāʾī's *Rauḍat al-ʿĀshiq* (before 635/1237) is a minor landmark as far as the discussion of terms in love theory is concerned. As pointed out in the previous chapter, it is the first (extant) work in the Arabic literature on the theory of profane love to give a systematic discussion of the nature of love, the names for it, and their derivation and meaning. Kisāʾī is also the first to use such a discussion as an introduction to the rest of the book. He confines himself to the discussion of fewer terms than the later Ibn al-Qayyim included. Allowing only eleven names for progressive degrees of love, he gives

13. *K. al-Maṣūn*, folio 29a–29b.
14. *Fihrist*, 133.

the meaning of each in terms of the developing emotions and conduct of the love-smitten. As happens also in other lists of this sort, several of the words actually mean a particular kind of longing for the beloved. Two of the eleven words cannot be found in Ḥuṣrī's (Marzubānī's) list of eighty, which gives some indication of the resources of Arabic for the subject of love. This may also have been a conscious exhibition of "one-up-manship," since Kisā'ī has given notice in the introduction to the book that he has read the previous books on love and intends to improve upon them in quality and balance of content, especially in giving this first chapter on the nature and names of love the kind of orderly and thorough treatment that will make it a suitable introduction to the rest of the book, which is on the "circumstances" of the lovers.

The next appearance of the list of words which Ḥuṣrī credited to Marzubānī is in the *Manāzil al-Aḥbāb wa Manāzih al-Albāb* of Shihāb ad-Dīn b. Salmān b. Fahd, where it occurs as part of a short section headed "The Exposition Conveying Information on the Names of *'Ishq* and Its Attributes." The section begins: "Amongst those given to it are those that Ḥuṣrī mentioned in his book; they are listed here: . . ." He reproduces Ḥuṣrī's list in part but omits about one-fourth of the terms from the latter part of the list. It is not clear from what he says whether he intended to abbreviate the list. It is possible that he had a corrupt manuscript of the *Kitāb al-Maṣūn* or that our manuscripts of the *Manāzil* are corrupt.[15]

The list of Ḥuṣrī (Marzubānī) appears again in Mughulṭāi's book *Al-Waḍīḥ al-Mubīn* and Mughulṭāi, who made it a policy to name authors and works all through his book, says that the list was taken from the *Kitāb al-Maṣūn*.[16] However, he gives the same reduced list

15. Of the four MSS of the *Manāzil* available to me at the time this question arose, three contained sixty-two names and attributes (Leiden Or. 1069, folio 16a–16b; Aya Sofya 4307, folio 8b; Top Kapı Saray, Ahmet III 2471, folio 13a) and one contained sixty-one (Leiden Or. 798, 12b–13a). Of the words missing from the original eighty, sixteen have dropped out in two groups of eight, leading one to think that at some point a copyist skipped two lines of eight words each. This would have been easy in a page full of words with no order or sense for the mind to follow.
16. *Wāḍiḥ*, 51–52.

of words[17] found in the *Manāzil*, not the eighty actually found in the *Kitāb al-Maṣūn*.[18] He follows the list with additions to it from several other sources, and quotes the commonest theories about the derivation of the words *ʿishq* and *ḥubb* from the concrete meanings originally associated with their roots.

Ibn Qayyim al-Jauzīya's handling of the lexical aspect of love theory in the *Rauḍat al-Muḥibbīn* excels all others before or after it. Like Kisāʾī (and perhaps Marzubānī) before him, he devotes the first chapters of his work to terminology. "People have given love nearly sixty names," he says, introducing a list of terms,[19] ". . . and more names, other than these, have been given, but they are not amongst its names. They are merely its consequences and the criteria for its existence, so we have not bothered to give them."[20] A comparison of his list with others would make it seem likely that the *Wāḍiḥ* of Mughulṭāi had already been written and that Ibn al-Qayyim used it to make up his own list. It is possible to reconstruct the steps by which he did that. From the list in the *Wāḍiḥ*, credited to Ḥuṣrī and probably copied from the *Manāzil*, Ibn al-Qayyim has pruned out some words that he did not consider acceptable as terms for love. He also added a few words which are among the most common for love and appear to have been omitted from the list of Ḥuṣrī (Marzubānī) because they were so obvious that they were overlooked, namely, *maḥabba*, *ʿalāqa*, *hawā*, and *shauq*. He tacked on to the end of the list seven of the words given by Mughulṭāi as additions to that of Ḥuṣrī and, with one exception, even wrote them in the same order that Mughulṭāi had given them. Though he shifted the position of a few words, apparently in order to bring out their

17. There are sixty words in Mughulṭāi's list as it appears in the Spies edition based on the two İstanbul MSS. The two words missing that were in the text of the *Manāzil* can be accounted for as copyist's errors.
18. Since Mughulṭāi quoted often from the *Manāzil* in the *Wāḍiḥ*, it would appear that he took this list second hand via the *Manāzil*, not directly from the *Kitāb al-Maṣūn*.
19. Actually, he gives in the list only forty-nine terms (Tübingen, Ma VI 217, folio 8a–8b; Chester Beatty, 3832, folio 8a–8b) or fifty (Lebanese MS, privately owned, used by the editor of the *Rauḍa* in preparing the printed text. See *Rauḍa*, text pages *jīm-dāl* and 14).
20. *Rauḍa*, 14.

importance or their association with other words in the list, the finished product is essentially an improved version of the list in the *Wāḍiḥ* of Mughulṭāi and enough of it is intact to reveal its origin, though the name Mughulṭāi is never mentioned in the *Rauḍa.*

Another reason for my belief that Mughulṭāi's book preceded Ibn al-Qayyim's is that Ibn al-Qayyim seems to have Mughulṭāi in mind when he says that people have given nearly sixty names to love but later criticizes the unnamed persons for including some words which were not, strictly speaking, names (*asmā'*) for love (*maḥabba*).[21] Mughulṭāi had in fact called them "names for love" (*asmā' al-'ishq*) and his list contained exactly sixty plus the proposed additions from Ibn as-Sikkīt, Abū Hilāl, and Tha'ālabī given after it.[22] The author of the *Manāzil,* the other possible though less likely source used by Ibn al-Qayyim, had presented the list as "attributes and names" (*ṣifāt, asmā'*) and Ḥuṣrī himself had introduced his list of eighty as "attributes (or traits, characteristics, *awṣāf*) and kinds (*ḍurūb*) of love (*'ishq*)."[23] Under this broader designation one can include without objection some of the terms which Ibn al-Qayyim rejected as being "consequences and criteria for its existence," not "names for love."

Ibn al-Qayyim devotes Chapter Two to discussing the derivation (or theories of the derivation) and meaning of each of the words in his list. He informs us, when he turns his attention to the fine analysis of each word, illustrating usages with passages of poetry and Scripture or Tradition, that he thinks some of these terms he has allowed to remain on the list still cannot be considered as names for love. It is more correct to call them symptoms or temporary effects of love. While it is true that, except for Mughulṭāi, his predecessors had been precise enough not to call their immense lists of terms "names for love," nevertheless, by gathering together "names" (or "kinds") and "attributes" in one great undifferentiated group reaching a total of sixty to eighty words, they were able to indulge to the maximum their pride in the copiousness of the Arabic language.

21. *Rauḍa,* 14.
22. *Wāḍiḥ,* 51–52.
23. *Manāzil* (Leiden Or. 1069), folio 16a. *K. al-Maṣūn* (Leiden Or. 1951), folio 29a.

One wonders why a chapter on etymology and meaning as complete as this was not written for an earlier work. Marzubānī's book may have been no less comprehensive in this respect, but we can only conjecture about that. If it was, there was a four-century interval between it and the *Rauḍat al-Muḥibbīn* during which no writer made full use of the material available in the dictionaries, collections of poetry, and Ḥadīth. Perhaps the reason is that forty pages of sustained discussion of derivation and meaning, however interesting, must be part of a book of proportionately solid content and quality. This was the case in the *Rauḍa*, but few other books approached that standard.

In the very short third chapter of his work, Ibn al-Qayyim goes into the controversial question of whether the various names for love are synonymous or not. This might seem an illogical question to raise when he has already made clear the exact shade of meaning of each word referring to love or to one of love's characteristic emotional states. The discussion turns out not to be related specifically to any of the words he has just defined in Chapter Two. Rather, it is a résumé of two theories current at that time about synonymity in the Arabic language. One school of thought denies the existence of synonymity, saying that if there are two words or names applied to one thing, there must, nevertheless, be some difference between the two words, whether we know what that difference is or not. Ibn al-Qayyim explains that, in his opinion, this could be true in the case of a single author. (Presumably this author would be one who was meticulous in applying a name or term to denote something particular and never used words interchangeably or inconsistently.) Ibn al-Qayyim himself holds that the second theory is the one that corresponds to reality, namely, that there must be synonymity where different individuals use different terms for naming the same thing and both terms gain equal acceptance among the members of one tribe. Conversely, he says, different individuals may apply the same term to different things named and the result in that case is homonymity. He explains that Arabic synonyms are of two types: words which are simple or pure synonyms with reference to the thing named, and words synonymous in so far as they both denote the same thing, but different in that they each single out a different attribute of this one thing.

Ibn al-Qayyim's extensive explanations of etymology and meaning are far from being a dull exercise in scholarship or an unnecessary diversion from the subject in order to display an academic fussiness. As he explains the ideas associated with some of these words, we are already deeply involved with the theory and psychology of love. Ideas about the nature of love, for example, are revealed in the discussion of the word *maḥabba*, derived from the root *ḥ-b-b*. Among his explanations is one that says the original sense was "purity" because the ancient Arabs knew the expression *ḥabab al-asnān*, "whiteness and brilliance of the teeth," (*ḥabab*, like *maḥabba*, being derived from the root *ḥ-b-b*); another that connects it with the idea of constancy and persistence as implied in the verb *aḥabba*, "the camel knelt down and stayed where it was"; and one that derives it from *ḥubb*, meaning "a spacious container which is filled up with something to the point where it will hold no more," since likewise the heart of the lover has no room in it for anything but his beloved.[24]

The imagined effects of love are revealed in the word *shaghaf*, "infatuation, amorousness, passionate love," said to de derived from the verb *shaghafa* "to strike, affect, or penetrate the *shaghāf* (pericardium)." Similarly, the word *khilāba* (root: *kh-l-b*) was said to mean "love that wheedles and coaxes or deceives with the tongue," so-called because it reaches one's *khilb*, a membrane of the liver,[25] or a membrane between the heart and the abdominal cavity.[26] Other words from the same root cited as conveying a similar sense were *khallāb*, "lying, deceiving," usually applied as an adjective to a person, and *khullab*, "lightning or clouds that deceive or disappoint because they bring no rain."

Even without having any direct knowledge of the content of

24. *Rauḍa*, 15–16.
25. See Lane, *s.v. kh-l-b* for this meaning. The liver was considered a seat of tender feeling, passion, or love. See the numerous quotations in *Wörterbuch der klassischen arabischen Sprache*, ed. J. Kraemer and H. Gätje, *s.v. k-b-d* (Weisbaden: Otto Harrassowitz, 1957) and also A. Merx, "Le rôle du foie dans la littérature des peuples sémitiques," *Floril. M. de Vogüé* (Paris: Imprimerie Nationale, 1909), 427–44.
26. Definition given by Ibn al-Qayyim (*Rauḍa*, 30) which may come from al-Aṣma'ī's *K. Khalq al-Insān* (in August Haffner's *Texte zur arabischen Lexikographie*) where the same definition occurs on page 218.

Arabic prose and poetry on love, one would receive the immediate impression, on reading such lists of terms for love as have been described, that according to the Arab point of view, love is often the cause of much unhappiness. A high proportion of the words express the woes of love—the longing, the pain, the grief, melancholy, confusion, and illness—rather than its pleasures. They outnumber the terms that convey the notion of quiet contentment, pleasurable excitement, or ecstatic joy.

The word *shauq* provides Ibn Qayyim al-Jauzīya with the occasion for a brief discussion of a favorite question of love theory: does union with the beloved diminish *shauq* or increase it? He quotes a line of poetry to support each view, and concludes that there are actually two kinds of *shauq*. One is the longing for one absent, that *shauq* that is sometimes defined as "the journeying of the heart towards the beloved." By definition, that kind of *shauq* finds peace only when the heart reaches its goal. The other kind is alluded to in the famous verse that says that *shauq* reaches its maximum on the day on which the tents of the tribe of the lover are pitched close to the tents of the tribe of the beloved. This is the *shauq* that is described as "the burning pain of love and its flaming fire."[27]

The fact that some authors took the trouble to demonstrate the resources of the language and to quote authoritative information on the meaning of the terms they used did not save Arabic theory of love from great confusion in the use of these terms. The character of these writings and their position vis-à-vis other intellectual concerns contributed to that semantic anarchy. Love theory was an occasional subject, taken up by one or, at most, a few writers in each generation. Each writer produced only one or two books on the subject, books that never wholly escaped the character of anthologies. The subject was never the exclusive preserve of any one discipline or of any single sect or school interested in arriving at a consistent set of assumptions and conclusions or employing a uniform terminology. The authors came from a variety of backgrounds, and, like many Muslim scholars, took pleasure in preserving and recounting, over nearly a millennium,

27. *Rauḍa*, 29. He makes no reference to the mystical connotations of the word.

an increasing number and variety of opinions, sometimes adding a few of their own. This passion for collecting, often without comment or analysis, leads to the appearance of several different uses of a term on one page without any note of that fact.

Of all the terms for love, the word *hawā* was probably subject to the widest variety of usage. In the first thirty-four chapters of Ibn al-Jauzī's *Dhamm al-Hawā*, the word occurs in the sense of "desire, concupiscence, or lust." It is said to mean both the instinctual drives and reactions that enable man to survive and to reproduce and an obsession with the desire for anything, whether power, learning, material wealth, or the gratification of one's sexual desires. In most passages it is unbridled sexual lust that is meant, but in any case, it is the kind of *hawā* that the theologians have made their concern, the cravings that threaten to overpower reason and draw one into their pursuit and away from God and the obedience to his laws. The word is burdened with the highly unfavorable connotations that it carries in Ḥadīth and the Koran, or that the commentators have given to it. From Chapter Thirty-Five onward, the word *hawā* occurs in many passages quoted and paraphrased from other authorities as a word for love in some degree, without the moralistic and negative overtones found in the earlier chapters. This is the *hawā* of poetry and belletristic literature, more limited in meaning and free from any suggestion that those who feel it are to be censured on moral grounds. Nowhere does Ibn al-Jauzī accord any recognition to the existence of such a difference in viewpoint and usage. He seems to intend that the reader should see *hawā*, wherever he meets it, through the eyes of a theologian.

Neither does he explain how *hawā*, the subject of his first thirty-four chapters, differs from *'ishq*, the subject of his later chapters.[28] He seems to have avoided any comparison of one term

28. A comparison of the standard definitions given by Ibn al-Jauzī for *hawā* (*Dhamm*, p. 12) and for *'ishq* (p. 293) does not clarify the difference. In the case of *hawā*, it is said to be the nature (*ṭab'*) of man which inclines toward what suits it (*mā yulā'imuhū*), whereas in *'ishq* it is the *nafs* (lower nature? spirit? self?) that "inclines very strongly toward a form (?) (*ṣūra*) which suits its nature, and, whenever the thought of it grows stronger, [the *nafs*] imagines attaining it and wishes for that, and from the intense preoccupation of the mind a sickness sets in." (Goldziher, in *ZDMG*, LXIX [1915], 196, once translated "*ṣūra*" in a similar context as "gestalt.")

with another. We have seen earlier that the chapters on *hawā* and those on *ʿishq* are completely independent. Since he adopts the negative, theological interpretation of *hawā* in the first thirty-four chapters, ignoring the literary (or secular), morally neutral use of the word, it would have been difficult to explain the relation between *hawā* and *ʿishq*. It is only the secular meaning of *hawā* that has an association, clearly apparent in the literary tradition, with the word *ʿishq*. Unlike *hawā*, the word *ʿishq* has no history of use in the Koran and Ḥadīth, let alone to denote something blameworthy.[29] Ibn al-Qayyim says that *ʿishq* is a word which the late poets are fond of using.[30] It has a purely secular use until the mystics take it up to express love of God, but Ibn al-Jauzī ignores that usage.

In the literary tradition, *hawā* and *ʿishq* appear to be used interchangeably very often. They may be paired in expressions like "*ahl al-hawā wa ʾl-ʿishq*" (literally, the people of *hawā* and *ʿishq*) and in the saying "*At-tatayyum nihāyat al-hawā wa ākhir al-ʿishq*" (Thralldom is the utmost degree of *hawā* and the last stage of *ʿishq*). However, *hawā* has also in some contexts been assigned a more specific meaning. In an attempt to be more precise about the degree of love which is represented by each term, writers have drawn up descriptions of the ascending degrees of love, beginning with inclination, liking, or good opinion, and proceeding to extreme obsession with feelings for the beloved. Ibn al-Jauzī quotes a number of such different schemes under the heading "The Degrees of *ʿIshq*." There *hawā* can be found as the sixth of eight degrees, the second of seven, and the third of seven. The word *ʿishq* itself occurs there as a "degree of *ʿishq*" usually denoting a stage of love one to three degrees more advanced than *hawā*.[31] In Kisāʾī's system, *hawā* is given as the last of eleven names for *ḥubb* or *maḥabba* and is said to subsume all the previous ten, which are said to be "varieties

29. The statement that it was never used in the Koran or Tradition comes from Ibn al-Qayyim (*Rauḍa*, 25). The one exception that he mentions, the martyrs-of-love tradition, does not count with him, since he denies its authenticity.
30. *Rauḍa*, 25.
31. *Dhamm*, 293–94.

of the species" (*anwāʿ li ʾl-jins*). This seems to mean that *ḥubb* is synonymous with *hawā* as far as Kisāʾī is concerned.[32]

Though commonly *ḥubb* and *maḥabba* are used interchangeably with *hawā* and *ʿishq*, they also appear in some graduated lists as a degree of love that is strong but not extreme like *hawā* and *ʿishq*. In other words, *ḥubb* and *maḥabba* may be used as general terms meaning "love" just as *ʿishq* and *hawā* are in some contexts, or they may occur as specific terms indicating a moderate or optimal degree of love. In general, the opinion of Jāḥiẓ that all *ʿishq* is *ḥubb* but not all *ḥubb* is *ʿishq*, because *ḥubb* is the broad term for love while *ʿishq* denotes a special kind of love, has prevailed.

32. Top Kapı Saray, Ahmet III 2373, folios 5b–18b.

PART 3

CENTRAL DOCTRINAL OR ETHICAL ISSUES

I

THE MARTYRS OF LOVE

The tradition about the martyrs of love first appears in the *Kitāb az-Zahra* of Ibn Dā'ūd:

> *Said Abū Bakr b. Dā'ūd: My father related to me a tradition saying: Suwaid b. Sa'īd al-Ḥadathānī related to us a tradition, saying: 'Alī b. Mushir related to us on the authority of Abū Yaḥyā al-Fattāt, who related on the authority of Mujāhid, who related on the authority of Ibn 'Abbās, who said: The Messenger of God—on him be blessing and peace—said: He who loves and remains chaste and conceals his secret and dies, dies a martyr. . . .*[1]

It would be tempting to associate this tradition with the manner in which Ibn Dā'ūd died. However, its appearance in the *Kitāb az-Zahra* does not seem to have particular significance, except retrospectively. He has nothing more to say about martyrs of love after quoting the tradition in passing, as it were, at the beginning of Chapter Eight, which carries the motto "He Who is [a?] *Ẓarīf*[2] Will Be Chaste." But the circle of scholars, mostly Mu'tazilī, who were Ibn Dā'ūd's friends, or at least acquaintances of his close friend Niftawayh, picked up and propagated the tradition along with

1. *Zahra*, 66. This is the end of the tradition as given in other sources. Here other words follow, but they appear to be the words of Ibn Dā'ūd or his father, not part of the tradition. "Al-Fattāt" should be "al-Qattāt." Cf. *Dhamm*, 326; *Wāḍiḥ*, 2; *Rauḍa*, 180.
2. Concerning the "*ẓarīf*" (pl. *ẓurafā'*), see above, p. 14 and Part 2, Chap. II, n. 8.

other fragments of pseudo-historical information and anecdotes having to do with love. On the evidence of *isnāds*, the tradition appears to have had a fairly wide circulation. Ibn Dā'ūd and his father figure in only one of ten versions of it given two centuries later by Ibn al-Jauzī in his book *Dhamm al-Hawā*.[3] Therefore, there seems to be no evidence that the tradition was the fiction of Ibn Dā'ūd or his father.[4] Neither, apparently, did it owe its popularity solely to that group of men who interested themselves in the oral and written transmission of such materials as compose the books on the theory of profane love, though they no doubt played the major role in its transmission to later generations. The names in the chains of transmitters are those that appear often in books like the *Maṣāri' al-'Ushshāq* and the *Dhamm al-Hawā*. Indeed, the question of the genuineness or spuriousness of its origin need not concern us at this point.[5] What is interesting is the measure of success it enjoyed. Whatever the original source of the text of the tradition, it is evident from the pages of these works on the theory of love that large numbers of sincere Muslims found the idea it represented to be both logical and appealing. Why did they? It would be well to look for the origins of the notion of martyrs of love and its possible connections with the growth of a body of ideas about martyrdom in general.

3. *Dhamm*, 326–29. Actually, the tradition appears twelve times in the printed edition, and Massignon (*Passion*, I, 175) speaks of the "douze isnâd différents" given by Ibn al-Jauzī. He consulted the MS Paris 1296, and the printed edition of the *Dhamm* is based on the Paris and Berlin MSS. I have not seen those MSS, but the edition reflects a copyist's double error. The text and the *isnād* of numbers seven and eight have been copied twice, except that the words "*thumma māta*" (then dies) have been omitted from the text of version ten (= version eight) causing the tradition to make no sense. This repetition seems to have escaped the attention of the editors. Since I noticed it only while preparing a late draft of this chapter, I have not had the opportunity to see the two MSS used in the edition nor to check the MSS found in İstanbul, which they did not use.

4. As we shall see, some scholars of tradition thought that Suwaid b. Sa'īd, the Iraqian on whose authority Ibn Dā'ūd's father transmitted the tradition, was responsible for it.

5. It is well known since the researches of Ignacz Goldziher that the majority of such formal traditions from the Prophet are spurious and that they were put into circulation for the first time several generations after his lifetime. For specialist and non-specialist alike, useful summaries and bibliographies on this subject may be found in the articles "Ḥadīth" by Th. W. Juynboll in *EI*[1] and by J. Robson in *EI*[2].

The concept of the martyr was handed down from the ancient Near East through the Hellenistic, Jewish Hellenistic, and Christian traditions to Islam, undergoing certain accretions as it went. A. J. Wensinck, though he does not mention the martyrs of love, has traced the development of the chief ideas concerning martyrs from their origins down to the Islamic period.[6] The central dogma originated in the primitive views on the fate of fallen warriors. The Jews of the Maccabean age adapted these and cognate ideas to monotheism and joined to them a Hellenistic notion, primarily Stoic, the idea of the ascetic philosopher, who with heroic patience clings to his divine calling and ethical principles. These two persons, the fallen warrior and the heroic philosopher, come under the common designation *μάρτυς*, and the abstract noun designating his behavior is *μαρτυρία*. Christianity later worked out this twofold concept of warrior and ascetic and handed it on to Islam, which made use of it in a manner parallel (even down to its details) but independent and in full harmony with its own developing doctrines.[7]

As in Greek, the Arabic word *shahīd* is used in the ordinary (theological) meaning of "witness" and in the later, technical sense of "martyr" or "witness unto death for the sake of the faith," the special or technical meaning.[8] *Shahīd* as "martyr" does not occur in the Koran, as Goldziher pointed out.[9] One of the verses later interpreted as a description of the reward of the martyrs reads:

Those who believe, and have left their homes and
striven with their wealth and their lives in
Allah's way are of much greater worth in Allah's
sight. These are they who are triumphant.
Their Lord giveth them good tidings of mercy from

6. "The Oriental Doctrine of the Martyrs," *Mededeelingen der Koninklijke Akademie van Wetenschappen te Amsterdam*, Afdeeling Letterkunde, Deel 53, Serie A, No. 6, 147–74. See also the brief summary in W. Björkman, art. "Shahīd," *EI*[1] or *SEI*, of the findings of Wensinck and of others.

7. Wensinck, 174.

8. In the ordinary meaning of "witness," it occurs approximately fifty times in the Koran.

9. *Muhammedanische Studien* (Hildesheim: G. Olms, 1961), II, 387.

Him, and acceptance, and Gardens where enduring pleasure will be theirs;
There they will abide forever. Lo! with Allah there is immense reward.[10]

The concepts of martyrdom and paradise, the two always in close relation, and the use of the term *shahīd*, in the meaning "martyr," developed with Muslim tradition and dogma. Moreover, when *jihād*, "holy war," literally, "striving [in the cause of God]," ceased to be the significant activity of Muslims, they began to ask whether the highest reward in Islam belonged only to those who waged war to propagate or defend Islam. Might not the fulfilling of the other duties of the believer be of equal merit? The next step, taken first by the Muslim mystics, was the proposition that all the works prescribed by Islamic Law had real meaning only when they were considered as outward symbols of inner, spiritual ideas. The true martyr according to this conception was the man who waged war not against infidels but against his own sensual nature, much as the Eastern Church recognized ascetics as martyrs. In this connection, Wensinck quotes from al-Ghazālī:

> *Everyone who gives himself wholly to God* (tadjarrada lillāhi) *in the war against his own desires* (nafs), *is a martyr when he meets death going forward without turning his back. So the holy warrior is he who makes war against his own desires, as it has been explained by the Apostle of God. And the 'greater war' is war against one's own desires, as the Companions said: We have returned from the lesser war unto the greater one, meaning thereby war against their own desires.*[11]

Long before Ghazālī, however, Ḥasan al-Baṣrī (d. 110/728) is supposed to have voiced a similar opinion. According to Ibn Qayyim al-Jauzīya, a man asked Ḥasan, "O Abū Sa'īd, which *jihād* is most

10. Koran, Sūra 9: 20–22, cf. 47: 4 and 61: 11 ff. Translation is that of Mohammad Marmaduke Pickthall, *The Meaning of the Glorious Koran* (New York: New American Library, 1953).

11. Wensinck, 155, citing al-Ghazālī, *Iḥyā' 'Ulūm ad-Dīn* (Cairo, 1302), II, 207.

meritorious?" He said, "Your battling against your *hawā*."[12] Ibn al-Qayyim adds that Ibn Taimīya said, "Fighting against your lower nature (*nafs*) and against *hawā* is fundamental to (or takes precedence over) the fighting of infidels and 'the hypocrites,' for a man cannot fight them until he first fights his *nafs* and its *hawā* (lusts). Then he may go out and wage war against them."[13]

The growth and spread of these ideas about the nature of martyrdom seem to have had two points of logical connection with the appearance of the tradition on the martyrs of love. The first is that one who falls violently in love, restrains his passions, remains upright and chaste, and consequently dies of love, would seem to be one who had battled against the lusts of the flesh and had "met death going forward." At least this seems to have been in the minds of those who considered in the first place that impassioned but pure love was not contrary to the teachings of Islam. Looking for the possible antecedents of this idea in Islam that ascetic mystics are the true martyrs, Wensinck observes that in the Eastern Church Ephraim Syrus recognized the moral martyrdom of those who remain steadfast in the strife against their own passions and counted Joseph and Susanna among the martyrs.[14] I might add that this information ties in directly with evidence in the Arabic books on the theory of profane love of the association between the ideal of chaste conduct and martyrdom in Islam, for there we find these same two persons held up as perfect exemplars of chaste, praiseworthy conduct and the willingness to face even death rather than to do what is wrong in the sight of God. Ibn al-Qayyim emphasized how every circumstance contributed to strengthen the desire Yūsuf (Joseph) felt for his seductress (the wife of the man who bought him from the caravan, Potiphar's wife in the Genesis version), yet he chose prison

12. The way in which the question is put implies either that the question of there being more than one kind of holy war was already being debated at that time or that later scholars put the words into Ḥasan's mouth.

13. *Rauḍa*, 472. "The hypocrites" or "those of weak or doubtful belief in Islam," Ar. *munāfiqūn*. See F. Buhl, art., "Munāfiḳūn," *EI*[1] or *SEI*.

14. Wensinck, 158–59, citing Ephraim Syrus, *Hymni et Sermones*, ed. Abbeloos and Lamy, III, col. 696.

rather than yield to sin.[15] When God later rewards Yūsuf with a powerful position, the woman comes humbly to him asking to become his lawful wife, and on his marriage night he says to her, "This is better than what you once wanted."[16] The story of Sausan the Devout, or Maisūna (Susanna) more or less follows the Biblical account.[17] In an interesting variant in the *Maṣāri' al-'Ushshāq* she is sentenced to be bound to a stone table (*maṣṭaba*), in accordance with what was said to be Jewish custom, in the expectation that fire would fall from Heaven and devour her. On the third day the young prophet Daniel comes and re-examines the testimony of the two Elders, entrapping them in their lie, whereupon fire from Heaven burns them up and Sausan is freed.[18]

However, the idea of martyrs of love may have been connected with a second facet of the developing doctrine of the *shahīd*: the tendency to consider death from certain other causes as equal to martyrdom in holy war. Among several traditions one of the most explicit says there are seven kinds of martyrs, apart from those who die "on the Path of God": the victims of epidemics, those dying of pleurisy or diarrhea (cholera is probably meant), those who are drowned, die in a fire, are struck by a falling house or wall, and finally, women who die in childbirth.[19]

These categories of martyrs all have one thing in common: they die prematurely or violently, recalling primitive Near Eastern beliefs that those who die violently receive a special place in the nether world.[20] Zurqānī, in his commentary on Mālik's *Muwaṭṭa'*, explains that some scholars hold that because these kinds of death are extremely painful God shows his grace to the Islamic community

15. *Rauḍa*, 318–21. The Koranic version of the story is Sūra 12, "Yūsuf."
16. *Rauḍa*, 441. On Haggadic elements in the Koranic story and later legendary additions to it, see B. Heller, art. "Yūsuf b. Ya'ḳūb," *EI*[1] or *SEI*. This is a post-Koranic addition not mentioned there.
17. Daniel 13, or The History of Susanna in editions with a separate Apocrypha.
18. *Maṣāri'*, I, 74. Cf. *I'tilāl* (Ulu Cami 1535), folio 25b; *Rauḍa*, 559.
19. See Wensinck, 172, citing Mālik's *Muwaṭṭa'*, II, 22. (The edition, not indicated, is probably that of Cairo, 1279–80.) For other traditions about the martyrs, see Wensinck, *A Handbook of Early Muhammadan Tradition* (Leiden: E. J. Brill, 1927), *s.v.* "'Martyrs."
20. Wensinck (page 173) gives examples from the Gilgamesh Epic.

by taking these deaths as an atonement for their sins, and as an addition to their wages so that he makes them attain the ranks of the martyrs. It also appears from Zurqānī's explanations that it was difficult for most Muslim interpreters to adapt these primitive concepts to other aspects of the doctrine of the martyrs.[21]

To die as a martyr of love likewise meant that one endured much suffering, and in any case one died prematurely. The agonies of the martyrs of love are treated with much compassion and great seriousness in the books on love. *Hawā*, or *ʿishq*, was also, of course, regarded as a disease, likely to be fatal. Since love-death combined in it both an ascetic denial of the flesh and a premature and painful end it must have seemed eminently logical that its victims should join the martyrs near the throne of God. I have so far been unable to find an explanation of the rationale of the doctrine in the writings on the theory of love or elsewhere in native tradition.[22] This need not surprise us. In keeping with the principle that if the Prophet said something, his authority was sufficient, those who accepted the tradition on the basis of the evidence of its soundness did not try to justify the substance of it with explanations of why it ought to be true.

The opponents of the tradition, on the other hand, kept silence neither about the *isnād* of the tradition nor its substance. Following the rules for Ḥadīth criticism, they found arguments for rejecting the majority of the versions of the tradition in circulation on grounds of doubts about the reliability of one transmitter, Suwaid b. Saʿīd, common to all these. Since, however, there existed by the time of

21. See Wensinck, 173. He cites *Muwaṭṭa'*, II, 23, margin. Zurqānī, a Mālikī *faqīh* (*GAL*, G. II, 318; S. II, 439) died 1122/1710.

22. Besides the particular associations with the idea of the ascetic and the painful death of the holy war martyr, there was the general tendency to claim the reward of the martyr for any death overtaking one while engaged in a laudable cause or activity. There is thus an interesting parallel between a late tradition given by Ghazālī in the *Iḥyā' ʿUlūm ad-Dīn* (Būlāq, 1289), page 6, which says that on Judgment Day the ink of the scholars shall be weighed with the blood of the martyrs and a saying attributed to Ibn al-Athīr in the *Wāḍiḥ*, page 8, who says, "The tears [*damʿ*] of the lover [*ʿāshiq*] and the blood [*dam*] of the victim of battle are like one another and equal in what they represent except that between them there is one difference: they differ from one another in color." There is a play on words, of course, between *damʿ* and *dam*.

Ibn al-Jauzī (if not earlier) two versions with technically unimpeachable *isnāds*, they were forced to come to grips with the text of the tradition itself. Guided by a consideration that actually ruled in all Ḥadīth criticism, they expressed the opinion that not only the credentials of some of the versions of the tradition but also the substance of the tradition was unacceptable to them; the Prophet could never have made such a statement. It was a sin, they declared, to conceive a passionate love for anything or anyone other than God himself. Therefore, there could be no martyrs of love, at least no martyrs of profane love, no matter how "pure" their love was alleged to be. Meanwhile, those who accepted the tradition were silent, standing their ground on its authenticity and apparently seeing no need to marshal any arguments in its defense.

Von Grunebaum has suggested that the concept of the martyr of love constitutes an original contribution of Arabic poetry. In it he sees the fusion of two themes from Greek and Hellenistic literature: the notion of the victim of love and the idea of the lover as fighter or soldier. He points out that Christian martyrology made extensive use of erotic phraseology and that the Arab world would have been familiar with Christian literature of this sort, suggesting, if I understand him correctly, that the converse would have been possible, i.e., the use of the martyr theme in erotic poetry. The transfer of the fighter-martyr concept to the battles of love appears to him "a very original, if bold and frivolous," innovation of Arabic literature of the later seventh century A.D.[23]

While it is possible that conventions and motifs of Hellenistic literature on love and the Greek novel were taken over in early Arabic literature, especially in poetry and in sentimental tales about unhappy lovers,[24] one should be careful to distinguish this literary motif from the doctrine set forth in the formal tradition in its different versions. Arabic poetry did not make martyrs of these persons; though their sufferings were depicted in vivid colors, the

23. *Medieval Islam* (2nd ed.; Chicago: University of Chicago Press, 1953), 316–17.
24. See Von Grunebaum, "Greek Form Elements in the Arabian Nights," *JAOS*, LXII (1942), 277–92, in which he also touches upon literature other than the Arabian Nights.

word *shahīd* is not at first specifically applied to them. While admittedly there is a great deal that remains unknown and undocumented concerning the first century and a half of the Islamic era, there is, as far as I know, not a word about martyrs of love until the appearance of the formal tradition, "He who loves passionately and remains chaste and dies, dies a martyr." Though a fondness for the theme of chaste love as celebrated in literature undoubtedly influenced those who accepted and propagated the tradition, the tradition itself was always treated seriously and made the subject of scholarly and highly technical discussions. After all the subtleties of Ḥadīth criticism had been applied to the fullest extent, the real ethical and moral issue was finally revealed. The question was: should *ʿishq* or *hawā* be considered a kind of tragic affliction to be borne nobly and ascetically as some good Muslims maintained, or was it a mistaken delusion brought about by the sinful disregard of what other Muslims held to be the clear teachings of Sacred Law? Since many serious scholars professed the opinion that there was an innocent passionate love and that its victims under certain circumstances might attain martyrdom, it seems necessary to consider these ideas as having their roots and justification in Islamic thought, and that probably the primary rationale for the existence of the martyrs of love is found in those two criteria, self-denial and painful death, in which they parallel or resemble the other categories of martyrs in Islam.

It seems worthwhile here to trace briefly the martyrs-of-love theme through the works on the theory of love to see how it fared. We have already mentioned the fact that Ibn Dāʾūd was the first to give the tradition in a book on love, and, in fact, it seems that he was the first author to quote it. However, though he himself allegedly died a martyr of love, he says nothing further on the subject. After him, as we learn from Shihāb ad-Dīn Maḥmūd b. Sulaimān's *Manāzil al-Aḥbāb*, Marzubānī wrote on the subject, or at least repeated several versions of the tradition in his now lost *Kitāb ar-Riyāḍ*.[25] Judging from the description of his book in the *Fihrist* of Ibn an-Nadīm and from the traditions which are given on his authority

25. See above, page 20.

in the *Maṣāriʿ al-ʿUshshāq*, he appears to have taken a positive attitude toward the martyrs-of-love doctrine.

In the fifth/eleventh century, Ibn Ḥazm in his *Ṭauq al-Ḥamāma* devoted a chapter entitled "Of Death" to the martyrs of love. "Sometimes," he says, "the affair becomes so aggravated, the lover's nature is so sensitive, and his anxiety is so extreme, that the combined circumstances result in his departure out of this transient world."[26] After repeating a version of the *ḥadīth* without its *isnād* and some verses that he had composed on the theme, he proceeds to tell the stories of six persons of his acquaintance whom he believed to be martyrs of love, including his brother's wife and one of his old friends. He offers no comment on the authenticity of the tradition or the moral issues involved.

The *Maṣāriʿ al-ʿUshshāq* of Abū Muḥammad Jaʿfar b. Aḥmad as-Sarrāj probably did more than any Arabic book to popularize the theme of tragic, passionate love. The word *maṣāriʿ* (broken pl. of *maṣraʿ*, verbal noun of the root *s-r-ʿ*) comes from a root which has the connotation of "throwing down to the ground." From this derive the meanings "to fall down in an epileptic fit," "to go mad," or "to be killed in battle."[27] The word is particularly appropriate in the title of this book, for it embraces almost all the afflictions described in its pages: the lovers faint, fall down in a spasm of rapture or painful longing, never to regain consciousness, or they go mad.

About a hundred years later, Abu 'l-Faraj ʿAbd ar-Rahmān b. al-Jauzī (d. 579/1200) in his *Dhamm al-Hawā* devotes three chapters out of fifty to the martyrs and those killed by love. Chapter Thirty-Eight on the martyrs, "The Reward of Those Who Loved Passionately and Remained Chaste and Concealed Their Secret," is a

26. *Ṭauq* (Arberry's translation), 220. Cf. Bercher's ed. and tr., 298.
27. The use of the nickname "Ṣarīʿ al-Ghawānī" (The One Felled by Beautiful Women), applied to the poets Qutāmī (d. 101) and Muslim (d. 208), is connected with the sense of *maṣāriʿ* in the book title. An anecdote purporting to explain how Harūn ar-Rashīd came to give Muslim this epithet occurs, in fact, in *Maṣāriʿ*, I, 37–38. See also Muslim b. Walīd, *Dīwān*, ed. Sāmī Dahhān (Cairo: Dār al-Maʿārif, 1376/1957), introd., pp. 17–19. The word *maṣāriʿ* occurs also in the titles of works on the *jihād*, e.g., the *Mashāriʿ al-Aswāq ilā Maṣāriʿ al-ʿUshshāq*, etc., by Ibn an-Naḥḥās ad-Dimashqī (d. 814). See *GAL*, G. II, 76; S. II, 83.

recital of ten versions of the tradition, differing mainly in their chains of transmitters.[28] After the ninth version, Ibn al-Jauzī gives a tradition[29] from Ibn al-Marzubān which reports that this scholar and *rāwī*[30] reproached an early transmitter of the tradition on the martyrs for attributing it to the Prophet. The transmitter was said to have backed down and attributed it only to Ibn al-ʿAbbās after that.[31] The chapter ends with a tradition which says that those who love most violently, or strongly, will be most rewarded. Nowhere in the chapter does Ibn al-Jauzī give any indication of his own attitude toward the tradition on the martyrs. On the face of it, it would seem that he accepts the substance of the tradition or at least has no serious objections to it. He neither rejects any of its credentials nor casts any doubt on them.

The lengthy Chapter Forty-One, "The Passionate Lovers Who Became Proverbial for Their Love" (and most of whom died of love), deals only with the most celebrated, beginning with the "most famous of the famous" (*ashhar al-mashhūrīn*), Majnūn Laila, followed by ʿUrwa b. Ḥizām al-ʿUdhrī, al-ʿAbbās b. al-Aḥnaf b. al-Aswad, Dhu 'r-Rumma, Tauba and his Laila al-Akhyalīya, Jamīl and Buthaina, and Kuthayyir ʿAzza. Ibn al-Jauzī takes care to give the source or credentials of everything he quotes and to relate all the reports about these persons' tribal descent, individual identity, and the circumstances of their lives and loves as well as different recensions of their poetry.

Chapter Forty-Seven, "Accounts of Ṯhose Whom *ʿIshq* Killed," seventy-odd pages on the less famous, even nameless, victims of love, is very similar to the chapter on the famous lovers except that the stories are shorter and the verses fewer. In about half the sixty-odd stories in the chapter, the *isnād* begins with the words "Shuhda

28. See note 3 and text.
29. The second *fa-ʿātabtuhū ʿalā dhālika* in the tradition is no doubt an erroneous repetition and should be deleted.
30. See above, p. 18.
31. *Dhamm*, 329. Mughulṭāi (*Wāḍiḥ*, 5–6) explains that al-Azraq, the transmitter reproached by Ibn al-Marzubān, was not a *ḥāfiẓ* (here: a man with a reliable memory for a large number of traditions who made a special effort to collect and transmit them). If he were, he would not have been led to doubt his own recollection of the *isnād* without demanding proof that it was incorrect.

bint Aḥmad informed us on the authority of Ja'far b. Aḥmad (or Abū Muḥammad as-Sarrāj) [who related] on the authority of . . ." We know from the preface of al-Biqā'ī's *Aswāq al-Ashwāq* that this woman scholar (d. 574) transmitted the *Maṣāri' al-'Ushshāq* of Ja'far b. Aḥmad as-Sarrāj with a certificate which contained his official permission to do so and testified to the correctness of her copy, and we also know from Ibn Rajab that Ibn al-Jauzī was one of those who received the text of the *Maṣāri'* from her.[32] By way of confirmation, most of these stories in the *Dhamm* bearing her name can be found in the *Maṣāri'*, though he does not mention that title or any other in his book. Since all traditions used in the *Dhamm al-Hawā* had been transmitted to him through authorized oral channels, he may have deemed this fact more important than the availability of a written text and may have considered quoting such a text unnecessary, or rather, he may have quoted it, adding to each item that part of the *isnād* which brought it up to his own day.[33] The fact that a few stories in this chapter in the *Dhamm al-Hawā* cannot be traced in the *Maṣāri'*, though they contain the names of Shuhda bint Aḥmad and Ja'far b. Aḥmad as-Sarrāj, may indicate either that the edition of the *Maṣāri'* available to me is not as complete as the text that Ibn al-Jauzī had or that he had additional stories transmitted from as-Sarrāj by Bint Aḥmad besides those in the authorized text of the *Maṣāri'*.[34]

On the other hand, there are stories which do not bear the names of Shuhda bint Aḥmad and as-Sarrāj but which can be found in almost identical form in the *Maṣāri'* though with different *isnāds*. Al-Kharā'iṭī, author of the *I'tilāl al-Qulūb*, who has already been mentioned, with as-Sarrāj, as an important contributor to the content of the *Dhamm al-Hawā*, appears in a number of *isnāds* in this chapter also, usually under the name Muḥammad b. Ja'far. These two important authors are only two of many persons whose names recur

32. See above, p. 26. Ibn Rajab, I, 100.

33. That is, the *isnād* in the written text plus the *isnād* as implied in the reading certificate, assuring the reliability of the text as personally transmitted to him by certain scholars.

34. As indicated earlier, the edition of the *Maṣāri'* used in this study is that of Beirut, 1378/1958, 2 vols.

scores of times as transmitters of material about love and lovers in the period from the third/ninth century to the time of Ibn al-Jauzī. The question, as yet largely unanswered, is: did any of these persons prominent as *rāwīs* write books on love theory, victims of love, or any of the traditional topics with which their names are associated as transmitters in the *Dhamm al-Hawā*, the *Maṣāri' al-'Ushshāq*, and their successors? The convention by which men like Ibn al-Jauzī list transmitters but not book titles as authorities for what they say leaves us in ignorance on this matter. We could hazard a guess that most of these *rāwīs* did not write books on the theory of love or one of its sub-topics, since otherwise they would have been quoted in at least one of the several later works which did cite some titles.

The martyrs of love reached the zenith of their literary glory when 'Alā' ad-Dīn Abū 'Abd Allāh Mughulṭāi wrote his monograph on them in the first half of the eighth/fourteenth century.[35] This monograph, *Al-Wāḍiḥ al-Mubīn fī Dhikr Man Ustushhida min al-Muḥibbīn*, The Clear and Eloquent Speaking of Those Lovers Who Became Martyrs, is divided into five parts, of which the first and part of the second provide a general scholarly, ethical, and philosophical introduction to the theory of profane love and to the doctrine of the martyrs of love in particular. Mughulṭāi subjects the various versions of the tradition to technical criticism, discussing and, in most cases, discounting the allegations that have been made against the credibility of the *isnāds*. As a specialist in the science of tradition who had taught the subject in the Ẓāhirīya in Cairo, he was familiar with all the arguments for and against the tradition and knew how to proceed with his own assessment.

The main portion of the book contains biographies of the martyrs of love, alphabetically arranged according to the name of the lover,

35. Probably not everyone would have explicitly labeled all these victims of love "martyr" as he did. It is one thing to believe in the tradition, but another entirely to assume the responsibility of loosely using the term *shahīd* with reference to a heterogeneous collection of victims of love whose credentials as martyrs, strictly speaking, were not uniformly good or even existent. Most of his *shuhadā'* had not been called that specifically when their stories appeared in earlier books on love. As-Sarrāj and Ibn al-Jauzī give the tradition but do not label every victim of love a *shahīd*.

or, if that is not known, the name of the authority who gives the story, the name of the tribe of the lover, or the term by which his nation or race is known. Thus a tale about an unknown "black man" (*rajul aswad*) comes as "*aswad*" under the letter *alif*, that of a nameless Turk (*rajul Turkī*) under *tā'*, and likewise the story of a lover of the tribe of Tamīm. Even the animal kingdom had its martyrs, like the poor duck (*baṭṭ*), under the letter *bā'*, who died of anguish within moments after its mate was slaughtered for the table.[36]

Around the time this monograph on the martyrs of love appeared, Ibn Qayyim al-Jauzīya delivered an attack upon the tradition in his *Rauḍat al-Muḥibbīn*.[37] As usual, he is fair enough to quote first a few of the more important authorities who accepted the tradition before calling to witness for his side other scholars who rejected it and whom he considers the stronger authorities on the subject of Ḥadīth criticism. Like most other critics, Ibn al-Qayyim points out that in nearly all of the chains of transmitters Suwaid b. Sa'īd[38] was the common transmitter and the only one of his generation. Technically, this weakened its credentials. In addition, he alleges, as others had before him, that Suwaid went blind at the end of his life, a handicap considered to cast doubt on traditions he may have transmitted afterwards. To counter these traditional allegations against the authority of Suwaid as a transmitter, Mughulṭāi had adduced testimony to the effect that, though Suwaid was the single transmitter of this tradition in his generation, he was considered to be very reliable by no less an authority than Aḥmad b. Ḥanbal,

36. *Wāḍiḥ*, 100. Cf. *Maṣāri'*, II, 291.
37. *Rauḍa*, 180–82.
38. Following the system outlined by J. Schacht (*Origins of Muhammadan Jurisprudence* [Oxford: Clarendon Press, 1953], Pt. II, Ch. 4), an analysis of the *isnāds* as they occur in the *Dhamm al-Hawā* shows that Suwaid b. Sa'īd was indeed almost certainly the inventor of the tradition. See Appendix. Biographies of Suwaid are given in al-Khaṭīb al-Baghdādī, *Ta'r. Bagh.*, IX, 228–32; Yāqūt, *Mu'jam al-Buldān* (Beirut: Dār Ṣādir, 1374–76/1955–57), II, 230b–231a; Ibn Ḥajar al-'Asqalānī, *Tahdhīb al-Tahdhīb* (Hyderabad: Dā'irat al-Ma'ārif an-Niẓāmīya, 1320), IV, 272–75 (No. 470); and Ṣafadī, *Nakt al-Himyān* (Cairo, 1329/1911), 162–63. He lived all his life in Iraq.

founder of the school of law of which Ibn al-Qayyim was an adherent. He also asserted that he transmitted the traditions that go under his name before he became blind.[39]

Ibn al-Qayyim disposes of one version which had a perfect *isnād*, technically speaking, by saying that it does not "smell" like a sound tradition and that "judgment in this matter belongs to the experts in tradition, not to the noses of those who are unfamiliar with it."[40] It could not possibly be genuine, because it was not the kind of thing that the Prophet would have said. He believes that the tradition that enumerates the martyrs, six categories in addition to the victims of the holy war, is sound and points out that the victims of chaste love are not among them. "Every victim of love could not possibly be a martyr," he says, "for he may have followed the whims of a passion that is deserving of punishment."[41]

From the discussions of Mughulṭāi, supporter of the tradition, and Ibn Qayyim al-Jauzīya, its harsh critic, we learn that Ibn al-Jauzī, who had said nothing himself in his chapter on the martyrs by way of rejecting the tradition, had elsewhere criticized at least one version of it. Ibn al-Qayyim says that Ibn al-Jauzī rejected versions related by Suwaid and put the tradition in his *Kitāb al-Mauḍū'āt*[42] (The Book of Fictitious, or Forged, Traditions), the *mauḍū'āt* being the most objectionable of traditions, rejected as absolutely false. Mughulṭāi, on the other hand, says that another version, one not transmitted through Suwaid, was labeled "weak" in Ibn al-Jauzī's *Kitāb aḍ-Ḍu'afā'* (Book of Weak Traditions).[43] Mughulṭāi says that Ibn al-Jauzī seems to have used a corrupt manuscript of the *Kitāb I'tilāl al-Qulūb*; a copyist's error in the *isnād* had led him to an incorrect conclusion about the tradition. In

39. *Wāḍiḥ*, 5. Cf. *Rauḍa*, 181.
40. *Rauḍa*, 182.
41. *Rauḍa*, 181. He is not accurate here, for, though Mughulṭāi, especially, used the term *shahīd* rather loosely, no writer on the subject of love, as far as I am aware, maintained that every victim of love was a martyr.
42. *GAL*, G. I, 503; S. I; 917.
43. Also in *GAL*,

the form in which it occurs in correct copies of the *I'tilāl,* the *isnād* is perfect.[44]

Ibn al-Qayyim's paragraphs on the martyr tradition have the appearance of being a direct refutation of what Mughulṭāi had written. The paragraph summarizing some of the traditional arguments in favor of the tradition appears to have been copied directly from Mughulṭāi's book. However, both men may have copied the summary of these arguments out of a standard text on traditions, and, if so, that would explain a word-for-word correspondence between them in places.[45] Ibn al-Qayyim does not treat the subject in his usual thorough manner, but hurries through it as though it were either a topic he did not relish or thought not worth any extended treatment. Though the tradition had long been controverted among specialists on tradition,[46] the controversy emerged in the pages of the literature on the theory of profane love only in the *Rauḍat al-Muḥibbīn* and the *Wāḍiḥ al-Mubīn.* For centuries, the tradition had been presented in these works as one of those dicta on love which was attractive and not especially controversial. In fact, it appears to have enjoyed wide acceptance as well as popularity, in spite of the doubts cast on it by some traditionists. The theme of the martyrs or victims of love was too thoroughly entrenched in the public regard. One wonders whether Ibn al-Jauzī was shrewd enough to realize this and chose therefore not to quibble over its origins or credentials in his *Dhamm al-Hawā.* His presentation of it as "The Reward of Those Who Love Passionately and Remain Chaste and Keep Their Secret" seems calculated to make constructive use of the tradition as an encouragement to the despairing young man to whom he addresses the book and an admonishment to bear his affliction with patience.

44. Since this question arose at a late stage of my research, I have not had the opportunity to consult MSS of these two works in Europe or İstanbul to see whether Mughulṭāi and Ibn al-Qayyim are both reporting correctly. Mughulṭāi himself wrote a supplement to Ibn al-Jauzī's *K. aḍ-Ḍu'afā'.* See *Wāḍiḥ,* 4; b. Taghr., Vol. 5, Pt. I, 179; Ibn Qutlūbughā, No. 236.

45. Compare *Wāḍiḥ,* 4–5 with *Rauḍa,* 180–81.

46. Among those who rejected it were Baihaqī and Jurjānī and among those who accepted it was Nawawī. See *Wāḍiḥ.* 1–7, and *Rauḍa,* 180–82. Also Massignon, *Passion,* I, 175, note.

After Ibn al-Qayyim's attack and Mughulṭāi's apologia, the later works, composed in the more light-hearted *adab* spirit, take a carefully moderate but positive attitude toward the martyrs-of-love tradition. Like most writers on profane love in the past, they accept the tradition, implicitly or explicitly. Al-Biqāʿī, for example, reports only one version of the tradition and does not discuss the authenticity of this or any other version,[47] while al-Anṭākī briefly summarizes the different versions and the arguments in support of its credibility and concludes by accepting it.[48]

The martyrs and victims of love occupy a large place in the pages of the late works, the greater number of their stories coming directly or indirectly from Jaʿfar b. Aḥmad as-Sarrāj's *Maṣāriʿ al-ʿUshshāq* and Mughulṭāi's *Wāḍiḥ al-Mubīn*. Ibn Abī Ḥajala in his *Dīwān aṣ-Ṣabāba* even follows Mughulṭāi's practice of heading many such stories with the word *shahīd*, or *shahīdān* (two martyrs), in bold letters.[49]

Even Marʿī b. Yūsuf of the eleventh/seventeenth century, a Ḥanbalī like Ibn Qayyim al-Jauzīya and devoted, like him, to the teachings of Ibn Taimīya, is ready to accept the tradition: he wrote, "Even if it is forged [in some versions] as some specialists in tradition allege, nevertheless, it is sound as transmitted by some [other] chains of transmitters."[50] This is consistent with the theory, set forth elsewhere in the book, that occasionally, when it is free of lust (*shahwa*), *ʿishq* can be truly praiseworthy (*mamdūḥ*), though in most cases and as the word is commonly understood, *ʿishq* is blameworthy (*madhmūm*).[51]

47. *Aswāq al-Ashwāq* (Haci Beşir Ağa 552), folio 4b ff.

48. *Tazyīn*, I, 23–25.

49. *D. aṣ-Ṣabāba* (Cairo ed.), Closing Chapter (*Khātima*): "Those Who Died of Love and Came before Their Lord," 216 ff.

50. ". . . *wa hādha 'l-ḥadīthu wa-in kāna mauḍūʿan kamā zaʿama bihī baʿḍu 'l-ḥuffāẓi lākinnahū saḥīḥun min baʿḍi 't-ṭuruq.*" *Munyat al-Muḥibbīn* (Talʿat, Adab 4648), folio 30a.

51. *Munyat al-Muḥibbīn* (Talʿat, Adab 4648), folio 12b.

II

THE GREAT DIVIDE: THE TWO SENSES OF "HAWA" AND THE COROLLARY ISSUE OF GHADD AN-NAZAR VS. THE NAZAR MUBAH

Now that we have approached the difference of opinion on this question from other directions, it will be clear that there are two fundamentally different attitudes toward *ʿishq* and *hawā* displayed in this literature, one predominantly positive, the other more negative or at least cautious. The first sees *ʿishq* as a complex and exceedingly interesting but mysterious human experience. Authors writing from this point of view describe *ʿishq*, analyze it, speculate upon it, and celebrate it in anecdote, story, and verse. They maintain a certain detachment by giving a comprehensive picture of it through the theories, opinions, and tales of men and women of very different background. Through the selection of their source material and by their treatment of the subject, they tend to emphasize the positive side of *ʿishq*, speaking of its virtues (*faḍāʾil*) and relating the stories of prophets, caliphs, and other great and good men who loved passionately.[1] Yet they do not overlook that dark and negative side

1. Kisāʾī, for example, in his *Rauḍat al-ʿĀshiq*, devoted Chapters Two to Five to the *faḍāʾil* of love and the famous men of the past who had been lovers.

of *'ishq* which is just as much a part of the literary tradition: suffering, violence, madness, and death. It is, in fact, the emotional heights and depths of *'ishq* which give it dramatic appeal as a literary subject, and which arouse the amazement, *'ajab*, of the reader. Here the dark depths of passion are essentially tragic rather than evil; as long as one conducts oneself honorably such love appears to be a noble adventure of the spirit or at least a noble form of suffering.

These writers avoid, ignore, or—in the case of Jāḥiẓ and Ibn Dā'ūd—deny the moral dilemmas which more strict and conservative Muslim authors see in passionate love. Writing in the more secular spirit of *adab* literature, they show the influence of a refined version of certain pagan Arab ideals, and Persian or Hellenistic ideas and values.[2] These continued to coexist with the more Islamicized ways of thinking and, in so far as they were not assimilated to Islamic thought, asserted themselves from time to time and were never wholly superseded.[3]

Men like Ibn al-Jauzī or Ibn al-Qayyim, the writers of the ethically oriented subtype of these works, hold the second, more negative or cautious view of *'ishq* and *hawā*. We have seen how they follow the pattern of the more secular works in most respects except that they cannot remain indifferent to the ethical issues. They take over much of the content of the more ordinary *adab* book on love theory but shape it to their own ends. They identify *'ishq* vaguely and indirectly with the term *hawā* as it is employed in the meaning of "desire" or "lust," either in the very general sense or in the more specialized sense of sexual desire, and an excessive preoccupation with these desires is implied. *Hawā* is not considered "absolutely blameworthy" (*madhmūm 'ala 'l-iṭlāq*) because without instinctive

2. Thus, for example, Jāḥiẓ discusses the psychological trauma wrought by *'ishq* wholly in terms of the pagan Arab concept of *murū'a* (the manly sense of honor): "*Ḥubb* is at the root of *hawā*, and *'ishq* branches off from *hawā*. *'Ishq* is that which causes a man to wander aimlessly about in a state of rapture or to die heartsick on his bed; and the starting point of all this is the bringing about of injury to his *murū'a* and his being filled with a feeling of submissiveness towards those who surround his beloved." ("Risāla fi 'l-'Ishqwa'n-Nisā'," *Majmū'at Rasā'il*, 161.)

3. See R. Walzer and H. A. R. Gibb, art. "Akhlāḳ," *EI*², Sect. i.

desires for such requirements as food, drink, and the sexual relationship, the species could not survive. These writers—and the Islamic theologians in general—find *hawā* blameworthy whenever it exceeds the degree necessary to acquire what is good for one.[4] It is evil primarily because such preoccupation with one's desires fills and corrupts the heart so that God does not have first place there. A man "follows his *hawā*" (*yatba'u hawāhū*) instead of following God and his Prophet. Secondly, they fear that the believer, carried away by his desire, will fall into serious sin.

It would seem that the literary, secular concept of *hawā* as "passionate love" is the older, essentially pagan notion. The seat of *hawā*, passionate love, is the heart or liver, judging from the etymological associations of the synonyms of *hawā* denoting the effect of love on these parts of the body and from the descriptions in poetry of the effects of *hawā* itself.

In the Koran and Tradition, the word *hawā* came to be used in the sense of "desire" and "object of one's desires" in contexts which implied that it was something of which God disapproves because it is an obstacle to obedience and devotion to him. *Hawā* in this sense becomes regularly associated with the "lower nature, or baser self, that incites to evil" (*an-nafs al-ammāra bi 's-sū'*)[5] and may overpower the essentially good "rational soul" or "intellect" (*'aql*)[6] which ought to have been relied upon to guide one to do right and to guard one against the seductions of *hawā*.

Ibn al-Jauzī and Ibn al-Qayyim, in their attempts to identify *hawā* in the pagan sense of "love" with *hawā* in the Islamic sense of "evil desire" and to caution against the pernicious effects of both *hawā* and *'ishq*, could point to the damning evidence offered by the popular theory which described *'ishq* and *hawā* (love) as humbling the lover before the beloved and causing "enslavement" (*ta'abbud*

4. See *I'tilāl*, folio 12a–12b; *Dhamm*, 12; *Rauḍa*, 463; *Munyat al-Muḥibbīn* (Tal'at, Adab 4648), folios 16a–19a.

5. See Koran, Sūra 12: 53. *Nafs* in this context is comparable to the Greek ψυχή as used in the Pauline epistles, often translated "the flesh." See E. E. Calverley, art. "Nafs," *EI*[1] or *SEI*, sect. I, A.

6. See *Dhamm*, Ch. I, "Concerning the *'Aql* and Its Excellence and What It Is." Also, *Rauḍa*, Introduction, and *Munyat al-Muḥibbīn* (Tal'at, Adab 4648), folio 18b.

or *tatayyum*) and bondage of the will. Since Islam by definition is spiritual submission (*islām*) to God, it was wrong, they argued, to be the spiritual slave or servant of a human being.[7]

How early such criticism of *hawā* came to be formulated I do not know. The first evidence of it appears in Ibn Dā'ūd's *Kitāb az-Zahra* where mention is made of those who reject *hawā*, and in Kharā'iṭī's use, in his *I'tilāl al-Qulūb*, of the traditions against *hawā* and against the first cause of *hawā*, looking at those who are not "lawful" to one.[8] Because of the great importance that the anti-*hawā* scholars place upon the corollary doctrine of *ghaḍḍ al-baṣar* (or *ghaḍḍ an-naẓar*), averting the eyes, it would appear that the conservative Sunnī critics against whom Jāḥiẓ directs his "Risālat al-Qiyān" represent this same group of anti-*hawā* scholars, mostly men of Ḥanbalī and Traditionist tendencies or allegiances. Let us assume, then, that the earliest document on the controversy in the writings on profane love is the "Risālat al-Qiyān" of Jāḥiẓ.

Those conservative Sunnīs had been criticizing Jāḥiẓ and his friends for their habit of gathering to enjoy the entertainments of the professional singing slaves, *qiyān* (sing. *qaina*). He defends himself by pointing out, in the pages of his *risāla*, that since God gave women to men to use and to enjoy, "a field for them to till,"[9] no man has more right than another over any particular woman except where Sacred Law steps in to prohibit what is illicit and to allow only what is licit in order to prevent confusion in parentage and the rights of inheritance.[10] All that is not prohibited in the Koran and the *sunna* of the Prophet has to be considered lawful, he argues,[11] and the fact that

7. Paradoxically, the influence of Islam may have transmuted pagan Arab passionate love to chaste 'Udhrī love which then became almost a religion of love and a blasphemy to zealous Muslims. For a discussion of the religious features of 'Udhrī love, see A. Kh. Kinany, *The Development of Gazal [sic] in Arabic Literature* (Damascus: Syrian University Press, 1951), pp. 270 ff.

8. *Zahra*, 4–5; *I'tilāl* (Ulu Cami 1535), folio 12a–12b, especially, on *dhamm al-hawā*, and folios 33a–41b on *ghaḍḍ an-naẓar*.

9. Koranic reminiscence, Sūra 2: 223.

10. Cairo ed., 56 (= Pellat, *Arabica*, X [1963], 124).

11. The difficulty which unfolds in this *risāla* with regard to the "*sunna* of the Prophet" is that Jāḥiẓ sees the *sunna* as being reflected in the customary practice of leading early Muslims which he illustrates with anecdotes about what they did and said, while his opponents see it reflected in traditions (*ḥadīth*) on the authority of the Prophet. Jāḥiẓ uses the anecdotes to "prove" that their *ḥadīth* is a forgery.

people consider something bad or good cannot be the basis for a *qiyās*[12] (to the effect that it is forbidden or allowed) as long as we do not derive from its being forbidden a proof that it is good and an indication that it is allowed.[13] His statement is negative, but the implication is that the reverse is also true: the fact that people consider it good or bad cannot be the basis for *qiyās* (to the effect that looking at women is forbidden) as long as we do not derive from its being allowed by Sacred Law a proof that it is bad and an indication that it is forbidden. He says that there is no reason for zealousness (or jealousy) except with regard to that which is *ḥarām* (literally, sacrosanct, except to one legally entitled), i.e., one's own wives and concubines. Aside from such specific terms of the law, women are in the same category as the perfumes and apples that men proffer to one another. If a man has several apples, he keeps one for himself and distributes the rest to those who are with him.[14]

Jāḥiẓ gives a number of well-known anecdotes to show that neither in pre-Islamic times nor under Islam, up to the day the veil was imposed solely on the wives of the Prophet, was it considered shameful for the most noble women to hold long intimate conversations with men and to exchange the numerous glances that must necessarily accompany any such occasion.[15] All this evidence, he says, gives the lie to the tradition reported by the "Ḥashwīya" (his conservative Sunnī critics, an epithet given them by the Muʿtazilīs)[16] according to which the first glance is licit but the second is illicit.[17] Kings and nobles have always had female slaves who wait upon them and who go into the government offices, as well as women who join the company of men and show themselves as attractive as possible in public.[18] Yet some persons have become so immoderate

12. *Qiyās* is legal reasoning from analogies, citing an existing parallel institution or decision. The Muʿtazilīs, of whom Jāḥiẓ was one, believed that acts are allowed (recommended, etc.) or forbidden because they are intrinsically good or bad.
13. Cairo ed., 57 (= Pellat, *Arabica*, X [1963], 125). The above translation differs somewhat from Pellat's.
14. Cairo ed., 57 (= Pellat, *Arabica*, X [1963], 125).
15. Cairo ed., 57–60 (= Pellat, *Arabica*, X [1963], 125–130).
16. See Part I, note 4.
17. Cairo ed., 60 (= Pellat, *Arabica*, X [1963], 130).
18. Cairo ed., 62 (= Pellat, *Arabica*, X [1963], 132).

in their views on the subject of looking at women that they have passed from zealousness to bad nature and narrowness of spirit so that prohibition of looking at women has become for them like an imperative obligation (*al-ḥaqq al-wājib*).[19]

He believes on the basis of the Companions' explanations of the Koran verse (Sūra 53: 32–33) about the "*lamam*" (commonly translated by words such as "trivial sins") that one can enjoy a considerable degree of physical pleasure with a woman without committing a "great sin."[20] He also attacks his conservative critics for believing that those who attend the entertainments of the *qiyān* are inevitably led to commit sin and must be fornicators. Judgments should be formed on the basis of the outward appearance of things, he reminds them. God has not charged the believer with the responsibility of passing judgment on hidden things or assessing the intentions of one's fellow men; what one doesn't see doesn't harm. One decides, for example, that a man is a Muslim on the basis of his apparent conduct, or that he is his father's son because he was "born on his bed."[21]

On the other hand, Jāḥiẓ minces no words on the faults of character, the vices, and the cynical treacheries which are implicit in the profession of the *qiyān*. They probably could not be chaste if they wanted to, for the conditions of their education and their work would militate against it. They have no chance to occupy their minds with sober, virtuous, or religious thoughts. He dissects their professional strategies, the seductions by which they lead several

19. Cairo ed., 62 (= Pellat, *Arabica*, X [1963], 133).
20. Cairo ed., 66 (= Pellat, *Arabica*, X [1963], 136–37). Cf. *'Uyūn al-Akhbār* (Cairo, 1925–30), IV, 100, where the libertine poet Waḍḍāḥ al-Yaman argues with his beloved, "When I said, 'Grant me a favor,' she smiled and replied, 'God prevent me from doing what is forbidden!' She granted me nothing until I implored her, telling her that God allowed some '*lamam*' [trivial sins]."
21. Cairo ed., 66–67 (= Pellat, *Arabica*, X [1963], 137). "Born on his bed" (*maulūd fī firāshihī*), from an early Arabic legal maxim of Islamic law positing the automatic legitimacy of all children born within a lawful union: *al-walad li 'l-firāsh* (the child belongs to the marriage bed), corresponding to and probably deriving from the maxim of Roman law, *pater est quem nuptiae demonstrant*. See Joseph Schacht, *An Introduction to Islamic Law* (Oxford: Oxford University Press, 1964), 21, 39.

men at once to conceive a grand passion for them and then manipulate their affections as they choose.[22]

Two points of view could hardly be further apart than those of Jāḥiẓ and his conservative Sunnī opponents. Jāḥiẓ, the man of letters, individualist, and Mu'tazilī rationalist, displays a latitudinarian, pleasure-loving, "live and let live" attitude. His critics, who in the perspective of subsequent history came to be called orthodox, cautiously tried to minimize the risks to the social and moral fabric of the community. Profoundly distrusting the self-possession and self-discipline of the average Muslim, they wished, by hedging against every possible slip due to weak human nature, to insure that there was no danger of transgressing the precepts of Holy Law. They were sure that sin would almost necessarily result from the activity of the wandering eye and the temptations of face-to-face encounter with unveiled women. Whereas Jāḥiẓ sought to light a fire and be warmed thereby, his conservative opponents would not so much as strike a spark, lest the fire, once lighted, burn the whole house down.

It is amusing that Jāḥiẓ chose to support his view that it was harmless to look at women by saying, "Up to our day, women who are daughters or mothers of the caliph or even of less exalted rank perform the circumambulation of the Ka'ba with their faces uncovered and that condition must be fulfilled in order that the pilgrimage be complete."[23] His teacher, al-Aṣma'ī, was reported to have told a witty anecdote which portrays his own temptation in that very circumstance at the holiest shrine of Islam:

> *During the circumambulation of the Ka'ba, I saw a girl who was like a wild cow and I began to watch her and to fill my eye with her beauties. Then she said to me, "Hey you! What is the trouble with you?" "What is it to you if I look at you?" I said.*
>
> *Then she recited:*
>
> *And you, when you sent your eye scouting for your heart*
> *one day,*

22. Cairo ed., 70–74 (= Pellat, *Arabica*, X [1963], 141–45).
23. Cairo ed., 58–59 (= Pellat, *Arabica*, X [1963], 127). ". . . or even of less exalted rank . . ." covers all women who make the circumambulation, since the requirement that a woman be unveiled during the pilgrimage is general.

> *Saw something over the whole of which you did not have*
> *power, nor with part of which were you able to rest*
> *content.*[24]

There is some evidence, in fact, largely in poetry and anecdotes, that the season of the pilgrimage was for some people a regular occasion for amorous adventures.[25]

This is the context in which the traditions against gazing at women and handsome youths came into circulation. To those who accepted such traditions they followed naturally on the Koran verse enjoining the men and women of Islam to behave modestly and chastely and including the advice that they "cast down their eyes."[26] In the tradition to which Jāḥiẓ alluded, one of the most important of these, the Prophet says to ʿAlī, "O, ʿAlī, do not follow one glance with another glance, for the first is allowed to you but the second is not."[27] Another tradition which is usually given in the same context is that in which Jarīr b. ʿAbd Allāh says, "I asked the Prophet—on him be blessing and peace—about a *naẓar al-faj'a* [an inadvertent look] and he advised me to turn my eyes away."[28] Ibn Qayyim al-Jauzīya explains:

> *The* naẓar al-faj'a *is the first glance, which occurs without any intention on the part of the person doing the looking. What the heart did not intend is not subject to punishment. But, if the person takes a second look by intent, he sins, and so the Prophet*

24. *Iʿtilāl* (Ulu Cami 1535), folio 33a; *Rauḍa*, 95.
25. For references in the *dīwāns* of the Ḥijāz poets and in the *K. al-Aghānī* to meetings on the occasion of the pilgrimage and especially at the Kaʿba, see R. Blachère, art. "Ghazal," *EI*², Sect. i, and Kinany, 206–8. Probably in connection with such activities during the pilgrimage, there exist a number of anecdotes in which various famous jurisconsults (*muftīs*) are asked, in verse, for an opinion on whether it would be permissible during the pilgrimage (or in Ramaḍān), when sexual abstinence is the rule, to embrace and kiss one's beloved. Invariably the *muftī* replies with a *fatwā* in verse declaring in a roundabout way that it could do no harm and that God is Merciful. Sometimes these anecdotes are followed by testimony that they are a lie and a slander of the *muftī* in question. (See *Iʿtilāl* (Ulu Cami 1535), folio 3b ff.; *Rauḍa*, 112 ff.; *Muwashshā*, 108.
26. Sūra 24: 30–31.
27. *Rauḍa*, 91. Cf. *Dhamm*, 86–87, three versions, and *CITM*, I, 261 (*Yā ʿAlī, lā tutbiʿ* . . . .).
28. *Rauḍa*, 95; *Dhamm*, 85. Cf. *CITM*, V, 71.

> *advised him in the case of a* naẓar al-faj'a *to turn his eyes away and not to continue looking, for continuing it is like repeating it [an allusion to the other tradition from 'Alī about not following one glance with another]. And he [the Prophet] advised anyone who felt sorely tried by a* naẓar al-faj'a *[i.e., was infatuated by, or felt strongly attracted to, the stranger] to remedy it by going home to his wife, and he said, "She [the wife] has the likes of what she [the stranger] has." And in that is consolation through the same species for [missing] what was desired. Also, looking stimulates the carnal appetite, so he advised him to decrease it by going to his wife.*[29]

In another tradition, the Companion al-Faḍl tells his brother Ibn 'Abbās:

> *I was seated on a camel behind the Messenger of God . . . while going from Jam' to Mina, and as he was driving along there came into view a bedouin with a beautiful daughter seated behind him in the saddle, and he drove along beside him. I was looking at her, and the Prophet—on him be blessing and peace—looked toward me and turned my face away from her face. Then I looked again, and he turned my face away [again] and he ended up doing that three times.*[30]

The fact that after Jāḥiẓ we see no such bold espousals of easy standards of social and sexual conduct and denials of the *ghaḍḍ al-baṣar* tradition based on the evidence of stories about the conduct of early Muslims can perhaps be laid to the triumph of the conservative Sunnīs late in Jāḥiẓ's lifetime, beginning with the reinstatement of Sunnism as the official interpretation of Islam by the Caliph Mutawakkil on his accession to the throne in 232/847 and the corresponding eclipse of the Mu'tazilīs. That there were more cautious and scholarly efforts to support a doctrine that allowed "looking"

29. *Rauḍa*, 94.
30. *Dhamm*, 83, with an *isnād* including Aḥmad b. Ḥanbal. Another version, without *isnād*, said by the author to be in "*aṣ-Ṣaḥīḥ*" is given in *Rauḍa*, 90. The editor notes that it occurs in "Bukhārī, Muslim, Tirmidhī, and others." However, according to the *CITM*, it occurs only in Ibn Mājā and Dārimī (*CITM*, IV, 6. "*Fa-tafiqa* . . .").

and easier standards of social and sexual conduct by the citing of Koran verses, Tradition, alleged statements of the heads of the four recognized schools of law, and commonly accepted principles of law, can be surmised from Chapters Eight and Nine of the *Rauḍat al-Muḥibbīn*. In these chapters, Ibn al-Qayyim sets up the advocates of such doctrines like so many straw men to be knocked down, reporting their teachings and providing evidence to prove them wrong.[31]

The traditions on averting the eyes enter some of the canonical collections of traditions in Jāḥiẓ's lifetime or shortly thereafter. Aḥmad b. Ḥanbal, great jurisconsult, leader of conservative Sunnī Islam, and contemporary of Jāḥiẓ, incorporated some of them in his celebrated collection, the *Musnad*. The particular tradition which Jāḥiẓ attacked is found there.[32] Aḥmad b. Ḥanbal's thought was entirely dominated by ethical preoccupations. He taught that one ought to avoid dubious things (*shubuhāt*) between the clearly marked limits of the licit and the illicit.[33] In this respect, Kharā'iṭī, Ibn al-Jauzī, and Ibn al-Qayyim were his true heirs. Though we do not know from the biographical sources to which school of law Kharā'iṭī claimed allegiance, his espousal of the doctrine of *ghaḍḍ al-baṣar* and the battle he waged against *hawā* (in which the two prominent Ḥanbalīs later followed him) indicated that he at least shared the Ḥanbalī interest in this subject.

We have already examined the historical position and structure of the books these men wrote, and we have contrasted their authors' ethical scrupulousness with the rather brazen and carefree attitude of Jāḥiẓ and the detached attitude, seasoned with a little piety, found in the typical *adab* book on the theory of profane love. Of the twenty-one chapters (thirty-five folios) on *hawā* (evil desire), Kharā'iṭī devoted the last four chapters to admonitions on averting the eyes. Using the content of the chapters in the *I'tilāl al-Qulūb*, Ibn al-Jauzī rearranged and expanded his treatment of the battle against *hawā* so as to emphasize more the importance of the eyes as the gate-

31. Some of them are identified as Mu'tazilīs and Ẓāhirīs, but in the case of others it is not stated whether they represent any particular theological or legal school.
32. See *CITM*, I, 261, "*Yā 'Alī, lā tutbi'* . . . ."
33. See H. Laoust, art. "Aḥmad b. Ḥanbal," *EI*².

way of dangerous sense impressions. With the addition of more traditions and anecdotal material, Kharā'iṭī's four and a half folios[34] on the dangers of looking are expanded to ten chapters, seventy-odd pages in the printed edition of the *Dhamm al-Hawā*.[35]

Both Kharā'iṭī's and Ibn al-Jauzī's treatment of the dangers of passionate love and of the roving eye lose some of their momentum after the authors reach the midpoint of their books because they abruptly give up the subject of *hawā* (evil desire), with which the traditions on averting the eyes seem to be closely associated, and shift to the subject of *'ishq*. Four hundred-odd pages after finishing his discussion of *ghaḍḍ al-baṣar* in connection with *hawā*, Ibn al-Jauzī comes back to the eyes again, this time in the chapter on "The Treatment of *'Ishq*,"[36] criticizing the old Arab custom according to which it was quite proper for a man to sit alone with "strange women" (i.e., women not their wives, concubines, or relatives within the prohibited degrees), converse with them, and look at them, trusting himself not to commit sin and contenting himself with looking and conversation. This practice, he argues, worked insidious harm to Majnūn Lailā and others like him, driving them mad and destroying them in the end. They erred, he says, in that such behavior is against both human nature and the Sacred Law. One glance cannot harm, but a repetition or allowing the eye to rest upon the person of interest will allow the eye to engrave the attractive image upon the heart.[37]

Ibn al-Qayyim made a much more effective case for averting the gaze by introducing the doctrine, not in connection with the traditions on *hawā* (evil desire) but as the prime preventive for the dangers and traumas of *'ishq* and *maḥabba*. (He relegates *hawā* to a single chapter near the end of the book.) He demonstrates through a lively discussion of the theory and psychology of love, using images current in poetry as illustrative material, the key role of the eye in bringing on catastrophic cases of love. His approach was better calculated

34. *I'tilāl* (Ulu Cami 1535), folio 33a ff.
35. *Dhamm*, 72–146.
36. *Dhamm*, 582.
37. *Dhamm*, 595.

to appeal to the average reader than Ibn al-Jauzī's more heavy-handed, lengthy, and repetitious book.

Furthermore, in devoting his undivided attention to a responsible, Islamic, code of conduct for the lover or potential lover, he tied up the relevant loose ends of love theory, making each of them support the code of conduct which he enjoined. One of the theoretical issues connected with *'ishq* or *hawā* (love) habitually discussed in the works on the theory of profane love was the question of whether *'ishq* was voluntary (*ikhtiyārī*) or involuntary (*iḍṭirārī*). Did its victims knowingly and willfully get themselves into that state or was it something that attacked them unawares, something they were powerless to prevent?[38] Some authorities claimed it might be involuntary, in which case the unfortunate *'āshiq* might even be forgiven the sins he committed under its compulsion. He was to be pitied rather than damned.[39] Such potentially dangerous ideas were aired even in the *Dhamm al-Hawā* without a clear formulation of the consequences of such a notion.[40] To all those who were prepared to accept his attractively presented and logical but rigorous doctrine, Ibn al-Qayyim closed this "escape clause" in love theory by elucidating certain instructive parallels between intoxication by alcohol and intoxication by love which show that they are very similar in their effects and in the way they may be avoided. While the drinker's intoxication is wholly beyond his control, proceeding unavoidably from the action of the alcohol in his body, there is one moment when he has complete freedom of choice as to whether he will become intoxicated: it is that moment when he can refuse to take the drink of wine. In just the same way, says Ibn al-Qayyim, a man may choose not to give a second glance to the person on whom his eye falls momentarily and unintentionally. At that moment he is in full possession of his fate and so it cannot be said that *'ishq* is involuntary or that a man is not responsible for falling victim to its intoxication.[41]

38. *Rauḍa*, Chapter Eleven.

39. See *Maṣāri'*, I, 12, for example, a passage often quoted by later authors.

40. *Dhamm*, 301.

41. See *Rauḍa*, Chapter Twelve, "Concerning the Intoxication of the Lovers." This differs, of course, from the Ṣūfī use of the simile of drunkenness. See I. Goldziher, *Vorlesungen über den Islam* (3rd ed.; Heidelberg: Carl Winter, 1963), 155.

Having firmly closed the door on irresponsibility, he opens another way out to the lover or potential lover: Arabic theory of love had long debated the question of whether or not "union" (*wiṣāl*) spoiled love and quenched the desire for the beloved. (The term meant either simply the enjoyment of one another's presence or sexual union, depending on the context.) A substantial segment of opinion said that sexual union spoiled love; the raptures of *ʿishq* were experienced only before marriage or outside of marriage. Ibn al-Qayyim argues that this is not true. On the contrary, he says, true love grows ever stronger and more delightful after lawful union; it is only sinful union that forever quenches *ʿishq* and turns it into bitterness and loathing. The Lord of All has made it work out this way and therefore the perfect remedy for the pangs of passionate love is in the complete union which the Lord allows.[42] Thus he constructed a coherent theory of profane love for the good Muslim by taking firm positions on two questions which the authors of the more secular works on the subject habitually left unanswered, merely presenting them as interesting and controversial matters for debate.

While Ibn al-Qayyim was making his case for averting the eyes as a preventive of *ʿishq*, he sharply attacked Ibn Dāʾūd and Ibn Ḥazm, adherents of the Ẓāhirī school of law, who, he alleged, held that one could freely enjoy looking at a person not "lawful" to one, though touching him or her was forbidden.[43] This possibly is not the first time that a legal scholar or traditionist had attacked Ibn Dāʾūd or perhaps both men on this score, but it is the first and only time this is done in the works on the theory of profane love. Seemingly, Ibn al-Qayyim's only evidence for believing that Ibn Dāʾūd held this view was the story related by Nifṭawayh, telling

42. See *Rauḍa*, Chapter Eighteen, "The Remedy for Love Is in the Perfect Union Which the Lord of All Allows." Ibn al-Qayyim also taught this remedy for *ʿishq* in his book *Al-Jawāb al-Kāfī li-Man Saʾala ʿan ad-Dawāʾ ash-Shāfī* (The Adequate Answer to Those Who Ask about Healing Remedies) (Cairo, n.d.). Before the existence or content of the *Rauḍat al-Muḥibbīn* was known to orientalists, I. Goldziher thought these portions of *Al-Jawāb al-Kāfī* sufficiently important and interesting to discuss them briefly in connection with books on love. The book is a monograph for those afflicted by *ʿishq* or by unsatisfied sexual desires, written in the form of a *fatwā*. (See Goldziher, *ZDMG*, LXIX [1915], 196.)

43. *Rauḍa*, 86, 116–17, 130–31.

how Ibn Dā'ūd became a "martyr of love" through "permitted gazing" (*an-naẓar al-mubāḥ*) at the friend with whom he was infatuated.[44] This story is apparently the *locus classicus* for that supposed Ẓāhirī doctrine. Evidently Ibn al-Qayyim thinks that, because he also was a Ẓāhirī, Ibn Ḥazm held the same view. It is probable also that Ibn al-Qayyim sees evidence of this in the stories that Ibn Ḥazm tells about himself and his contemporaries in the *Ṭauq al-Ḥamāma*,[45] for he says that Ibn Ḥazm allowed a scandalous freedom in looking at strange women and in having love affairs with them.[46] Yet, along with this evidence in the *Ṭauq* that Ibn Ḥazm did not hold the doctrine of *ghaḍḍ an-naẓar*, there is also some indication there that Ibn Ḥazm had not yet switched allegiance to the Ẓāhirī school of law or at least was not as strict in his views as he later was.[47] Also, Ibn Ḥazm's *Kitāb al-Akhlāq wa 's-Siyar*, a book on morals and ethics written later in his life, seems to indicate that at that time, at least, Ibn Ḥazm held that averting the eyes was part of continence or chasteness, *'iffa*:

> *The definition of continence is that one averts the eyes and all the organs of sense from objects not allowed to one. All that exceeds this is debauchery and what falls short of it, to the point of holding oneself back from what God . . . allows, is weakness and impotence.*[48]

The chasteness of Ibn Ḥazm was said to be proverbial, but at the same time he was profoundly antiascetic and antimystical as regards the lawful pleasures of the flesh, as this definition of his clearly indicates.[49]

44. See *Ta'r. Bagh.*, V, 162–63 and above, p. 10–11. Ibn al-Qayyim quotes from the story in *Rauḍa*, 116–17 and 180–81.

45. Ibn al-Qayyim says Ibn Ḥazm "traveled this (Ẓāhirī) path in his *Ṭauq al-Ḥamāma*" (*Rauḍa*, 117).

46. *Rauḍa*, 86.

47. See Goldziher, *ZDMG*, LXIX (1915), 201 ff.

48. Edited and translated by Nada Tomiche (Beirut: Commission International pour la Traduction des Chefs-d'Œuvre, 1961) (Collection UNESCO d'Œuvres Représentatives, Série Arabe). See paragraph 91, pp. 33–34 of the French text and pp. 30–31 of the Arabic text.

49. See references on page 33, note 4, and page 34, note 1, of the French text.

Another point to consider is that the scandalous conduct which Ibn al-Qayyim sees in the *Ṭauq al-Ḥamāma* pervades the whole book. Since Ibn Ḥazm was reported to be almost the only Andalusian scholar in his generation adhering to the Ẓāhirī school (if, indeed, he was a Ẓāhirī when he wrote the book), the alleged liberal Ẓāhirī doctrine of "permitted looking" cannot be stretched to account for all that is said and done in the stories and anecdotes which supposedly portray actual events and escapades in the lives of friends and contemporaries all over al-Andalus. The story, for example, in the chapter on "Those Who Fell in Love at First Sight" tells how the poet Yūsuf b. Harūn ar-Ramādī (d. 403/1012) followed a slave girl out of Cordova toward the suburb, and when she turned to rebuke him, he protested that he was hopelessly in love with her. When she warned him that he would gain nothing by continuing to follow her, he said that he would be content, then, to look at her. "That is permitted (*mubāḥ*) to you," she replied. Though parts of his book might be thought to express particularly the author's own views (the chapter, for instance, on "Signaling with the Eyes"), the *Ṭauq al-Ḥamāma* contains much evidence that stolen glances and even stolen pleasures[50] were fairly common among the Muslim aristocracy of Ibn Ḥazm's time, most of them good and devout believers, according to his accounting. If his book is an accurate portrayal of life and manners in al-Andalus, as has generally been assumed, one wonders whether social behavior and customs were much freer there than in the orient, or whether, if there had been an Ibn Ḥazm in Ibn al-Qayyim's own city, we should have learned that actual social behavior and public morals were about the same in Damascus.[51]

50. See, for example, the story of the young man of good family on an outing with relatives, who had a delightful time with a slave girl with whom he was madly in love when he was ordered to shelter her under a large raincoat (or rain cover) during a sudden storm. (*Ṭauq*, chapter on the "Reunion of Lovers" = Bercher ed., 168–69.)

Actually, Ibn al-Qayyim's own book and every book on the theory of profane love contain stories in which the principal actors must have done some forbidden "looking" and which might sound as risqué as Ibn Ḥazm's stories if their traditional, rather laconic, and stylized language were changed for the lively style and personal detail found in the *Ṭauq al- Ḥamāma*.

51. These questions also raise others which take one far beyond the scope of this chapter. It seems that those principally concerned with, or most committed to, the

The books after the *Rauḍat al-Muḥibbīn* are nearly all of the more typical *adab* type of work on love theory; their authors do not trouble themselves over the battle against *hawā* and the terrible consequences of "looking." Their authors also have certain mystical affinities, as I have indicated in my introductory description of these works and their authors. Perhaps that partially explains their approach, for they are doubtless in the habit of thinking of the positive spiritual potentialities of human love. The one exception, of course, is the Ḥanbalī Marʿī b. Yūsuf, who echoes in a mild way the ideas of his Ḥanbalī predecessors, though he too seems to have been won over to mysticism in some degree.

ghaḍḍ al-baṣar doctrine were Ḥanbalīs. Ibn al-Jauzī and Ibn al-Qayyim insist that it is a command of the Sacred Law, the *Sharīʿa*. However, Hellmut Ritter seems to think that orthodoxy, in general, demands it. (He would include in that designation the four recognized schools of law, presumably.) He says that in an earlier generation any Turk who was speaking to a strange woman would stare the entire time at the ground. As surviving evidence of the effect of this doctrine on social behavior, he cites the behavior of Hajivad in one of the Karagöz shadow plays. (See Ritter, *Der Islam*, XXI [1933], 85.) While the traditions enjoining such behavior occur in the canonical collections, I would point out that the Ḥanafī school of law, the official one of the Ottoman Empire, seems to have interpreted them less strictly than the Ḥanbalīs and less strictly than the social behavior described by Ritter would lead one to think. The *Hidāya* of al-Marghīnānī (d. 593/1196) says, "A man may not look at a strange woman except in the face, hand, or foot. . . . If, however, a man be not secure from the impulse of lust, it is not allowable to look even at the face of a woman, except in cases of absolute necessity." (tr. Charles Hamilton, *The Hedaya* [Lahore: New Book Co., a reprint of the edition of 1870, 1957], page 598.) Mālikī, Shāfiʿī, and Ḥanbalī legal handbooks consulted so far do not treat the question of "looking"; it would be interesting to learn what the consensus of the Mālikīs and Shāfiʿīs on this subject may have been, though that might not necessarily explain actual social practice in al-Andalus, where they predominated. There is evidence in the *Rauḍa*, Chapters 8 and 9, that those who sought for various reasons to allow looking or freer standards of social and sexual behavior presented alleged opinions of Mālik and Shāfiʿī to support their cases. Ibn al-Qayyim, however, denied that Mālik or Shāfiʿī ever gave the opinions attributed to them.

CONCLUSION

If one looks back over the nine centuries of this literature which began with Jāḥiẓ in the third/ninth century and ended with Marʿī b. Yūsuf and as-Salaṭī in the eleventh/seventeenth, three phases in its development can be discerned. In the first phase, the third through the fifth Islamic centuries (ninth–eleventh centuries A.D.), the time of Jāḥiẓ, Muḥammad b. Dā'ūd aẓ-Ẓāhirī, al-Washshā', al-Kharā'iṭī, al-Marzubānī, al-Ḥuṣrī, Ibn Ḥazm, and as-Sarrāj, the literature of profane love comes in a variety of forms and with a variety of emphases. It is this very variety that leads one at first, perhaps, to doubt whether one is dealing with a group of texts that are in any way related.

In the second phase, the sixth through the eighth Islamic centuries, the authors base their writings on the tradition that has been laid down in its essentials in the first phase. Now certain tendencies in form and content already discernible in the first phase become predominant and form the traditional type of work on this subject. The twofold division of content first clearly apparent from the evidence about Marzubānī's lost book but visible also, though less clearly, in the *Kitāb az-Zahra* and the *Ṭauq al-Ḥamāma* becomes the model for the more comprehensive and better-organized works of this second phase. Besides this fundamental division of content found in most works, the ethically oriented subtype introduces a further division of subject matter necessitated by including a discussion of *hawā* in the sense of "evil desire."

The third and last phase, which covers the ninth through the eleventh Islamic centuries, is that of the "superanthology" or "anthology of anthologies" which reworks the contents of the works of the middle phase as well as as-Sarrāj's *Maṣāriʿ al-ʿUshshāq*. Though the emphasis is now clearly on providing works of entertainment, and consequently on the anecdote and the verse quotation rather than on theoretical questions, these anthologies are no less comprehensive than some of the works belonging to the two preceding periods. Moreover, they show the influence of earlier works on the subject in the arrangement of the chapters: an introduction to such matters as the nature of love, its causes, and its terminology, followed by chapters on the various *aḥwāl* of the lovers.

After reading a number of the Arabic works on the theory of profane love and following the history of this type of literature from century to century, a contemporary Western reader may experience a degree of disappointment at the perennial reappearance of a great deal of traditional material, retold at intervals to a new generation by a new writer. However justified this feeling might be, one must remember that the medieval Arab Muslim view of literature (taking the word "literature" here in a wide sense and including all but purely scientific works) was rather different from our own. According to Von Grunebaum it was based on two hypotheses, both essentially Aristotelian. One dealt with the role of imagination and the other with form and content.[1] Literature did not exist for invention or for purposes of self-expression. Medieval Islam, generally following Aristotelian psychology, viewed imagination as one of the animal faculties, and theology confirmed this low estimate with its dark view of human creativeness. Reason, on the other hand, was appreciated, though not without reservations imposed by theological considerations. Literature was to serve as the archive of the community; it was to instruct and delight, or, according to another saying, enchant and convey wisdom.[2] The writer was expected above all to display comprehensive and detailed erudition, and if he wrote poetry he must follow the detailed rules and conventions that tradition imposed. As long as it was achieved within the framework of these rules, originality (as contrasted with invention or imagination) was highly regarded.

1. Von Grunebaum, "The Nature of the Arab Literary Effort," *JNES*, VII (1948), 116–22, or, better, the much expanded and recast version of his study to be found in *Comparative Literature*, IV (1952), 323–40, with the title "The Aesthetic Foundations of Arabic Literature" and provided with wide-ranging references to Classical, Arabic, and European literature.

2. Von Grunebaum, *JNES*, VII (1948), 117, citing sayings of the Caliph 'Umar I and the Prophet.

As to the second part of the basic concept of literature, form in literature was considered an entity in itself and we rarely find consistent theories about its relation to content. Beauty is seen as something that may be imparted at will to the material through technical means and from the outside, as it were, as a kind of ornament or embroidery. Originality under these conditions is often viewed as the improved rendering of traditional material, perhaps by its elaboration and reshaping, and literary progress is a series of improvements or elaborations on existing themes.

In Arabic literary criticism, all discussions of originality move around poetry and rhymed prose. However, the fundamental concepts or attitudes expressed there seem to apply broadly to the composition of these *adab*-like books on the theory of profane love. Just as in poetry, it can be said that the author strives, within limits imposed by the existence of an established tradition of form and content, to make his own book more meritorious than those of his predecessors, in this case by exercising his own tastes in the choice and arrangement of the available raw materials.

Another traditional way to achieve something new is to collect whatever one considers unusual in prose and poetry. In an effort to outdo his predecessors, and to add something to his work, the writer on love theory looks for the surprising (*ʿajīb*), extraordinary (*nādir*), and strange (*gharīb*) rather than for what was original, in our sense of the word.[3] He therefore ransacks the old books for their most rare and amazing treasures, and then, to make his work timely and to further justify his efforts at composition, he adds stories and poetry from recent times. Thus, for example, Ibn Abī Ḥajala (eighth/fourteenth century) in his *Dīwān aṣ-Ṣabāba* includes verses from the relatively recent poet Ṭughrāʾī (d. 515/1121)[4] as well as stories about "the men of this time who were sorely afflicted with love through

3. Von Grunebaum compares this notion with the manner in which the writers of the European *secentismo* sought to evoke *maraviglia*. He thinks this is explained by the fact that the *secentismo* and the Arab esthetic ideal were both influenced by Aristotelianism. See Von Grunebaum, *JNES*, VII (1948), 119, or, preferably, *Comparative Literature*, IV (1952), 328–29.

4. *GAL*, G. I, 247–48; S. I, 439–40. He held several high offices under Malikshāh and his son Muḥammad, hence the epithet Ṭughrāʾī (Chancellor).

seeing a woman or a boy."[5] In addition, he repeats the chapter headings, stories, and poetry that had been part of the repertory for perhaps five hundred years.

The authors who, from our point of view, are most original are Ibn Ḥazm and Ibn Qayyim al-Jauzīya. Both men achieved their originality by means not envisioned in the tradition of the ordinary *adab*-type book on profane love or by the medieval Muslim theory of literature. Ibn Ḥazm achieved it by rejecting the oriental tradition in so far as it demanded both the imitation of the traditional model and the quoting of predecessors or the repetition of old familiar stories of the lovers of the distant past. Ibn al-Qayyim achieved it through the conclusions he drew from the traditional material he used. Instead of merely rearranging and refining the corpus of material on this subject, he builds it into a consistent theoretical edifice expressing an Islamic theory (and doctrine) of love. To accomplish this, he must take exception to many widespread and popular theories about love which had been current in this literature for hundreds of years. He had to give a new interpretation to stories, anecdotes, and poems which most of his predecessors had been content to arrange under subject headings. However heterogeneous the material that he brought together might be, it always serves to support his theological and ethical doctrines, the most important of which is that human love finds its ultimate fulfillment and its most sublime expression only in marriage, and in single-minded love for God expressed in obedience and devotion.[6] It is not the fact that Ibn al-Qayyim was both a man of letters and a theologian which makes him interesting, for this combination is by no means unusual and may, in fact, be considered typical of medieval Islam. Rather it is the way in which he made one side of his scholarly personality serve the other.

By offering an outline of the historical development of the group of works in which Ibn al-Qayyim's book belongs and thus putting

5. Chapter 39, *Dīwān aṣ-Ṣabāba*.
6. See *Rauḍa*, 290 ff., where he teaches that the heart is spacious enough to accommodate both Godward love and the love of those servants of God who are good and suitable objects for one's affection.

it in the proper context, I hope I have succeeded in bringing out the distinctive contribution of this great scholar. As a study devoted to the internal development of the Arabic literature on the theory of profane love, and therefore primarily concerned with demonstrating the relationships between many works and the relatively homogeneous and coherent character of the group, this study could not treat individual works exhaustively. Neither could it concern itself with broad questions—however interesting or urgent—peripheral to the effort of showing the nine-hundred-year evolution of this branch of literature. Among such matters awaiting further research and discussion are the relations between the theory of profane love and the ideas of the Muslim mystics on divine love, as well as the points of agreement or contrast between the theories of the Arabs and those of medieval and Renaissance European writers. In short, this study is only a first step in an arduous but fascinating series of investigations.

APPENDIX

REMARKS ON THE CHARACTER AND RELEVANCE OF SOME WRITINGS NOT TREATED IN THIS STUDY

"OF CARNAL LOVE AND FAMILIARITY, WITH A SUMMARY ACCOUNT OF PLEASURE," CHAPTER FIVE OF THE "AṬ-ṬIBB AR-RŪḤĀNĪ" (THE SPIRITUAL PHYSICK) OF AR-RĀZĪ (RHAZES)

In this attractive book on personal ethics, Abū Bakr Muḥammad b. Zakarīyā' ar-Rāzī (251/865–313/925)[1] writes as a physician and philosopher who is also well grounded in literature and literary fashion. Basing himself on Platonic philosophy, he roundly condemns passionate love as a calamity which men of high purpose and those pressed by the urgencies of worldly or other-worldly concerns avoid. It is idle, soft, effeminate men who, chasing after pleasure, fall prey to it. Those who indulge in reading lovers' tales, reciting delicate and amorous verses, and listening to sad music are especially vulnerable.

He criticizes passionate love as being—in the eyes of the Platonic philosopher—no proper pleasure at all, for it does not meet the definition of pleasure as being the restoration of that original state of nature which was expelled by the intrusion of some sort of pain. Also, lovers are worse than the beasts in their lack of self-control. In the fifteenth chapter, "On Sexual Intercourse," he rates the sexual appetite as the foulest and most disgusting of the appetites in the view of the rational soul, the true man. It is also the one appetite

1. *GAL*, G. I, 233–35; S. I, 417–21. A. J. Arberry has made an English translation of *Aṭ-Ṭibb ar-Rūḥānī, The Spiritual Physick of Rhazes* ([Wisdom of the East Series] London: John Murray, 1950).

whose gratification is not necessary to the survival of the individual. Love is foolish, he says, because lovers experience sorrow precisely where they think they will find joy, and the last and most bitter of sorrows, parting from the beloved, is certain to come someday, a Platonic teaching echoed also in the treatise of the Ikhwān aṣ-Ṣafā' on love, analyzed later in this Appendix.

Several paragraphs are devoted to refuting the oft-repeated arguments in favor of love and to poking fun at those who advanced them. (He proves them to be ignorant persons, because, among other things, they do not understand or appreciate any sciences except grammar and lexicography and even in those they are confused.) The views ascribed to the partisans of love seem to correspond with those of Ibn Dā'ūd and al-Washshā' and lead me to think that it is these gentlemen and their ilk, the "*ẓurafā*'"[2] which he has in mind. He was a contemporary of these two men and for two periods of time lived in the same city, Baghdad.

AN ACCOUNT OF A LEARNED DISCUSSION OF LOVE IN MAS'ŪDĪ'S "MURŪJ ADH-DHAHAB"

While dealing with the history of the Barmakids and describing a gathering of scholars held at Baghdad in the presence of the Vizier Yaḥyā b. Khālid, Mas'ūdī (d. ca. 345/956) gives several pages of theories of profane love.[3] He purports to quote the explanations given by thirteen eminent men about the nature, cause, effects, and

2. See above, page 102, note 8, for the special significance of "*ẓurafā*'" here, as signifying an "in-group" of "refined people" adhering to certain ideas about dress, conduct, life-style, etc. These remarks on the relevance of the *Aṭ-Ṭibb ar-Rūḥānī* were added shortly before press time. More time would be required, and more space than should be alloted here, to provide the textual quotations showing that ar-Rāzī had these men in mind and was paraphrasing them. The first parallel to be cited, however, would be Ibn Dā'ūd's remarks on the kind of person who has an affinity for *hawā* (*Zahra*, 4–5).

3. *Murūj*, VI, 368–87.

so forth, of love. He himself adds the theories of Hippocrates, "certain philosophers," Galen, "several persons concerned with astronomy and astrology," some Ṣūfīs, heterodox propagandists, and lastly Plato. Mas'ūdī concludes by referring the reader to his *Akhbār az-Zamān*, where he says he has given all the arguments and opinions current on this subject among various groups.[4] This account by Mas'ūdī confirms the impression one gets from the works on love theory contemporary with it[5] that, as early as the third century, love was a widely discussed topic and that many aspects of it were considered.

"RISĀLAT MĀHĪYAT AL-'ISHQ" OF THE IKHWĀN AṢ-ṢAFĀ'

The Essay on the Nature of Love, one of the *rasā'il* that make up the encyclopedia of the Brethren of Purity,[6] written in the middle of the fourth/tenth century, is straightforward and informative in style, and orderly and coherent in form, bearing some resemblance, in fact, to modern encyclopedia articles. Though the *Rasā'il* were probably well known[7] and, except for the Ismā'īlī elements in them, generally acceptable to orthodox readers, this *risāla* is not cited or mentioned in later works on the theory of profane love. The reason may be that the essay is brief and general and would not, therefore, have been of particular interest. Though it is written to accord with the

4. *Akhbār az-Zamān*, 10 vols., his major work, does not survive. A one-volume work of that title, attributed to Mas'ūdī (ed. and tr. B. Carra de Vaux [Cairo, 1930]), has nothing on love theory. Alfred von Kremer (*Sitzungsberichte der Akademie der Wissenschaften zu Wien*, Bnd. IV [1850], 207–11) described the contents of a MS of the *Akhbār az-Zamān* (Historical Annals) which he saw in Aleppo in 1850 and which he evidently considered complete. However, his rather detailed description does not indicate that this MS contained any discussions of love theory.

5. See the chronological table (Table I) showing the life spans of authors of works on the theory of profane love following this section.

6. *Rasā'il Ikhwān aṣ-Ṣafā wa Khillān al-Wafā* (*sic*) (Cairo, 1347/1928), III, 260–85. See *GAL*, G. I, 213–14; S. I, 379–80. See also Y. Marguet, art. "Ikhwān al-Ṣafā'," *EI*[2].

7. See *EI*[1], *s.v.* "Ismā'īlīya." (Also in *SEI*.)

Ismā'īlī system of philosophy, some of the quotations and other statements in it duplicate material found in earlier works such as Jāḥiẓ's two essays, the *Kitāb az-Zahra,* and the *I'tilāl al-Qulūb.* In fact, the content does not differ very much from other writings on love by non-Ismā'īlīs until the last paragraphs which speak in terms of Ismā'īlī doctrines. As in other essays of the Brethren, there are vague references to the Greek philosophers and physicians, for Ismā'īlī philosophy is based to some extent on Aristotle and neo-Pythagorean and other early speculations. (However, any essay on love—Ismā'īlī or not—might contain a few such references.) The chief conclusion of the essay about *'ishq* is that a better and more enduring object of ardent love is the eternal Maker who created those other passing and temporal objects of love. It does not condemn *'ishq*; it merely points out that human love is subject to change, that the lover can become bored with his love, and that, in any event, he is doomed to eventual separation from the earthly beloved. Therefore, it is ignorance to crave only created things and not the Creator.

ABŪ ḤAYYĀN AT-TAUḤĪDĪ'S "RISĀLAT AṢ-ṢADĀQA WA 'Ṣ-ṢADĪQ"

The Treatise on Friendship and the Friend by Abū Ḥayyān at-Tauḥīdī (born ca. 310–20/922–32, died perhaps 414/1023)[8] parallels some of the early books on love in its form and content. It is a collection of anecdotes, traditions, verses, and dicta on friendship and the friend, some quite bitter and pessimistic. Where the subject matter is "love of a brother in God," love of friends, and such matters as could be dealt with in the comprehensive books on love theory, there is some duplication of material. An example is the famous

8. *GAL,* G. I, 244; S. I, 435–36. See S. M. Stern, art. "Abū Ḥayyān at-Tauḥīdī', *EI*². *Risālat aṣ-Ṣadāqa wa 'ṣ-Ṣadīq,* ed. Ibrāhīm al-Kailānī (Damascus: Dār al-Fikr, 1964).

tradition from the Prophet, "Souls are troops and those who recognize one another seek one another's company, and those who do not, clash."[9] As in the books on profane love, quotations attributed to al-Aṣmaʿī reporting what "an Arab" said are prominent. These bedouins always come forth with words on the subject that are vivid and profound and show great sensitivity.

While there are these similarities between Abū Ḥayyān's book and the books on love, there is also a sharp contrast, for any discussion of *ʿishq* in this book portrays it in a bad light as a treacherous bringer of bitterness and misery. A number of quotations in it compare the lovers and their passionate attachment to each other with the friendship of friends and find the latter much the better and more desirable relationship.[10]

IBN SĪNĀ'S "RISĀLA FĪ MĀHĪYAT AL-ʿISHQ"[11]

This essay of Ibn Sīnā (Avicenna) d. ca. 426/1037) is a philosophical treatise on the nature of love in which love is conceived as the universal principle of being, animate and inanimate. His philosophy of love owes something to Plato, Aristotle, Plotinus, and the Peripatetics.[12] Still, the treatise shows originality. It ought to be studied in comparison with the short sections that deal with a kind of cosmic love or universal love in the *Rauḍat al-Muḥibbīn* and the *Tazyīn al-Aswāq* by someone equipped to detect their sources and the affinities of these notions with those of earlier philosophical schools.

9. See above, Part 2, Chap. 1.
10. *Aṣ-Ṣadāqa wa 'ṣ-Ṣadīq*, pp. 31, 102–03, 129, 157–61.
11. Ahmet Ateş, ed. and tr., *Risāla fī Māhīyat al-ʿIshq*, Aşkın Mâhiyati Hakkında Risâle (İstanbul Üniversitesi Edebiyat Fakültesi Yayınlarından," No. 552; İstanbul: İbrahim Horoz Basımevi, 1953); also in an abridged version in French in A. A. F. Mehren, tr., *Traités mystiques d'Avicenne* (Leiden: E. J. Brill, 1894). English tr. and introd. by E. L. Fackenheim, *Mediaeval Studies*, VII (1945), 208–28.
12. How much he owes to them and to which tendencies he is most indebted seems to be a matter of controversy. See Hilmy Ziya Ülken's preface to Ateş's edition.

These passages in the *Rauḍa* and the *Tazyīn* also speak of *maḥabba* or *ʿishq* as a pervasive principle or force acting throughout all creation, and used to explain many natural phenomena, among them the motions of the planets and the attraction of gravity.

There is some reason to believe that Ibn Sīnā's treatise was written between 426 and 428. It may be one of his last works and a product of the period when his philosophical system was most developed.[13] According to Massignon, Ibn Sīnā sees *ʿishq* as "l'Emanation Nécessaire de Dieu qui fait mouvoir harmonieusement toutes les créatures dans un entrelac de cycles sphériques, comme Platon, et l'avicennisant Dante."[14] The term *ʿishq* is taken up from the usage of the Hallajians and the school of Baṣra before ʿAbd al-Wāḥid b. Zaid (second/eighth century), but Massignon points out that Ibn Sīnā does not use it as they did to mean "l'Essence même de Dieu."[15]

Since Ibn Sīnā deals with *ʿishq* as a universal principle, in the course of his discussion he ultimately comes to *ʿishq* as the feeling of one person for another, but his discussion is brief and abstract and has little in common with the approach of the traditional book on the theory of profane love.

A CHAPTER ON LOVE IN NUWAIRĪ'S "NIHĀYAT AL-ARAB FĪ FUNŪN AL-ADAB"

In this encyclopedia by Abu 'l-ʿAbbās Aḥmad b. ʿAbd al-Wahhāb an-Nuwairī (d. 732/1332),[16] the greater part of Chapter Three of

13. Ateş, p. viii.
14. Massignon, "Avicenne, philosoph, a-t-il été aussi un mystique?" *Opera Minora*, II, 467.
15. Massignon, "Interférences philosophiques et percées metaphysiques dans la mystique Hallagienne: Notion de 'l'Essentiel Désir'," *Opera Minora*, II, 246–47. *Opera Minora*, II, 467. See also above, Part 2, Chap. III, for a previous reference to the usage of the Hallajians.
16. *GAL*, G. II, 139–40; S. II, 173–74. The title of the encyclopedia might be translated: The Utmost That Could Be Desired in the Varieties of Literature. A currently available edition is published in Cairo by the Mu'assasa al-Miṣrīya al-ʿAmma li 't-Ta'līf wa 't-Tarjama wa 't-Ṭibāʿa wa 'n-Nashr, n.d. [1964–?].

Part One of the Second *Fann* is devoted to love theory. I have found that all this material, from the beginning of Chapter Three through the section on the temporal and eternal punishment due for sodomy (*al-lūṭīya*), is material copied out of the *Dhamm al-Hawā* of Ibn al-Jauzī. Several times he cites Ibn al-Jauzī and his book in such a way that one would think that only that immediate passage was taken from Ibn al-Jauzī, whereas, in fact, everything else is, too. In most cases, Nuwairī drops the *isnāds* found in the *Dhamm*, and he sometimes alters the order of the presentation. However, the copied segments are word for word the same, except for some introductory lines at the beginning of a new subject where he may abbreviate slightly the words of introduction provided by Ibn al-Jauzī. *If* Nuwairī's entire work is of this kind, it is an extreme example—even for late medieval Arabic literature—of a compilation of previous compilations, done with no effort beyond the work of copying, and one would have to be very broad-minded to think that he deserves the immortality he has gotten.

TABLE I

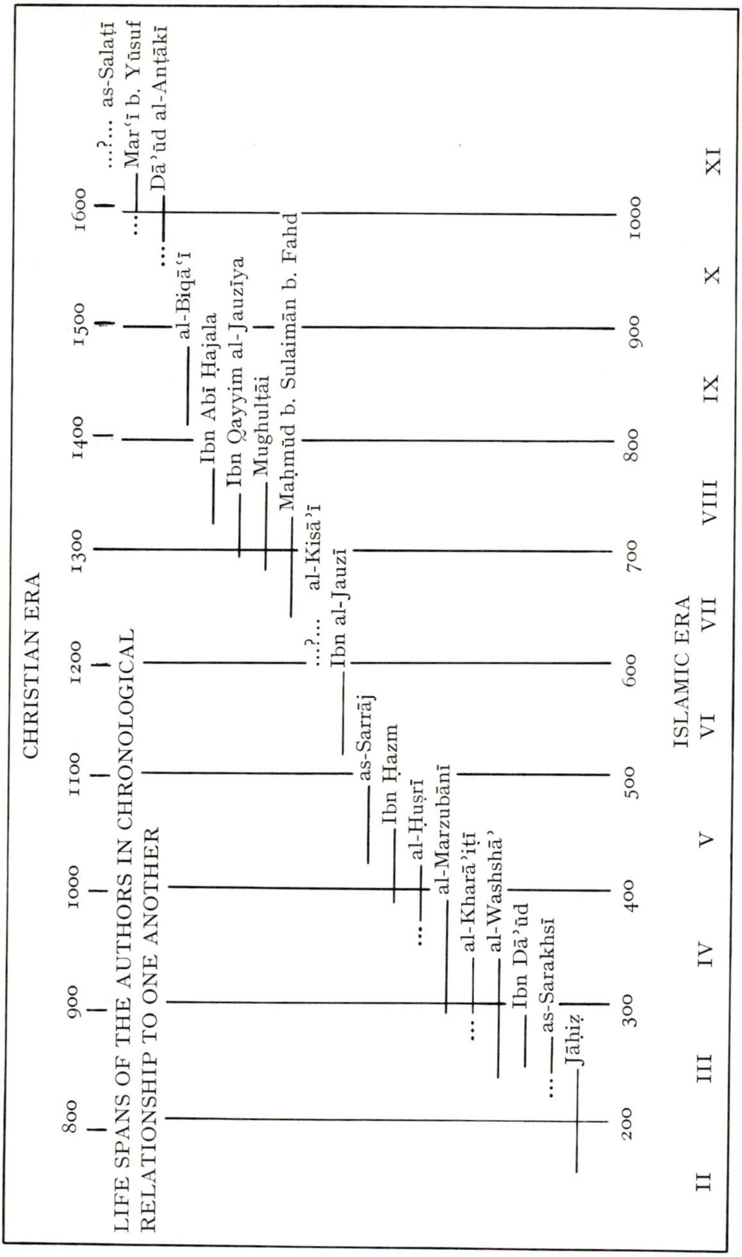
LIFE SPANS OF THE AUTHORS IN CHRONOLOGICAL RELATIONSHIP TO ONE ANOTHER
CHRISTIAN ERA
800
900
1000
1100
1200
1300
1400
1500
1600
ISLAMIC ERA
200
300
400
500
600
700
800
900
1000
II
III
IV
V
VI
VII
VIII
IX
X
XI
Jāḥiẓ
as-Sarakhsī
Ibn Dā'ūd
al-Washshā'
al-Kharā'iṭī
al-Marzubānī
al-Ḥuṣrī
Ibn Ḥazm
as-Sarrāj
Ibn al-Jauzī
...?...
al-Kisā'ī
Maḥmūd b. Sulaimān b. Fahd
Mughulṭāi
Ibn Qayyim al-Jauzīya
Ibn Abī Ḥajala
al-Biqā'ī
Dā'ūd al-Anṭākī
Mar'ī b. Yūsuf
...?... as-Salaṭī

TABLE II

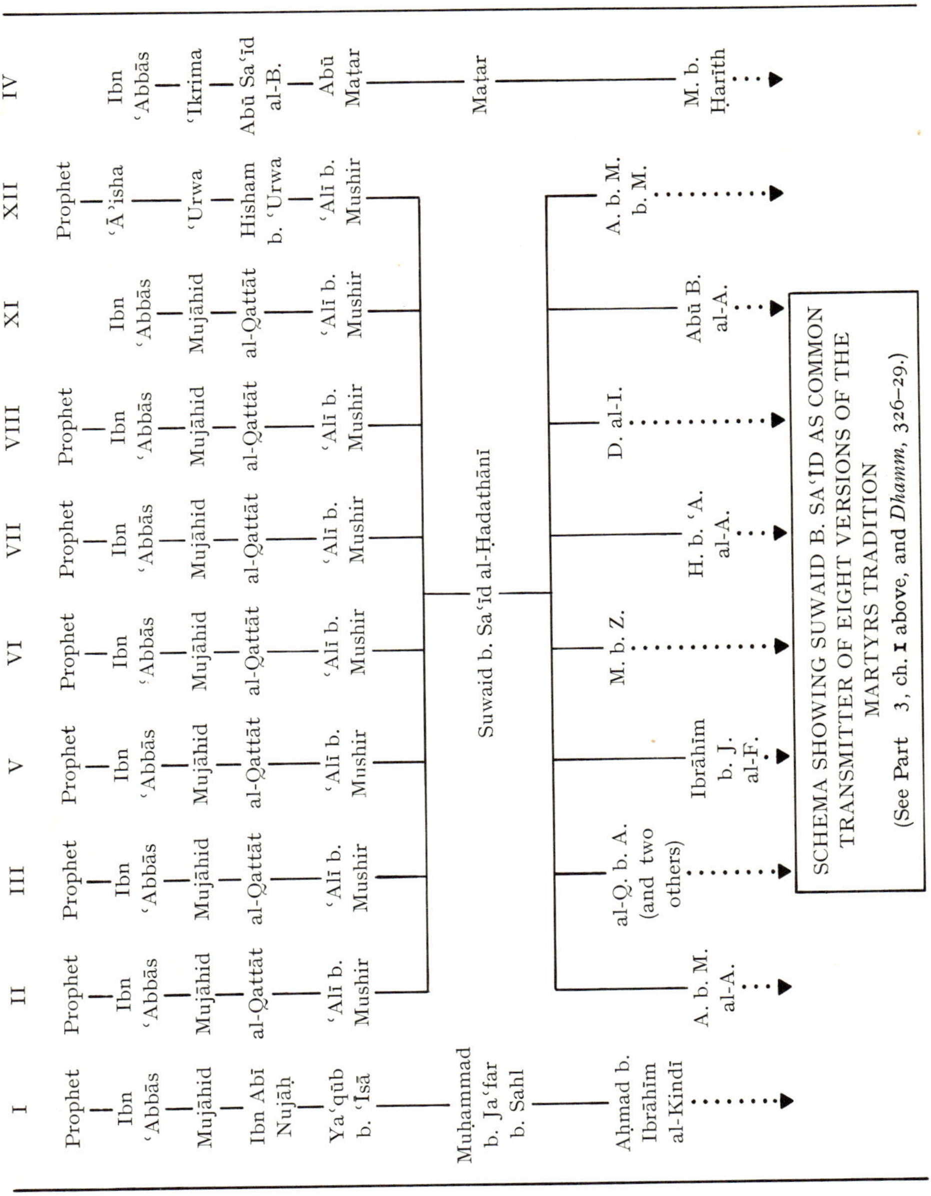

SCHEMA SHOWING SUWAID B. SA'ĪD AS COMMON TRANSMITTER OF EIGHT VERSIONS OF THE MARTYRS TRADITION

(See Part 3, ch. **1** above, and *Dhamm*, 326–29.)

BIBLIOGRAPHY AND ABBREVIATIONS

And. = *al-Andalus.*
al-Anṭākī, Dā'ūd b. 'Umar. *Tazyīn al-Aswāq bi Tafṣīl Ashwāq al-'Ushshāq.* 6 vols. Beirut: Dār Makshūf, 1957–58.
al-Anbārī = *Nuzhat al-Alibbā'.* See Ibn al-Anbārī.
Arnaldez, R. "Ibn Ḥazm," *Encyclopaedia of Islam,* New edition.
As'ār al-Aswāq fī Ash'ār al-Ashwāq. MS Tunis, Bibliothèque Nationale de Tunisie 176 *mīm.*
———. MS Tunis, Bibliothèque de la Faculté des Lettres 4272.
al-'Ayyāshī, Abū Sālim 'Abd Allāh b. M. b. Abū Bakr. *Ar-Riḥla al-'Ayyāshīya.* (Abbreviated al-'Ayyāshī, *Riḥla.*) 2 vols. Fās, 1316.
BEO = *Bulletin d'études orientales.*
Bercher, L. "A propos du texte du 'Ṭauq al-Ḥamâma' d'Ibn Ḥazm," *Mélanges William Marçais,* 1950, pp. 29–36.
———. "Ibn H'azm et son 'T'auq al-h'amâma'," *Bulletin des études arabes,* VII (1947), 3–6.
al-Biqā'ī, Burhān ad-Dīn Abu 'l-Ḥasan Ibrāhīm b. 'Umar. *Aswāq al-Ashwāq fī Maṣāri' al-'Ushshāq.* MS İstanbul, (Süleymaniye) Esad Efendi 2724.
———. ———. MS İstanbul (Süleymaniye), Haci Beşir Ağa 552.
———. ———. MS İstanbul (Süleymaniye), Reisülküttab 745.
b. Khall. = Ibn Khallikān, *Wafayāt al-A'yān.*
Blachère, R., and Bausani, A. "Gh̲azal," *Encyclopaedia of Islam,* New edition.
b. Ma'ṣūm, *Sulāfat al-'Aṣr* = Ibn Ma'ṣūm, *Sulāfat al-'Aṣr fī Maḥāsin A'yān al-'Aṣr.*
Bonebakker, Seeger A. *Some Early Definitions of the Tawrīya and Ṣafadī's Faḍḍ al-Xitām 'an at-Tawrīya wa-'l-Istixdām.* ("Columbia University Publications in Near and Middle East Studies," Series A, No. VIII.) The Hague: Mouton and Co., 1966.
Bouyahia, Ch. "al-Ḥuṣrī," *Encyclopaedia of Islam,* New edition.
Bräunlich, E. *Islamica,* VI (1934), 343–48. (Review of A. R. Nykl's edition of *Kitāb az-Zahra.*)
Brockelmann, C. "Beiträge zur Kritik und Erklärung von Ibn Ḥazm's *Ṭauq al-Ḥamāma,*" *Islamica,* V (1932), 462–74.
———. *Geschichte der arabischen Litteratur.* 2nd ed. 2 vols. (Abbreviated as G. I and G. II.) Leiden: E. J. Brill, 1945–49. 3 supplementary vols. (Abbreviated as S. I, S. II, and S. III.) Leiden: E. J. Brill, 1937–42.

———, and Vernet, J. "Al-Anṭākī," *Encyclopaedia of Islam*, New edition.

b. Taghr. = Ibn Taghrībirdī, *An-Nujūm az-Zāhira.*

Calverley, E. E. "Nafs," *Encyclopaedia of Islam*, and also in the *Shorter Encyclopaedia of Islam.*

CITM = *Concordance et indices de la tradition musulmane.* See under Wensinck.

adh-Dhahabī, Muḥammad b. Aḥmad. (*Tadhkirat al-Ḥuffāẓ*) *Liber classium virorum qui Korani et traditionum cognitione excelluerunt*, auctore Abu Abdalla Dahabio. In epitomen coegit et continuavit Anonymus [Arabice]. Ed. H. F. Wüstenfeld. Göttingen: Vandenhöck and Ruprecht, 1832–34.

Dhamm = Ibn al-Jauzī, *Dhamm al-Hawā.*

D.K. = Ibn Ḥajar al-'Asqalānī, *Ad-Durar al-Kāmina.*

Donaldson, E. Talbot. "The Myth of Courtly Love," *Ventures: The Magazine of the Yale Graduate School*, V, No. 2, 16–24.

EI^1 = *The Encyclopaedia of Islam.* 4 vols. and Supplement. Leiden: E. J. Brill, 1913–38.

EI^2 = *The Encyclopaedia of Islam.* New edition. Leiden: E. J. Brill, 1954– .

[Essay on love, anonymous and untitled.] MS İstanbul (Top Kapı Saray), Ahmet III 3483, folios 238a–240b.

Fackenheim, E. L. "A Treatise on Love by Ibn Sina," translated, with an introduction, *Mediaeval Studies*, VII (1945), 208–28.

Fawāt = al-Kutubī, *Fawāt al-Wafayāt.*

Festschr. Kahle. See Kahle.

Fihrist = Ibn an-Nadīm, *al-Fihrist.*

Flügel = Ibn an-Nadīm, *Fihrist*, Ed. Flügel. See Ibn an-Nadīm.

Flügel, Gustave. *Concordantiae Corani Arabicae.* Lipsiae: Caroli Tauchnitii, 1842.

——— ed. *Corani Textus Arabicus.* Lipsiae: Ernesti Bredtii, 1893.

GAL = C. Brockelmann, *Geschichte der arabischen Litteratur.* See Brockelmann.

García Gómez, Emilio. "El 'Ṭawq' de Ibn Ḥazm y el 'Dīwān al-Ṣabāba'," *al-Andalus*, VI (1946), 65–72.

———. "Un precedente y una consecuencia del 'Collar de la Paloma'," *al-Andalus*, XVI (1951), 309–30.

Gerhardt, Mia. *The Art of Story-Telling.* Leiden: E. J. Brill, 1963.

Ghazi, M. F. "Un groupe social: 'Les Raffinés' (*Ẓurafā'*)," *Studia Islamica*, XI (1959), 39–71.

Goldziher, Ignacz. *Die Zâhiriten, ihr Lehrsystem und ihre Geschichte.* Leipzig: Otto Schulze, 1884.

———. *ZDMG*, LXIX (1915), 192–207. (Review of the Petrof edition of the *Ṭauq al-Ḥamāma* of Ibn Ḥazm.)

Haywood, John A. *Arabic Lexicography*, Its History, and Its Place in the General History of Lexicography. 2nd edition, photomechanical reprint. Leiden: E. J. Brill, 1960.

Heller, B. "Yūsuf b. Ya'ḳūb," *Encyclopaedia of Islam*, and also in the *Shorter Encyclopaedia of Islam*.

Ḥuff. = adh-Dhahabī, *Tadhkirat al-Ḥuffāẓ*, ed. Wüstenfeld. See adh-Dhahabī.

al-Ḥuṣrī, Abū Isḥāq Ibrāhīm b. 'Alī b. Tamīm. *Kitāb al-Maṣūn fī Sirr al-Hawā al-Maknūn*. MS. Leiden, Or. 1951.

Ibn Abī Ḥajala, Shihāb ad-Dīn Abu'l-'Abbās Yaḥyā. *Dīwān aṣ-Ṣabāba*. Cairo, 1308. (On the margin of the *Tazyīn al-Aswāq* of Dā'ūd al-Anṭākī.)

———. ———. MS Cairo, Adab 112.

———. ———. MS Cairo, Adab 1843.

———. ———. MS İstanbul (Süleymaniye), Haci Beşir Ağa 527.

———. ———. MS İstanbul (Süleymaniye), Haci Mahmud Efendi 5145.

———. ———. MS İstanbul (Süleymaniye), Reisülküttab 970.

———. ———. MS Milan (Ambrosiana), Caprotti F 175.

Ibn al-Anbārī, 'Abd ar-Raḥmān b. Muḥammad. *Nuzhat al-Alibbā' fī Ṭabaqāt al-Udabā'*. Bulāq, n.d.

Ibn Dā'ūd, Abū Bakr Muḥammad b. Abī Sulaimān. *Kitāb az-Zahra*. (The complete work of 100 chapters.) MS Turin, Biblioteca Reale, ms. arabo 68. (Microfilm.)

———. *Kitāb al-Zahrah*, The First Half. Ed. A. R. Nykl in collaboration with Ibrāhīm Tūqān ("Studies in Ancient Oriental Civilization," No. 6). Chicago: University of Chicago Press, 1932.

Ibn Fahd, Shihāb ad-Dīn Maḥmūd b. Sulaimān (or Salmān). *Manāzil al-Aḥbāb wa Manāzih al-Albāb*. MS İstanbul, Aya Sofya 4307.

———. ———. MS İstanbul (Top Kapı Saray), Ahmet III 2471.

———. ———. MS Leiden, Or. 1069.

———. ———. MS Leiden, Or. 798.

Ibn Ḥajar al-'Asqalānī, Aḥmad b. 'Alī b. Muḥammad. *Ad-Durar al-Kāmina fī A'yān al-Mi'a ath-Thāmina*. 2nd ed. Hyderabad: Dā'irat al-Ma'ārif al-Uthmānīya, 1373/1954.

Ibn Ḥazm, Abū Muḥammad 'Alī b. Aḥmad b. Sa'īd. *Kitāb al-Akhlāq wa 's-Siyar*. Ed. and tr. Nada Tomiche (Collection UNESCO d'Œuvres Représentatives, Série Arabe). Beirut: Commission pour la Traduction des Chefs-d'Œuvre, 1961.

———. *Ṭauq al-Ḥamāma fi 'l-Ulfa wa 'l-Ullāf*. Ed. D. K. Petrof. Leiden: E. J. Brill, 1914.

———. ———. Ed. Ḥasan Kāmil aṣ-Ṣayrafī. Cairo: Al-Maktaba at-Tijārīya, 1369/1950.

———. ———. English translation by A. R. Nykl. *A Book Containing the*

Risāla Known as the Dove's Neck-Ring about Love and Lovers. Paris: Paul Geuthner, 1931.

———. ———. Spanish translation by E. García Gómez. *El Collar de la Paloma*. Madrid: La Sociedad de Estudios y Publicaciones, 1952.

———. ———. German translation by Max Weisweiler. *Halsband der Taube, über die Liebe und die Liebenden*. Leiden: E. J. Brill, 1944.

———. ———. Italian translation by Francesco Gabrieli. *Il Collare della Colomba, sull'amore e gli amanti*. Bari: Giuseppi Laterza e Figli, 1949.

———. ———. English translation by A. J. Arberry. *The Ring of the Dove*, a Treatise on the Art and the Practice of Arab Love. London: Luzac, 1953.

———. ———. Russian translation by A. Salie. *Ožerele golubki*. Moscow and Leningrad, 1933.

———. ———. Arabic and French text, ed. and tr. by Leon Bercher. *Le Collier du Pigeon ou de l'Amour et les Amants*. Algiers: Editions Carbonels, 1949.

Ibn al-ʿImād, ʿAbd al-Ḥayy b. Aḥmad. *Shadharāt adh-Dhahab min Akhbār Man Dhahab*. 8 vols. Cairo: Maktabat al-Qudsī, 1350–51/1931–32.

b. Iyās, *Ta'rīkh Miṣr* = Ibn Iyās, *Badā'iʿ az-Zuhūr fī Waqā'iʿ ad-Duhūr*.

Ibn Iyās, Abu 'l-Barakāt Muḥammad b. Aḥmad. *Badā'iʿ az-Zuhūr fī Waqā'iʿ ad-Duhūr*. Bulāq, 1311.

Ibn al-Jauzī, ʿAbd ar-Raḥmān b. ʿAlī. *Dhamm al-Hawā*. Ed. Muṣṭafā ʿAbd al-Wāḥid. Cairo: Dār al-Kutub al-Ḥadītha, 1381/1962.

Ibn Kathīr = Ibn Kathīr, *Al-Bidāya wa 'n-Nihāya*.

Ibn Kathīr, Ismāʿīl b. ʿUmar. *Al-Bidāya wa 'n-Nihāya*. 14 vols. Cairo: Maṭbaʿat as-Saʿāda, 1351–58/1932–39.

Ibn Khallikān, Shams ad-Dīn Aḥmad b. Muḥammad b. Ibrāhīm. *Wafayāt al-Aʿyān*. Ed. Ferdinand Wüstenfeld. 2 vols. Göttingen: Rudolph Deuerlich, 1839.

Ibn al-Khaṭīb, Lisān ad-Dīn Muḥammad b. ʿAbd Allāh. *Rauḍat at-Taʿrīf bi 'l-Ḥubb ash-Sharīf*. MS İstanbul (Süleymaniye), Esad Efendi 2724.

Ibn Maʿṣūm, ʿAlī Khān b. Aḥmad b. Muḥammad. *Sulāfat al-ʿAṣr*. Cairo, 1334.

Ibn an-Nadīm, Abu 'l-Faraj Muḥammad b. Isḥāq b. Yaʿqūb. *Kitāb al-Fihrist*. Ed. G. Flügel. 2 vols. Leipzig: F. C. W. Vogel, 1871–72.

Ibn Qayyim al-Jauzīya, Shams ad-Dīn Abū ʿAbd Allāh Muḥammad b. Abī Bakr. *Akhbār an-Nisā'*. Cairo: Maṭbaʿat at-Taqaddum, 1307.

———. *Al-Jawāb al-Kāfī li-Man Sa'ala ʿan ad-Dawā' ash-Shāfī*. Cairo, n.d.

———. *Rauḍat al-Muḥibbīn wa Nuzhat al-Mushtāqīn*. Ed. Aḥmad ʿUbaid. Cairo: Maṭbaʿat as-Saʿāda, 1385/1956.

———. ———. MS Dublin, Chester Beatty 3832.
———. ———. MS Tübingen 186. (Microfilm.)
Ibn Quṭlūbughā, Zain ad-Dīn Qāsim b. ʿAbd Allāh. *Tāj at-Tarājim fī Ṭabaqāt al-Ḥanafīya*. Ed. G. Flügel. ("Abhandlungen für die Kunde des Morgenlandes," Bd. II, No. 3.) Leipzig: Deutsche Morgenlandische Gesellschaft in Kommission bei F. A. Brockhaus, 1862.
Ibn Rajab, Abu 'l-Faraj ʿAbd ar-Raḥmān b. Shihāb ad-Dīn Aḥmad. *Kitāb adh-Dhail ʿalā Ṭabaqāt al-Ḥaṇābila*. 2 vols. Ed. Muḥammad Ḥāmid al-Fiqqī. Cairo: Maṭbaʿat as-Sunna al-Muḥammadīya, 1372/1953. (Abbreviated "Ibn Rajab" in some places.)
Ibn Sīnā, al-Ḥusain b. ʿAbd Allāh. *Risāla fī Māhīyat al-ʿIshq*. Aşkin Mâhiyati Hakkında Risâle. Ed. and tr. Ahmet Ateş. ("İstanbul Üniversitesi Edebiyat Fakültesi Yayınlarından," No. 552.) İstanbul: İbrahim Horoz Basımevi, 1953.
Ibn Taghrībirdī, Abu 'l-Maḥāsin Yūsuf. *An-Nujūm aẓ-Ẓāhira fī Mulūk Miṣr wa 'l-Qāhira*. Vol. V, Part 1. Ed. William Popper. ("University of California Publications in Semitic Philology," Vol. V, No. 1.) Berkeley: University of California Press, 1932.
al-Ifrānī, Abū ʿAbd Allāh Muḥammad Ṣaghīr b. al-Ḥājj Muḥammad. *Ṣafwat Man Intashar min Akhbār al-Qarn al-Ḥādī ʿAshar*. Fās, n.d. (Abbreviated "al-Ifrānī, *Ṣafwa*.")
Ikhwān aṣ-Ṣafā'. *Rasā'il Ikhwān aṣ-Ṣafā (sic) wa Khillān al-Wafā (sic)*. Ed. Khair ad-Dīn az-Zirkilī. Introd. by Ṭāhā Ḥusain. 4 vols. Cairo, 1347/1928.
Irshād = Yāqūt, *Irshād al-Arīb*.
b. Iyās, *Taʾrīkh Miṣr* = Ibn Iyās, *Badāʾiʿ az-Zuhūr*. . . . See Ibn Iyās.
JA = *Journal Asiatique*.
Jāḥiẓ, Abū ʿUthmān ʿAmr b. Baḥr. "Risāla fi'l-ʿIshq wa 'n-Nisāʾ," *Majmūʿat Rasāʾil* (With *Kitāb al-Bukhalāʾ* in one vol.). Cairo: Maṭbaʿat al-Jumhūr, 1323/1905.
———. "Risālat al-Qiyān," *Thalāth Rasāʾil*. Ed. J. Finkel. Cairo: Maṭbaʿat as-Salafīya, 1382/1962–63.
JAOS = *Journal of the American Oriental Society*.
JNES = *Journal of Near Eastern Studies*.
[Kahle, Paul]. *Studien zur Geschichte und Kultur des nahen und fernen Ostens*. Paul Kahle zum 60. Geburtstag . . . Herausg. von W. Heffening und W. Kirfel. Leiden: E. J. Brill, 1935.
al-Khaṭīb al-Baghdādī, Abū Bakr Aḥmad b. ʿAlī. *Taʾrīkh Baghdād*. 14 vols. Cairo: Maṭbaʿat as-Saʿāda, 1349/1931.
al-Kharāʾiṭī, Abū Bakr Muḥammad b. Jaʿfar. *Iʿtilāl al-Qulūb*. MS Bursa, Ulu Cami 1535.
Kinany, A. Kh. *The Development of Gazal (sic) in Arabic Literature: Pre-Islamic and Early Islamic Periods*. Damascus: Syrian University Press, 1951.

al-Kisā'ī, Aḥmad b. Sulaimān b. Ḥumaid. *Rauḍat al-'Āshiq wa Nuzhat al-Wāmiq*. MS İstanbul (Top Kapı Saray), Ahmet III 2373, folios 1–163b.

Kopf, L. "Religious Influences on Medieval Arabic Philology," *Studia Islamica*, V (1956), 33–59.

al-Kutubī, Ibn Shākir. *Fawāt al-Wafayāt*. 2 vols. Bulāq, 1299/1882.

Lane = Edward W. Lane, *An Arabic-English Lexicon*.

Lane, Edward W. *An Arabic-English Lexicon*. Book I, Parts 1–8 and Supplement. Ed. Stanley Lane-Poole. London: Williams and Norgate, 1863–93.

Laoust, Henri. "Aḥmad b. Ḥanbal," *Encyclopaedia of Islam*, New edition.

———. *Essai sur les doctrines sociales et politiques de Taḳī-d-Dīn Aḥmad b. Taimīya*, canoniste Ḥanbalite né à Ḥarrān en 661/1262, mort à Damas en 728/1328. ("Recherches d'archéologie, de philologie et d'histoire," t. X.) Cairo: Institut français d'archéologie orientale, 1939.

———. "Ibn al-Djawzī," *Encyclopaedia of Islam*, New edition.

———. "Ibn Ḳayyim al-Djawziyya," *Encyclopaedia of Islam*, New edition.

———. "La biographie d'Ibn Taimīya d'après Ibn Kaṯīr," *Bulletin d'Études Orientales de l'Institut Français de Damas*, IX (1942–43), 115–162.

Lévi-Provençal, E. "En relisant le 'Collier de la colombe'," *al-Andalus*, XV (1950), 335–75.

Lewin, B. "al-Aṣma'ī," *Encyclopaedia of Islam*, New edition.

Loosen, Paul. "Die Weisen Narren des Naisābūrī," *Zeitschrift für Assyriologie*, XXVII (1912), 184–229.

Manāzil = Shihāb ad-Dīn Maḥmūd b. Sulaimān b. Fahd, *Manāzil al-Aḥbāb wa Manāzih al-Albāb*.

Marçais, W. "Observations sur le texte du 'Ṭawq al-Ḥamāma' d'Ibn Ḥazm," *Mémorial Henri Basset* ("Publications de l'Institut des Hautes-Études Marocaines," Nos. 17, 18), II, 1928, pp. 59–88.

Mar'ī b. Yūsuf b. Abū Bakr b. Aḥmad al-Karmī. *Munyat al-Muḥibbīn wa Bughyat al-'Āshiqīn*. (Attribution on title page: Yūsuf b. Mar'ī al-Ḥanbalī.) MS Cairo, Tal'at, Adab 4648.

Maṣāri' = as-Sarrāj, *Maṣāri' al-'Ushshāq*.

Massignon, Louis. "Avicenne, philosophe, a-t-il été aussi un mystique?" and "Interférences philosophiques et percées metaphysiques dans la mystique Hallagienne: Notion de 'l'Essentiel Désir'," *Opera Minora*. Ed. Y. Moubarac. (Collection "Recherches et documents.") Beirut: Dar al-Maaref-Liban, 1963. Vol. II, pp. 466–69, 226–53.

———. *La Passion d'al-Hosayn-ibn-Mansour al-Hallaj, Martyr Mystique de l'Islam*. 2 vols. Paris: Paul Geuthner, 1922. (Abbreviated "Massignon, *Passion*.")

al-Mas'ūdī, 'Alī b. al-Ḥusain. *Murūj adh-Dhahab*. Les Prairies d'Or. Ed. and tr. C. Barbier de Meynard et Pavet de Courteille. 9 vols. Paris: Imprimerie Nationale, 1861–77.

al-Maṣūn = al-Ḥuṣrī, *Kitāb al-Maṣūn fī Sirr al-Hawā al-Maknūn.*

Mughulṭāi, 'Alā' ad-Dīn Abū 'Abd Allāh. *Al-Wāḍiḥ al-Mubīn fī Man Ustushhida min al-Muḥibbīn*. Ed. O. Spies. Vol. I (Vol. II never published). ("Bonner Orientalistische Studien," 18. Heft; herausg. von P. Kahle and W. Kirfel.) Stuttgart: W. Kohlhammer, 1936.

———. ———. MS İstanbul (Süleymaniye), Şehit Ali 2160.

———. ———. MS İstanbul (Süleymaniye), Fâtih 4143.

al-Muḥibbī, Muḥammad al-Amīn b. Faḍl Allāh. *Khulāṣat al-Athar fī A'yān al-Qarn al-Ḥādī 'Ashar*. 4 vols. Cairo, 1284–90/1868–74.

Murūj = Mas'ūdī, *Murūj adh-Dhahab.*

Nallino, C. A. *Oriente moderno*, XIII (1933), 490. (Review of A. R. Nykl's edition of *Kitāb az-Zahra.*)

Nelson, John Charles. *Renaissance Theory of Love*: The Context of Giordano Bruno's *Eroici furori*. New York: Columbia University Press, 1958.

an-Nīsābūrī, Abu 'l-Qāsim al-Ḥasan b. Muḥammad b. Ḥabīb. *'Uqalā' al-Majānīn*. Damascus, 1343/1924.

Nykl, A. R. "Nuevos datos sobre el 'Kitāb al-Zahra'," *al-Andalus*, IV (1936), 147–54.

O.M. = *Oriente moderno.*

Pellat, Charles. "al-Djāḥiẓ," *Encyclopaedia of Islam*, New edition.

———. *Arabisches Geisteswelt*. Dargestellt von Charles Pellat auf Grund der Schriften von al-Ǧāḥiẓ. Unter Zugrundlegung der arabischen Originaltexte aus den französischen Übertragen von Walter W. Müller. ("Die Bibliothek des Morgenlandes") Zürich: Artemis Verlag, 1967.

———. *Le milieu baṣrien et la formation de Ǧāḥiẓ*. Paris: Adrien-Maisonneuve, 1953.

———. "Les esclaves-chanteuses de Ǧāḥiẓ," *Arabica*, X (1963), 121–47.

———. (ed. and tr.). *The Life and Works of Jāḥiẓ*: Translations of Selected Texts. Tr. from the French by D. M. Hawke. ("The Islamic World") Berkeley and Los Angeles: University of California Press, 1969.

Pérès, H. "La poésie arabe d'Andalousie et ses relations possible avec la poésie des troubadours," *L'Islam et l'Occident*, 1947, pp. 109–30.

Pickthall, Mohammed Marmaduke. *The Meaning of the Glorious Koran.* New York: New American Library, 1953.

Plato: Lysis, Symposium, Gorgias. Tr. W. R. M. Lamb. ("Loeb Classical Library," No. 166.) Cambridge: Harvard University Press, 1961.

al-Qādirī, Abū 'Abd Allāh Muḥammad b. aṭ-Ṭayyib. *Nashr al-Mathānī li-'Ahl al-Qarn al-Ḥādī 'Ashar wa 'th-Thānī.* Fās, 1310. (Abbreviated "al-Qādirī, *N.M.*".)

Rauḍa = Ibn Qayyim al-Jauzīya, *Rauḍat al-Muḥibbīn wa Nuzhat al-Mushtāqīn.*

Ritter, H. (ed.). *Kitāb Mashāriq Anwār al-Qulūb wa Mafātīḥ Asrār al-Ghuyūb* by Ibn ad-Dabbāgh. Beirut: Dār Ṣādir wa Dār Bairūt, 1389/1959.

———. "Philologika VII: Arabische und persische Schriften über die profane und die mystische Liebe," *Der Islam,* XXI (1933,) 84–109.

Rizzitano, U. "Il *Dīwān aṣ-ṣabābah* dello scrittore magrebino Ibn Abī Ḥaǵalah," *Rivista degli studi orientali,* XXVIII (1953), 35–70.

Robson, J. and Rizzitano, U. "Ibn Abī Ḥadjala," *Encyclopaedia of Islam,* New edition.

Rosenthal, Franz. *Aḥmad b. aṭ-Ṭayyib as-Saraḫsī.* ("American Oriental Series," Vol. 26.) New Haven: American Oriental Society, 1943.

———. "From Arabic Books and Manuscripts VIII: As-Saraḫsī on Love," *Journal of the American Oriental Society,* LXXXI (1961), 222–24.

RSO = *Rivista degli studi orientali.*

Ṣafadī = aṣ-Ṣafadī, *Al-Wāfī bi 'l-Wafayāt.*

aṣ-Ṣafadī, Ṣalāḥ ad-Dīn Khalīl b. Aibak. *Faḍḍ al-Khitām 'an at-Tawrīya wa-'l-Istikhdām.* MS İstanbul, Köprülü 1351.

———. *Al-Wāfī bi 'l-Wafayāt.* Teil 1: Ed. H. Ritter. Teil 2–4: Ed. S. Dedering. ("Biblioteca Islamica," Vol. 6.) İstanbul; Millî Eğitim Basımevi, 1931– .

as-Sakhāwī, Muḥammad b. 'Abd ar-Raḥmān. *aḍ-Ḍau' al-Lāmi' fī A'yān al-Qarn at-Tāsi'.* 12 vols. Cairo, 1353–55/1934–36.

as-Salaṭī, Muḥyī ad-Dīn b. Taqī ad-Dīn. *Ṣabābat al-Mu'ānī wa Ṣabbābat al-Ma'ānī.* MS Dublin, Chester Beatty 4990.

———. ———. MS Princeton, Yahuda 5168, folios 76a–101a. (Parts of Chapters One and Two.)

Sallefranque, C. "Périples de l'amour en Orient et en Occident (Les origines arabes de l'amour courtois)," *L'Islam et l'Occident,* 1947, pp. 92–106.

Sam'ānī = as-Sam'ānī, *Kitāb al-Ansāb.*

as-Sam'ānī, 'Abd al-Karīm b. Muḥammad. *Kitāb al-Ansāb.* ("E. J. W. Gibb Memorial Series," Vol. XX.) Leiden: E. J. Brill, 1912.

as-Sarrāj, Abū Muḥammad Ja'far b. Aḥmad b. al-Ḥusain. *Maṣāri' al-'Ushshāq.* Ed. Karam al-Bustānī. Beirut: Dār Bairūt wa Dār Sādir, 1378/1958.

SEI = *The Shorter Encyclopaedia of Islam.* Ithaca: Cornell University Press, 1961.

Shaukānī = as-Shaukānī, *Al-Badr aṭ-Ṭāli'.*

as-Shaukānī, Muḥammad b. 'Alī. *Al-Badr aṭ-Ṭāli' bi-Maḥāsin Man ba'd al-Qarn as-Sābi'*. With supplement by Muḥammad b. Muḥammad b. Yaḥyā Zabbāra al-Yamanī. 2 vols. Cairo: Maṭba'at as-Sa'āda, 1348/1929.

Sh.Dh. = Ibn al-'Imād, *Shadharāt adh-Dhahab*.

Spies, Otto. "Al-Mughulṭā'ī's Spezialwerk über 'Martyrer der Liebe'," *Studien zur Geschichte und Kultur des nahen und fernen Ostens*. (= *Festschr. Kahle*. See under Kahle.) pp. 145–55.

as-Suyūṭī, Jalāl ad-Dīn 'Abd ar-Raḥmān. *Bughyat al-Wu'āt fī Ṭabaqāt al-Lughawīyīn wa 'n-Nuḥāt*. Cairo: Maṭba'at as-Sa'āda, 1326/1908. (Abbreviated "Suyūṭī, *Bughya*.")

Suyūṭī, *Interpr.* = as-Suyūṭī, *Ṭabaqāt al-Mufassirīn*.

as-Suyūṭī, Jalāl ad-Dīn 'Abd ar-Raḥmān. *Ṭabaqāt al-Mufassirīn*. Ed. Albert Meursinge. Leiden: S. and J. Luchtmans, 1839.

Ta'r. Bagh. = al-Khaṭīb al-Baghdādī, *Ta'rīkh Baghdād*.

Ṭauq = Ibn Ḥazm, *Ṭauq al-Ḥamāma*.

at-Tauḥīdī, Abū Ḥayyān 'Alī b. Muḥammad b. al-'Abbās. *Risālat aṣ-Ṣadāqa wa 'ṣ-Ṣadīq*. Ed. Ibrāhīm al-Kailānī. Damascus: Dār al-Fikr, 1964.

Vadet, Jean-Claude. "Ibn Dāwūd," *Encyclopaedia of Islam*, New edition.

———. "Littérature courtoise et transmission du *ḥadīṯ*," *Arabica*, VII (1960), 140–66.

Van Arendonk, C. "Ibn Ḥazm," *Encyclopaedia of Islam*, Supplement, and also in the *Shorter Encyclopaedia of Islam*.

Von Grunebaum, Gustave E. "Avicenna's *Risâla fî 'l-'Išq* and Courtly Love," *JNES*, XI (1952), 233–38.

———. *Medieval Islam*: A Study in Cultural Orientation. 2nd ed. Chicago: University of Chicago Press, 1953.

———. "The Aesthetic Foundation of Arabic Literature," *Comparative Literature*, IV (1952), 323–40.

———. "The Nature of the Arabic Literary Effort," *Journal of Near Eastern Studies*, VII (1948), 116–21.

Wāḍiḥ = Mughulṭāi, *Al-Wāḍiḥ al-Mubīn fī Dhikr Man Ustushhida min al-Muḥibbīn*.

Walzer, Richard, and Gibb, H. A. R. "*Akhlāḳ*," *Encyclopaedia of Islam*, New edition.

———. *Greek into Arabic*: Essays on Islamic Philosophy. ("Oriental Studies," Vol. I; edited by S. M. Stern and Richard Walzer.) Oxford: Bruno Cassirer, 1962.

al-Washshā', Abu 'ṭ-Ṭayyib Muḥammad b. Isḥāq. *Kitāb al-Muwashshā*. Ed. Rudolph E. Brünnow. Leiden: E. J. Brill, 1886.

Watt, W. Montgomery. *Islamic Philosophy and Theology*. ("Islamic Surveys," Vol. I.) Edinburgh: Edinburgh University Press, 1962.

Wellek, René, and Warren, Austin. *Theory of Literature*. 2nd ed. New York: Harcourt, Brace & World, 1955.

Wensinck, A. J. *A Handbook of Early Muhammadan Tradition*. Leiden: E. J. Brill, 1927.

———, Mensing, J. P., and Brugman, J. *Concordance et indices de la tradition musulmane*. Leiden: E. J. Brill, 1936– .

———. "The Oriental Doctrine of the Martyrs," *Mededeelingen der Koninklijke Akademie van Wetenschappen te Amsterdam*, Afdeeling Letterkunde, Deel 53, Serie A, No. 6, pp. 147—74.

Wüst., *Gesch.* = Wüstenfeld, *Die Geschichtschreiber der Araber und ihre Werke*.

Wüstenfeld, Ferdinand. *Die Geschichtschreiber der Araber und ihre Werke*. ("Abhandlungen der königlichen Gesellschaft der Wissenschaften zu Göttingen," Bnd. 28, 29.) Göttingen: Dietrichsche Verlags-Buchhandlung, 1882.

Yāfiʿī, *Mir. al-Jan.* = al-Yāfiʿī, *Mirʾāt al-Janān wa ʿIbrat al-Yaqzān*.

al-Yāfiʿī, ʿAbd Allāh b. Asʿad b. ʿAlī. *Mirʾāt al-Janān wa ʿIbrat al-Yaqzān*. Hyderabad, 1337–40/1918–21.

Yāqūt ar-Rūmī. *Irshād al-Arīb ilā Maʿrifat al-Adīb*. 2nd ed. Ed. D. S. Margoliouth. 7 vols. ("E. J. W. Gibb Memorial Series," VI.) London: Luzac and Co., 1925.

ZA = *Zeitschrift für Assyriologie*.

Zahra = Ibn Dāʾūd, *Kitāb az-Zahra*.

Zambaur = Zambaur, *Manuel de généalogie*. . . .

Zambaur, E. de. *Manuel de généalogie et de chronologie pour l'histoire de l'Islam*. Bad Pyrmont: Orientbuchhandlung Heinz La Faire, 1955. (Reprint of edition of 1927.)

ZDMG = *Zeitschrift der Deutschen morgenländischen Gesellschaft*.

INDEX

Note:—Titles of works are not indexed; reference is by author's name only. Page numbers in boldface type indicate main discussions of entries.

al-ʿAbbās b. al-Aḥnaf 72, 109
Abbott, Nabia 61
ʿAbd al-Wāḥid, grandfather of Ibn Abī Ḥajala 38
ʿAbd al-Wāḥid, Muṣṭafā 27
ʿAbd al-Wāḥid b. Zaid 146
Abū Bakr, Caliph 27
Abu ʾl-Faḍl al-ʿAbbās b. Sulaiman 21
Abū Ḥanīfa 23
Abū Hilāl al-ʿAskarī 86, 90
Abū Tammām 12
Abū ʿUbaida 84
Abū Yaḥyā al-Qattāt 99
Abū Zaid al-Maghribī 39
Adab 14, 76
Adab literature 67, 80–82, 132, and *passim*
Adīb 14
Aḍūd ad-Daula, Caliph 17
Ahlwardt, W. 49
Aḥmad b. Ḥanbal 112, 125, 126
Aḥmad b. Muḥammad b. al-Jasūr 24
Aḥwāl (sing. *Ḥāl*) xv, 19, 30, 32–33, 39, 67, **68–70,** 73, 78–79, 80, 134
Akhbār (sing. *Khabar*) 16, 17, 79
ʿĀʾisha 34, 55
ʿAlī 124, 125
ʿAlī b. Mushir 99
al-ʿAlmāwī 35
Anecdotes, use of as a source 60–62
al-Anṭakī, Dāʾūd **42–45,** 49, 62, 82, 115, 145–146
ʿAql 5, 29, 78, 119
Arberry, A. xii, xvi, 108, 141
al-Ardistanī, Abū Bakr Muḥammad 26
Arendonk, C. van 23, 24
Aristophanes 80
Aristotle 66, 144, 145
Arnaldez, R. 23
"Art of love" xvi
Asʿār al-Aswāq fī Ashʿār al-Ashwāq xv, **45–46**
al-Ashʿarī 15, 23
Asin Palacios, M. 23
al-Aṣmaʿī xvi, 64, 83–84, 92, 123, 145
Ateş, Ahmet 145, 146
Aṭibbāʾ 64–66
al-Azraq 109
ʿAzza 59

Badīʿ 61
Baihaqī 114
Bausani, A. 58
Bercher, L. xii, 108, 131
al-Biqāʿī 26, **41–42,** 43, 44, 45, 46, 77, 110, 115
Björkman, W. 101
Blachère, R. 58, 124
Bonebakker, S. A. v, 44, 45
Bouyahia, C. 21, 22
Brockelmann, C. xii, xvi, 39, 42, 47
Brünnow, R. E. 13, 14, 15, 20, 71
Buhl, F. 103
al-Buḥturī 12
Bukhārī 125
Buthaina 109

Calverly, E. E. 5
Carra de Vaux, B. 143
Codera, F. 72
Companions (*aṣḥāb*) 56, 57
"Courtly love" 14

Dahhān, Sāmī 108
ad-Dailamī 66
Daniel, Prophet 104
Dante 146
Dārimī 125
Dāʾūd aẓ-Ẓāhirī, father of Muḥammad b. Dāʾūd 99–100
De Goeje, M. J. 21, 22, 28
Dhahabī 35, 36
Dhu ʾr-Rumma 109
Donaldson, E. Talbot 14
Dualists 65–66
Duhmān, Muḥammad Aḥmad 38

Ephraim Syrus 103

Fackenheim, E. L. 145
al-Faḍl, Companion of the Prophet 125
Fanā' 37
Farrā' 63
Fatwā 9
Fihrist. See Ibn an-Nadīm
Finkel, J. 4
Freytag, G. W. 56
Fuqarā' 38

Gabrieli, F. xii
Galen 12, 143
García Gómez, E. xi, xii, 14, 15, 23, 24, 46, 47, 69, 70, 79
Gardet, L. 69
Gätje, H. 92
"Genre", use of term xiii–xiv
Gerhardt, Mia I. 61
Ghaḍḍ al-baṣar (*ghaḍḍ an-naẓar*) 120–126, 127, 130, 131–132
Ghazal 58
al-Ghazālī 102, 105
Ghāzī, M. F. 14, 71
Gibb, H. A. R. 58, 84, 118
Goldziher, I. xi, xii, xv, 100, 101, 128, 129, 130
Griffini, E. 30, 32
Grunebaum, G. E. von vi, xv, 14, 15, 24, 40, 72, 106, 134, 135

Ḥadīth, use of as a source **16**, 28, **54–57**, 94, 95, 105–107, 112, 120, and *passim*
Haffner, A. 83, 84, 92
Hajivad 132
al-Ḥajjāj 23, 59
Ḥāl. See Aḥwāl
Ḥalāl 54
al-Ḥallāj 9, 71
Hallajians 146
Hamilton, Chas. 132
Ḥanafīs 132
Ḥanbalīs 48, 76
Ḥaqīqat al-ʿishq xvi
al-Ḥaqq al-wājib 122
Ḥarām 54
Harūn ar-Rashīd 108
Ḥasan al-Baṣrī 102–103
Ḥashwīya 4, 121
Hawā 4, 10, 16, 29, 30, 63, 65, 69, 71, 75, 77, 78, 81, 85, **94–96**, 103, 105, 107, **117–132**, and *passim*
Hawke, D. M. 3
Haywood, John A. 63, 64, 83, 84
Heller, B. 104
al-Ḥimyarī 47
Hippocrates 66, 143
Ḥiss 5
Holy Law. *See Sharīʿa*
Houtsma, M. Th. 21, 22, 33
Ḥubb 18, 63, 85, 86, 87, **95–96,** 118
Ḥubb ʿUdhrī 71. *See also* ʿUdhrī love
Ḥukamā 64–66
Ḥukamā' al-awā'il 7
Ḥunain b. Isḥāq 66
al-Ḥusnī, Jaʿfar 35
al-Ḥuṣrī xv, 20, **21–22,** 32, 71, 72, 74, 87, 88, 89, 90, 133

ʿIbāda 37
Ibn ʿAbbās, Companion of the Prophet 20, 99, 109, 125
Ibn Abī Ḥajala 32, **38–41,** 44, 45, 48 49–50, 115, 135
Ibn Abī Uṣaibiʿa 8
Ibn al-ʿArabī 41, 63
Ibn al-Athīr 105
Ibn aḍ-Ḍabbāgh xii–xiii
Ibn Dā'ūd, Abū Bakr Muḥammad vi, xii, 7, **8–13,** 15, 16, 17, 18, 22, 58–59, 65, 69–72, 73, 80, 86, 99–100, 107, 118, 120, 129–130, 133, 142, 144
Ibn Duraid, Abū Bakr 17, 22
Ibn Fahd. *See* Shihāb ad-Dīn Maḥmūd b. Sulaimān (Salmān) b. Fahd
Ibn al-Fāriḍ, ʿUmar 39, 41, 42, 43–44
Ibn al-Furat, Vizier 9
Ibn Ḥajar al-ʿAsqalānī 35, 36
Ibn Ḥayawayh 17, 18
Ibn Ḥazm, Abū Muḥammad ʿAlī xi, 11, 15, **23–25,** 48, 69–72, **79–80,** 108, **129–131,** 133, 136
Ibn al-ʿImād 36
Ibn Jāmiʿ, Muḥammad, aṣ-Ṣaidalānī 9, 71, 86
Ibn al-Jauzī 7, 16, **27–29**, 48, 54, **76–79,** 81, 85, 94–95, 100, 106, 108, 110, 111, 113, 114, 118–120, 126, 127, 128, 147
Ibn Jubair 28
Ibn Kathīr 35, 36
Ibn Khair al-Ishbīlī 72
Ibn Khaldūn 40
Ibn Khallikān 26
Ibn al-Khaṭīb 40

Ibn Mājā 125
Ibn al-Marzubān 18, 109
Ibn an-Nadīm 18–19, 72, 87, 107
Ibn an-Naḥḥās ad-Dimashqī 108
Ibn Qayyim al-Jauzīya vi, xii, xvi–xvii, 16, 24, 32, 33, **34–38,** 48, 49, 54, 59–60, 63, **80–82,** 87, 89–93, 95, 102, 103, **112–115,** 118–120, 124, 126. **129–132,** 136, 145–146
Ibn Rajab 31, 35, 110
Ibn Rustah 6
Ibn Saʿīd al-Ballūṭī 24
Ibn Sayyid an-Nās 33
Ibn Shādhān, Abū Bakr 17, 18
Ibn Shuhaid, Abū ʿĀmir 79
Ibn Sīda 63
Ibn as-Sikkīt 90
Ibn Sīnā (Avicenna) 24, **145–146**
Ibn Suraij 9
Ibn Taghrībirdī 36
Ibn Taimīya 36, 37, 38, 39, 47, 115
Ibrāhīm Maimūnī 47
ʿIffa 130
Ikhwān aṣ-Ṣafāʾ 142, **143–144**
al-Irbilī, Aḥmad b. Zafar 38
ʿIshq **3–4,** 7, 29, 32–33, 48, 49, 59–60, 63, 64, 65, 75, 78, 81, 85–86, **94–96,** 105, 107, 115, 117–120, **127–129,** 144, 145, 146, and *passim*
Islām, as submission to God 120
Ismāʿīlīs 143–144
Isnāds, use of 16, 17–18, 43, 72, 77–78, 85, 100, 105–106, 110, 111, 112–113, 113–114, and *passim*
Ittiḥādīya 39

al-Jāḥiẓ **3–4,** 8, 22, 59, 68, **84–86,** 118, **120–126,** 133, 144
Jamīl 109
Jarīr b. ʿAbd Allāh 124
al-Jauharī 63
Jawād, Muṣṭafā 35
Jihād 102
Joseph (Yūsuf) 103–104
Jurjānī 114
Juynboll, Th. W. 100

al-Kailānī, Ibrāhīm 144
Kampman, A. A. vi
Karagöz 132
Khabar. See Akhbār
Khalīl b. Kaikaldī al-ʿAlāʾī 34
al-Kharāʾiṭī **15–16,** 17, 54, 72, **74–78,** 110, 113–114, 120, 126, 127, 133, 144
al-Khaṭīb al-Baghdādī 17
Khilāba 92
Khulla 48
Kinany, A. Kh. 120, 124
al-Kindī 7, 65
al-Kisāʾī, Aḥmad b. Sulaimān **30–31, 68–69,** 73, 87–88, 95–96, 117
Kitāb al-Aghānī 12
Kopf, L. 57
Koran, use of as a source 30, **54–57,** 94, 95, 101
Koran passages cited: (9:20–22, 47:4, 61:11 *ff.*) 102, (*Sūra* 12) 104, (12:53) 119, (2:223) 120, (53:32–33) 122, (24:30–31) 124
Kraemer, J. 92
Kremer, A. von 143–144
Krenkow, F. 17
Kuthayyir ʿAzza 59, 109

Lailā al-Akhyalīya 109
Lamam 122
Lamb, W. R. M. 80
Lane, E. W. 43, 49
Laoust, H. 37, 38, 126
Levi Della Vida, G. 84
Lévi-Provençal, E. xii, 47
Lewin, B. 64
Lexicographers, use of as a source, **62–64,** 72–73
"Literature", use of term xiii–xiv
Loosen, P. 26
Lory, C., 39
Love in God, or for God's sake 32, 144
Löwenthal, A. 66

Maḥabba 48, 49, 75, 86, 92, **95–96,** 127, 146
Maḥabbat al-ʿaql 20
Maḥabbat ar-rūḥ 20
Māhīyat al-ʿishq xvi
Majnūn Lailā 109, 127
Mālik b. Anas 23, 104, 132
al-Malik al-Ashraf Abu ʾl-Muẓaffar 30
Malikshāh 135
al-Manṣūr (Almanzor) 23
Maqqarī 23
Marçais, W. xii

al-Marghinānī 132
Marguet, Y. 143
Mar'ī b. Yūsuf **46–48,** 115, 132, 133
Martyrs of love 10–11, 20, 33, 80, 81, **99–115**
al-Marzubānī xv, **16–20, 72–74,** 80, 85, 87, 88, 89, 91, 107, 133
Massignon, L. 7, 9, 12, 39, 69, 71, 86, 100, 114, 146
Mas'ūdī 65, **142–143**
Matn 16
Mehren, A. A. F. 145
Merx, A. 92
Moubarac, Y. 7
al-Mubarrad 13, 85
Mughulṭāi 16, 18, 19, 22, 32, **33–34,** 42, 44, 50, **80,** 86, 88–90, 109, 111, 112, 113, 114, 115
Muḥammad, the Prophet. *See* Prophet
Muḥammad, son of Malikshāh 135
Muḥibbī 43, 46, 47
Muḥyī ad-Dīn Yūsuf b. al-Jauzī, 35
Mujāhid 99
Müller, Walter W. 3
Murū'a (or *murūwa*) 14, 76, 118
Muslim, Traditionist 125
Muslim b. Walīd 108
Mu'taḍid, Caliph 8
Mutawakkil, Caliph 125
Mutayyam (pl. *mutayyamūn*, *-īn*) 18, 19, 80
Mu'tazilīs 17, 99, 121, 125, 126
al-Muẓaffar 23
Mystical love xi, xiii, 27, 37, 40, 47, 76, 82, 86

Nafs 5, 29, 33, 49, 103, 119
Nafs nāṭiqa 5
Nafzāwī xvi
Nallino, C. A. 11
Nasīb 58
"Nature of love" xvi
Nawawī 114
Naẓar al-faj'a 124–125
an-Naẓar al-mubāḥ 129–132
Nelson, J. C. xv
Nifṭawayh 10–11, 17, 18, 71, 72, 99, 129
an-Nīsābūrī, Abu 'l-Qāsim 26, **73–74**
an-Nu'aimī, 'Abd al-Qādir b. Muḥammad 35
an-Nuwairī 146–147
Nykl, A. R. xii, 10, 11, 24, 69

Pedersen, J. 35
Pellat, C. 3, 4, 85, 86, 120, 121, 122, 123
Peripatetics 145
Petrof, D. K. xi
"Phenomenology of love" xv–xvi
Philologists, use of as a source **62–64,** 72–73
Philosophers and physicians, use of as a source 64–66
"Philosophy of love" xv
Pickthall, M. M. 102
Plato 12, 80, 143, 145, 146
Plotinus 145
Poetry, use of as a source **57–60,** 72, 84
Potiphar's wife 103–104
Prophet (Muḥammad) 11, 16, 31, 43, **54–57,** 86, 99, 102, 113, 124, 134, 145
"Psychology of love" xv–xvi
Ptolemy 12
Pythagoras 66

Qalb 5
al-Qannaujī 44
Qiyān (sing. *qaina*) 4, 8, **120–123**
Qiyās 121
al-Qummī, 'Alī b. Ayyūb 17, 18
Qur'ān. *See* Koran
Quṭāmī 108

Rabin, C. 84
Rāwī 7, 17–18, 73, 110–111, and *passim*
ar-Rāzī (Rhazes) 141–142
Ribera Tarrago, J. 72
Ritter, H. xii–xiii, xv, 132
Rizzitano, U. 38, 50
Robson, J. 38, 100
Rosenthal, F. 5–6, 7, 8, 40
Rūḥ 5

Sacred Law. *See Sharī'a*
Ṣafadī 35
Sakhāwī 41
as-Salaṭī, Muhyī ad-Dīn b. Taqī ad-Dīn Abū Bakr, xv, 18, **48–50**, 133
Salie, A. xii
as-Sarakhsī 4, **5–8,** 68
as-Sarrāj 18, **25–27,** 41, 42, 44, 71–72, 74, 76, 77, 100, 104, 108, 110, 115, 133
Sauvaire, H. 35
Ṣayrafī, Ḥasan Kāmil xii

Schacht, J. vi, 112, 122
Shāfiʿī 132
Shaghaf 92
Shahīd (pl. *shuhadā'*) **101–107**, 111, 113, 115. *See also* Martyrs of love
Shahwa 115
Sharāra, ʿAbd al-Laṭīf xv
Sharīʿa 37, 107, 121, 123, 132
Shaukānī 35
Shauq 93
Shawāhid 56–57
Shihāb ad-Dīn Maḥmūd b. Sulaimān (Salmān) b. Fahd 18, 20, 22, **31–33**, 42, 44, 48, 74, 85, 88–89, 90, 107
Shiʿīs 17
Shuhda bint Aḥmad 26, 109–110
Spies, O. 18, 89
Stendhal 39
Stern, S. M. 66, 144
Stetkevych, J. vi
Stories, use of as a source 60–62, and *passim*
Ṣufīs 37–38, 39–40
aṣ-Ṣūli 7, 17
Sulūw 71
"*Sunna* of the Prophet" 120
Sunnīs 4, 86, 125
"Superanthology" 82
Susanna 43, 62, 103–104
Suwaid b. Saʿīd 56, 99, 100, 105, 112, 113
as-Suyūṭī 27, 36, 41

Taʿabbud 119–120
aṭ-Ṭabarī, Ibn Jarīr 9
Tatayyum 95, 119–120
Tauba 109
at-Tauḥīdī, Abū Ḥayyān 144–145
Tawriya 44
Thaʿālabī 90
Thaʿlab 13
"Theories" of love xvi
"Theory", use of term xv–xvi
Thousand and One Nights 61
at-Tilimsānī, ʿAfīf ad-Dīn 44
Tirmidhī 125
Tomiche, N. 130
Traditions. *See* Ḥadīth
Ṭughrā'ī 135
Ṭūqān, Ibrāhīm xii, 10

ʿUbaid, Aḥmad xii
ʿUdhra 29, 33
ʿUdhrī ideals 75
ʿUdhrī love 14, 29, 120
Ülken, Hilmy Ziya 145
ʿUmar I, Caliph 134
ʿUmar b. Abī Rabīʿa 24
Union with God 37, 44
ʿUrwa b. Ḥizām al-ʿUdhrī 109

Vadet, J.-C. v, 8, 75, 76, 77, 78
Vernet, J. 42

Waḍḍāḥ al-Yaman 122
Walzer, R. 66, 118
Warren, Austin xiv
al-Washshā' 4, 8, **13–15**, 17, 70—71, 72, 133, 142
Watt, W. Montgomery 37
Weisweiler, M. xii
Wellek, René xiv
Wensinck, A. J. 32, 101, 102, 103, 104, 105
Wiṣāl 129
Wright, W. 8
Wüstenfeld, F. 46, 47

Yaḥyā b. Khālid, Vizier 142
Yāqūt 26
Yūsuf. *See* Joseph
Yūsuf b. Harūn ar-Ramādī 131
Yūsuf b. Yaḥyā b. Marʿī 46, 47

Ẓāhirīs 8–9, 23–24, 126, 129–131
Ẓarf 14, 71
Ẓarīf (pl. *ẓurafā'*) 14, 30, 68, 71, 99, 142
Zoroastrians 65–66
Zuhair al-Madīnī 19
Ẓurafā'. *See Ẓarīf*
Zurqānī 104–105